"From now on any comprehensive study of Ancient Mexican civilization must start from (and with) your discoveries. " Octavio Paz, leading Mexican intellectual, scholar, poet.

"**AMAZING**! ... The exactness of the reasoning! The rigor of the demonstrations! ... Absolutely convincing ... beautifully written ... deeply moving! ... I could not leave the book until I had finished it."-Claude Levi-Strauss, College de France.

"**SPARKLES WITH POETIC SIMPLICITY**! . . . Will take its place as one of the foremost interdisciplinary analyses of a deeply significant cultural complex . . . [it is] characterized by a profound psychological insight."--Richard Evans Schultes, Harvard University.

"**WASSON'S BOOKS STAND OUT AS REAL CLASSICS**! . . . [They] have caused the histories of India, Greece, and now Mexico to be reconsidered."-Michael Aldrich, The Fitz Hugh Ludlow Memorial Library.

"**PURE GOLD**! ... Interweaving science, artistry, and an almost uncanny sense of where hidden veins of pure gold lie... [the book] adds another novel and major chapter to our knowledge of the history of Early Man. "-Huston Smith, Syracuse University.

THE WONDROUS MUSHROOM

Mycolatry in Mesoamerica

by
R. Gordon Wasson

ISBN 9780872865921

TABLE OF CONTENTS

Mycolatry; (mĪ·col'a·tre) nov. verb.: Worship of a mushroom; specifically, worship of entheogenic mushroom species in proto- and prehistory as a means for communicating in grave circumstances with the Almighty Powers.

Mushroom: This word today covers widely different areas in different circles of the English-speaking world. In Great Britain many apply it only to the cultivated marketplace mushroom Agaricus (or Psalliota) hortensis, also perhaps Agaricus campestris; others, to any edible species including the morels and even the truffles; others, to any fleshy-capped fungus, whether edible or inedible; others try to apply it only to the Basidiomycetes, which excludes e.g. the morels. Mycologists tend to broaden the field. In this book ' mushroom' embraces all the higher fungi, whether Basidiomycetes or Ascomycetes, with conspicuous fruiting bodies.

Entheogen; nov. verb.: 'God within us', those plant substances that, when ingested, give one a divine experience, in the past commonly called 'hallucinogens', 'psychedelics', 'psychotomimetics', etc etc, to each of which serious objections can be made. A group headed by the Greek scholar Carl A. P. Ruck advances 'entheogen' as fully filling the need, notably catching the rich cultural resonances evoked by the substances, many of them fungal, over vast areas of the world in pro to- and prehistory. See journal of Psychedelic Drugs Vol 1 t.1-2, 1979, pp 145-6. We favor the adoption of this word. Early Man, throughout much of Eurasia and the Americas, discovered the properties of these substances and regarded them with profound respect and even awe, hedging them about with bonds of secrecy. We are now rediscovering the secret and we should treat the ' entheogens' with the respect to which they were richly entitled. As we undertake to explore their role in the early history of religions, we should call them by a name unvulgarized by hippy abuse.

PRELUDE

From the beginning the entheogenic mushrooms have interested me solely for their role in Early Man's religious life. My wife Valentina Pavlovna and I discovered, in the course of decades of observation and study, the division of European peoples between mycophobes and mycophiles and this, plus an abundance of linguistic and folkloric evidence, led us to make (to ourselves only) the bold surmise that mushrooms (of all plants!) had once played a center-stage part in the worship of our remote ancestors - we knew not how nor why nor which mushrooms. Then, crossing the Urals, we discovered the mycolatry that had prevailed in the northern belt of peoples bordering on the Arctic Ocean, all the way to the Bering Strait. So, our surmise was vindicated and our goal was reached, or so we thought.

But more discoveries were to come. On the eve of World War II there were ethnomycological stirrings in the study of the cultural entity known to anthropologists as Mesoamerica - an area from Nicaragua west and north to a wavy line that runs across Mexico north of Mexico City, an area marked by distinctive cultural traits even though it embraced peoples speaking a multitude of languages.

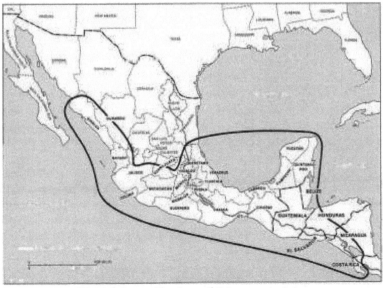

Fig 1 Map of 'cultural' Mesoamerica

We learned of these stirrings only in 1952 but from then on, we pursued them hard. On the night of 29 June 1 95 5 in a remote Indian village of Oaxaca I achieved our goal: I participated with a handful of Mazatec Indians in a shamanic mushroom agape and caught from them, young and old, the awe and reverence that has always imbued these gatherings. In Life, 13 May 1 957, I published an account of our adventure and at the same moment we brought out, my wife and I, our two-volume work, Mushrooms Russia & History, detailing the chronicle of our pursuit up to that date.

I have often taken the sacred mushrooms, but never for a 'kick' or for 'recreation'. Knowing as I did from the outset the lofty regard in which they are held by those who believe in them, I would not, could not, so profane them. Following my article in Life a mob of thrill-mongers seeking the 'magic mushrooms' descended on Huautla d e Jimenez - hippies, self-styled psychiatrists, oddballs, even tour leaders with their docile flocks, many accompanied by their molls – upsetting and abusing the quiet tenor of life in what had been, _superficially at least, an idyllic Indian village. Countless thousands elsewhere have taken the mushrooms (or the synthetic pills containing their active agent) and the chatter of some of them fills the nether reaches of one segment of our 'free press'. I deplore this activity of the riffraff of our population but what else could we have done? Had we refrained from presenting to the world the facts as we knew them to be, a novel and I think a major chapter in Early Man's cultural history, not only in Mexico, would have perhaps vanished unnoticed. (In this book I define 'Early Man' as humankind before there was reading and writing.) We knew and weighed the objections: had not our shaman Maria Sabina said that to give out photographs of her performance 'would be a betrayal'?

My wife and I were solely responsible for the present development of what we were the first to call ethnomycology. Wherever we have studied the story of Early Man, we have discovered entheogenic mushrooms in use, hedged about with awesome beliefs and trappings of the Holy. Of course, there are many other entheogens, but I think the p art these have played in Early Man's history has been for each of them geographically circumscribed. The use of mushrooms, if I am right, spread over most of Eurasia and the Americas, and as Stone Age Man has emerged into the light of proto-history these strange fungi may well have been the primary secret of his sacred Mysteries. To document this belief of ours (and held only by us) seemed worthwhile, and to dissect the corpus of a still living culture, i.e. in Mesoamerica, where the mushrooms played their traditional role, was an opportunity to be quickly seized. In the successive chapters of this book I present a picture of the sacred mushrooms in Mesoamerica that is quite other than the world has known. Before the Conquest they were a major element in public celebrations. Ample evidence also exists that they played a widespread shamanic role i n private gatherings, and I will show that this use can be traced back for centuries, in all likelihood for many millennia. The Conquest put an abrupt end to the public celebrations. The private gatherings, by reason of their privacy and in spite of harassment by the Inquisition, have survived to this day. But from 1726 until 1915 we have discovered only trifling mention of them in public prints or documents: the world had virtually forgotten them.

We will show that in 1953, when we embarked on our Mesoamerican inquiries, many of the leading authorities in such studies were ignoring the sacred (or entheogenic) mushrooms.

As I read the pre- Conquest Nahuatl poetry, at last made accessible to us in the version given to us by Father Garibay, the poets speak eloquently and repeatedly of the exalted status in which mushrooms were held: 'Tell us, oh Priests, whence come these inebriating flowers?' to which the Priests, via the poet, reply: ' From God's house in Heaven. ' (There emerges from the pre-Conquest poetry of the Nahua a hierarchy of quality for the entheogens, the mushrooms figuring in the highest class, the daturas in the lowest. As we shall see, 'flowers' is a figure of speech for all of the superior ones.)

The mushrooms transport one for the nonce to heaven, where all the senses unite in a joyous symphony shot through with an overwhelming feeling of caritas, of peace and affection for the fellow communicants.

This touched an acutely sensitive nerve in the newly arrived Catholic missionaries and we catch a taste of their panic, their indignation and fury, in these words, wholly misleading as we will see later, of Fray Toribio de Benavente called Motolinia:

They had another way of drunkenness that made them crueler and it was with some fungi or small mushrooms, which exist in this land as in Castilla; but those of this land are of such a kind that, eaten raw and being bitter, they drink after them or eat with them a little bees' honey ; and a while later they would see a thousand visions, especially serpents, and as they would be out of their senses, it would seem to them that their legs and bodies were full of worms eating them alive, and thus half rabid they would sally forth from the house, wanting someone to kill them ; and with this bestial drunkenness and travail that they were feeling, it happened sometimes that they hanged themselves, and also against others they were crueler. These mushrooms they called in their language teunanacatlth,

9

which means 'flesh of god', or the devil whom they worshipped; and in this wise with that bitter victual by their cruel god were they houseled.

[For the Spanish original, vide Memoriales, UNAM, Mexico, 1971, p 32]

Here is indeed odium theologicum.

In short, for the friars the Nahua' celebrated an appalling simulacrum of Holy Communion with these mushrooms. One can imagine the many trembling confabulations of the friars as they would whisper together how to meet this Satanic enemy. The teonandcatl struck at the heart of the Christian religion. I need hardly remind my readers of the parallel, the designation of the Elements in our Eucharist: 'Take, eat, this is my Body...', and again, 'Grant us therefore, gracious Lord, so to eat the flesh of thy dear Son . . . and to drink His blood... '. But the truth was even worse. The orthodox Christian must accept on faith the miracle of the conversion of the bread and wine into God's flesh and blood: that is what is meant by the Doctrine of Transubstantiation. By contrast the sacred mushroom of the Aztecs carries its own conviction: every communicant will testify to the miracle that he has experienced.

The friars were conscientious chroniclers of Mesoamerican culture and they have left us many long and absorbing accounts of Indian life and of the New World
that they were the first to study. But about the sacred mushrooms they are sparing of words or, as in the famous Badianus manuscript, silent. Nor are the inebriating mushrooms even mentioned (contrary to what the title would lead one to expect) in Problemas y Secretos Maravillosos de las Indias, by Juan de Cardenas, published in 1591 in Mexico. The best of the churchmen are neutral, but all their testimony is hearsay sometimes mixed with prejudice: they neither ingested them nor witnessed their ingestion, if we judge by their writings. The testimony of their informants, insofar as we possess it, must be read with caution: the witnesses used by Bernardino de Sahagun were the most honorable, intelligent, and well-informed natives that could be found and they occupied a privileged position with the friars that they would fain keep. They knew what the friars would have them say about the entheogens. When these informants testify in Nahuatl about the mushrooms, their words occasionally disclose an embarrassing torque between, on the one hand, what the friars expected them to say and, on the other, their strong leaning in favor of the truth: but their words always wind up on the side of the friars.

Another source of information lies in the Proceedings of the Holy Office of the Inquisition, now housed in the Archivo General de la N acion: for the sixteenth and seventeenth centuries they give us a taste of what was happening in the humble-

1. At the time of the Conquest Mesoamerica was dominated by the Nahua, native speakers of the Nahuatl language, the lingua franca of the area, and the Nahua were dominated in turn by the Nahuatl-speaking Aztecs living in an island city in the Valley of Mexico called Tenochtitlan, now known as Mexico City. The prestige of the Nahua ran far beyond the confines of Mesoamerica. The distinguished Ojibway Keewaydinoquay calls my attention to an Ojibway legend that starts with these ringing words:

> *Mewija shabwasong Nahuwahinawinnini.*
> *Long Jong ago, far away to the South, in the land of the*
> *people called Nahua . . .*

The Ojibway are an Algonkian people living in the Great Lakes area. Until I told her Kee had never known who the Nahua were.

-homes of the indigenas, as the Indians are called today, of mestizo families, and in that part of the creole world living in intimacy with the indigenas. The coverage of the Inquisition was spotty, as one would expect, but would have permitted an historian of imagination to surmise the truth. We now know, thanks to our own soundings of the Indian world in the highlands of the States of Oaxaca, Puebla, Ve racruz, and Mexico, and thanks also to the mycologists, anthropologists, and linguists who have followed our trail, how widespread and firm a hold until recent times the mushrooms have had on the imaginations and practices of the indigenous world of monoglot Indians. The public celebrations of pre-Conquest times are long since gone for good, but the midnight veladas continue even now in lowly homes, in rancherias, a major feature in the lives of the Indians. They continue today, but as the country is fast opening up, this unique survival of a practice going back to the Stone Age is disappearing.

The Indians of Mesoamerica, as I have said, discovered the amazing properties of the entheogenic mushrooms. The friars learned of them from the Indians and tell us a little about them by hearsay. They were re-discovered in our times by a dramatic event: A United States Government botanist of established reputation, William E. Safford, on 4 May 1 9 1 5 in a formal address delivered before the Botanical Society of Washington, D. C., said that he had searched for inebriating mushrooms and found none. As was not uncommon in those days in botanical and ethnological circles, he was contemptuous of the herbal knowledge of the Indians and said they had confused the dried cactus peyote (Lophophora Williamsii) buttons with mushrooms. (It is the fate of some worthy scientists and scholars to be remembered for the blunders they make.) Later in that year his address was published, lavishly illustrated and documented, with the express approval of the Department of Agriculture, in the journal of Heredity. Most of those who listened to him or read him learned of the supposed existence of inebriating mushrooms only to learn in the same breath that they had never really existed. His paper was a major effort on his part, but contrary to his expectation, sometime later a still small voice of an obscure ethnobotanist in Mexico, Blas Pablo Reko, made itself heard, faintly, persistently, protesting that the mushrooms were still being used in the State of Oaxaca, and little by little other voices joined his – Robert J Weitlaner, Jean Bassett Johnson, and the Harvard botanist Richard Evans Schultes. In 1938 Schultes took back to Harvard from Huautla de Jimenez specimens of the mushrooms and Johnson with his companions succeeded in enlisting a shaman for a midnight session. This session turned out to be one where grains of corn were used for divination. There was no singing and the mushrooms were ingested by the shaman alone.

World War II broke out. All thought of the mushrooms dried up until Valentina Pavlovna and I, approaching the subject from a far different angle, turned up in Huautla in the middle 1950's. We had been alerted by two articles that Schultes had published following his field trip, by the pencil sketch of a ' mushroom stone' that our printer Giovanni Mardersteig had found in the Rietberg Museum of Zurich, and later by an extraordinary letter written to us by Eunice V. Pike, a Protestant missionary to the Mazatecs.

And so, it came about that Safford's resounding blast in 1 9 1 5 served as the catalyst that triggered the investigation among our ethnobotanists, starting Mesoamerican studies on their way to a just appraisal of the part played by the entheogenic mushrooms in pre- Conquest history. In 1971 Benjamin Keen published his The Aztec Image in Wes tern Thought in which he presented, in a fascinating way, the attitude of successive generations and of different segments of each generation toward the Aztec civilization. He mentions the 'magical mushrooms' only once in 600 pages and they are not even cited in his index. Keen was right: the mushrooms have played no part in the world's appraisal of Mesoamerican culture. In the first instance the Catholic clergy were responsible for playing down and misrepresenting this major element in the complex pattern of Mesoamerican life. But I believe the mushrooms were ignored for an additional reason: the deep-seated mycophobic strain in the West-European elements that have studied or observed the Nahuatl culture, a latent mycophobia, a subliminal rejection, that runs through much of Western civilization and that dates from a time in prehistory when the cult of assorted entheogenic mushroom species was superseded by other religious foci and ultimately by the Christian religion. I only cite this as a possibility here but will return to the theme later.

When we first went down to Mexico in 1 953, we felt certain, my wife and I, that we were on the trail of an ancient and holy Mystery and we went as pilgrims seeking the Grail. To this attitude of ours I attribute such success as we have had. It was not easy. For four and a half centuries the rulers of Mexico, men of Spanish blood or at least of Spanish culture, have never entered sympathetically into the ways of the Indians, and the Church regarded the worship of the sacred mushroom as an idolatry. The Protestant missionaries of today are naturally intent on carrying the Gospel to the Indians, not on absorbing the religion of the Indians. Nor are most Mesoamerican anthropologists good at this sort of thing. Their frequent failure to enter into the religious life of the peoples they study, their frequent inability to cope with the higher reaches of the cultures that absorb their attention, reveal a disconcerting lacuna in their work, an anthropological fact about the anthropologists that should alert the rest of us.'

1. L M. Lewis, Professor of Anthropology in the London School of Economics, draws attention also to the frequent inability of anthropologists to sense the religious aspect of the people they are studying; see Ecstatic Religion, a Pelican book published in London by Penguin Books in 1971, p. 14 and lacer. Similarly, P. Gelling and Hilda Ellis Davidson: The Cha riot of the Sun, pp 5-6, J M. Dent Sons, Ltd, 1969.

For more than four centuries the Indians have kept the divine mushroom close to their hearts, sheltering it from desecration by white men, a precious secret. We know that today there are many shamans who carry on the cult, each according to his lights, some of them consummate artists, performing the ancient liturgy in remote dwellings before minuscule congregations. With the passing years they will die off, and, as the country opens up, the cult is destined to disappear. They are hard to reach, these shamans. Almost invariably they speak little or no Spanish. To them, performing before strangers seems a profanation. They will refuse to meet with you, much less discuss the beliefs that go with the mushrooms and perform for you. Perhaps you will l earn the names of a number of renowned shamans and your emissaries will even promise to deliver them to you, but then you wait and wait and they never come. You will brush past them in the marketplace and they will know you but you will not know them. The cobbler across the way may be the very man you are seeking: you may p ass the time of day with him, yet never learn that he is the shaman you need. In the writings on shamanism, I have never seen mentioned this reluctance of the gifted shamans to perform before outsiders. Yet it seems unlikely that such reluctance is confined to the mountains of Oaxaca, for it is the natural response of a believing religious leader to the importunities of non-believers and thrill-mongers. A Catholic priest will scorn to say Mass expressly to satisfy the curiosity of non-believers. In some accounts of shamanic performances held in various parts of the world I have asked myself what category of shaman we are dealing with: they behave like the charlatans in Huautla, eager to perform for outsiders but who are embusteros, farsantes, frauds. They have leaped into existence to meet the demands of the visitors following in our trail. The true shaman believes in the mushrooms, believes in himself, and believes in the handful of poor Indians who constitute his following.

The genuine shamans, as I have said, shun contact with strangers. But this is not so with the 'laymen ', especially the elderly men and women of a village. They do not initiate a conversation with you about the mushrooms. But after you have made a good impression on them and won their confidence, then l ate in the evening, by the light of a fire and *velas*, if you bring the conversation around to the sacred mushrooms, it is astonishing how freely they discuss them, how they will stay up late full of the subject, and how glad they are to meet a stranger who shows a sympathetic and lively interest in the miraculous 'little things' . Though Sahagun and many other sixteenth century friars gave leads aplenty, our anthropologists have traditionally shown no curiosity about them.

Not that the shamanism as practiced in Oaxaca has been unaffected by four centuries and more of contact with Christianity: Catholic elements blend with the pagan mushroom rite and the Indians see no incompatibility. Maria Sabina, our now famous shaman, sings chants that are full of Christian locutions - names of saints, the Lord's Prayer in Spanish that she has learned by rote, etc. These Christian locutions in her singing jostle with the forces of nature, with professions of humility, and later in the session with bold assertions of her authority. The mushrooms are the 'dear little children', *'nti'xti'*, the 'clowns', *'sa'se'*, but at the climax of the *Velada* they pronounce dread judgement with the voice of Jesus Christ! '

The synthesis is complete. When I have been present she has always begun her performance with a cheap chroma of the Santo Nino, the 'Holy

Child', on the altar in front of her. But when she has inverted a flower over the last wick and thus extinguished it, from then on, the proceedings take place, pagan-fashion, on the floor, the habitual practice of the American Indian. We are now in darkness. There can be no question: her verses come down to her from a rite that Ruiz de Alarcon reported to us in the early seventeenth century and of necessity, her singing and the verses being inseparable, her music dates also from the same remote period. They are of great antiquity, pre- Cartesian, going back surely for millennia.

Maria Sabina, herself an eminent shaman of the mushroom rite, is a church member in good standing. She has belonged to the Asociacion del Sagrado Corazon de Jesus, and has been not only a member - socia - but a captain of ten, a celadora. The Church has ceased to fight the mushrooms. It is even rumored, perhaps falsely, that in some remote parishes the priest himself has officiated at the mushroom rite. It was not always so. In the sixteenth and seventeenth centuries, when the secular arm placed itself at the disposal of the Church, the Inquisition saw to it that those who used the mushrooms suffered the harsh rigors of the l aw. Curiously, the Church did not dispute the efficacy of the mushrooms, their capacity to reveal the truth. But the Church said the mushrooms were the Devil's minions and so the idolatrous practices invoking them had to be extirpated.

To win the confidence of the Indians and to gain access to a superior shamanic performance one must possess two qualities in high degree: patience and tact, and then in addition a bountiful measure of luck. Our first stroke of fortune was winning the cooperation of the late Robert J. Weitlaner, Austrian-born engineer who gave up that profession to study the Indians. He led us by the hand on our first excursion on muleback into the Sierra Mazateca and later he accompanied us on m any other explorations. For ten years we had repeated recourse to him, tapping his immense knowledge of the Indians, their ways, their languages, their history. His patience, good humor, and joie de vivre, in the sierra and in Mexico City, were unfailing. But above all else we learned from him how to handle ourselves with the Indian.

The Indians are simply living by the conventions of an orally transmitted culture such as our own forebears lived by not so long ago - not long ago as compared with the long stretch of time that our ancestors have been on the earth. When you visit the Indian villages, you make allowances for this time lag. You do not treat them as inferiors or children. You do not treat them kindly as though they were equals. (The Indians are quick to see through you.) Weitlaner taught us to treat the Indians as

15

equals: a secret simple yet elusive. As the poet said, truly 'this is the famous stone that turneth all to gold '.

1. *Mazatec is a tonal language with 4 tones, 1 being the highest. There are also glides from one tone to another, the glides being represented by two or, rarely, three digits. '?' represents a glottal stop, as in the Scottish pronunciation bott'l.*

2. *See Maria Sabina and Her Mazatec Mushroom Velada, by Wasson et al, Harcourt Brace Jovanovich, Inc., New York, 1974; pp xxv ff. In the Zapotec country on the Pacific Coast, far removed from Huzutla, speaking of Aristeo Matias, the shaman, in 1957 I wrote: 'His chanting was low and feeble, and of course in Zapotec, but I h ad the impression that his singing was identical to what the Senora h ad sung with magisterial authority in the Mazatec country.' Mushrooms Russia & History, p. 314. The Zapotec and Mazatec languages are perhaps unrelated, and if related, only most distantly so.*

I am repeatedly asked what the future holds for our entheogenic mushrooms and the other entheogens. My interest being in proto-history and Early Man, this question is beyond the scope of my inquiry. Whether chemists and therapists will find some lasting use for the extraordinary substances that we have discovered in these strange pl ants, I will not predict. Today we know, as Early Man did not, that the active agents are certain chemicals with a precisely defined molecular structure. Early Man thought they were miracle plants that spoke to him with the voice of God. In these times we cannot accept this, though there is a possibility that these chemicals in some way unlock the door to extrasensory perception in some people. The awe and reverence that these plants once evoked seem to me gone for good. Their utilization for 'recreation' is, certainly, a passing fad. The world offers too many opportunities for exciting explorations and discoveries to justify any such activity on a large and lasting scale.

More than fifty years have passed since Valentina Pavlovna a n d I started on mushrooms. She was a Russian, a Muscovite, and a practicing pediatrician in New York. I began life as a newspaper man and after almost ten years switched to banking, where I stayed for more than thirty-five years, retiring for age on 30 June 1963. Neither of us was qualified in any of the disciplines that the pursuit of our avocation called for. Neither of us was a mycologist nor even a botanist, nor archaeologist, nor anthropologist, nor folklorist, nor in the technical sense a linguist, nor had we made of literature or history any special study. I suppose most persons would call us deeply religious, though we did not really adhere to any creed. She was a member of the Russian Orthodox Church and I am an

Episcopalian; my father having been a minister. We began our inquiries among our friends and almost before we knew it our circle of friends began to expand. As questions arose we directed them, at first by letter, to those best qualified to answer them, and on our far-ranging travels we sought the acquaintance of those who seemed to be promising sources of information. This we did with unremitting zeal. Many of our new friends were academicians, others were amateurs in the original meaning of that word, but many were humble people often unlettered and these included some of our most opened the doors for me to the Slovakian mushroom vocabulary, my excellent friend Nicholas Kazenchak. My wife died on 31 December 1958 late in the evening and after her death I carried on alone.

In this book the attentive reader will observe that I avoid certain words commonly used in treating our subject. We do not call the entheogens 'narcotics': the etymology from 'narcosis', sleep, is so obvious that the word is inappropriate and misleading for substances that keep one, willy-nilly, wide awake. We refrain from using 'witch doctor', a denigrating term for the herbalist who in his day knew the plant world well and has taught our medical profession many secrets, some of major importance. Nor do I speak of the peoples who are my subject as 'barbarians' or 'savages', as used to be our wont, epithets of contempt that will become anyone in our day to apply to other peoples. We of the twentieth century have earned a prior lien on those titles of dishonor.

I cannot even guess how many advisers and informants we have had. If we have contributed something to man's understanding of his past, we may fairly say, I think, that this is due to our not being specialists and to our faculty for tapping information from all sources, of low and high degree. We often said to each other that we were only rapporteurs digesting as best we could what our sources had to say. Naturally there are half a dozen counsellors who loom large in our thinking, who indeed were indispensable to us in making headway. Conspicuous among them is Roger Heim to whom this book is dedicated.

What guardian angel had me in his keeping when, after the Second World War, I ascended the steps of Professor Heim's laboratory in Paris to meet him for the first time, a stranger, an American, an ignoramus in the intricate, the vast, the exacting discipline that was his! At once he made me feel at home and soon he came to share our enthusiasm for ethnomycological inquiries. (At that time, we had no inkling of our future Mexican discoveries.) With Valentin a Pavl ovna and our daughter Masha, in the early '50's, we made an excursion together to Serignan near Orange in the Rhone Valley, to the home of Henri Fabre (his ' harmas') where we selected the Fabre watercolors that we reproduced with infinite care in *Mushrooms Russia & History*. Roger Heim was electrified by our discoveries in the seasons 1953, 1954, and 1955 in Mexico and he accepted at once my suggestion that he join us on field trips to the Mazatec country, the Mixeria, and the Chatino enclave in 1956, 1959, and 1961. When we brought out early in 1959 our joint work, *Les Champignons hallucinogenes d u Mexique*, it was he who, without my knowledge, dedicated it to the memory of Valentina Pavlovna, and who in its pages and also in his *Revue de Mycologie* carried to a successful conclusion a minor but vexatious mycological polemic that threatened to disturb the even tenor of our work. Later, again on my initiative, we made two extraordinarily fruitful field trips, one to the Kuma people below Mount Hagen in New Guinea in 1963 and the other in 1967 to the Simlipal Hills and thereabouts in Orissa (India) and the Santal Parganas in Bihar. Altogether our trips, our thick files of correspondence, our many publications vastly enriched Valentina Pavlovna's life and mine.

For upwards of forty years Roger Heim was the chief in Paris of the *Laboratoire de Cryptogamie* and the editor of the *Revue de Mycologie*. From 1951 to 1965 he also bore the burden of the direction of the Museum National d'Histoire Naturelle, that renowned center for advanced teaching and research in biological studies, one of the glories of French culture, and for a term he was also President of the Academie des Sciences. But these titles to academic distinction, though themselves of the highest order, do not tell the whole story. Vast as is his learning and experience in field and laboratory, sound as is his judgement in the vexed problems that beset mycologists, formidable as he is in polemic, it is as a rare human being that I best remember him. Patient with the beginner, inspiring as a teacher, model of generosity toward others, prodigious worker, classical stylist in the French language, who could be more delightful whether in his published writings, or in his correspondence,
or as a companion in the field? In the presence of Roger Heim, the timeworn conflict between science and the humanities fades away. One senses that the field of science for him is merely the New World that civilized man, the exponent of the humanities, is exploring and assimilating. It is an honor for me to be privileged to record thus publicly our debt to this beloved friend, this distinguished French scientist and Academician.

Chapter 1 tells the story of the all-night shamanic vigil of Mesoamerica where the divine mushrooms (or other entheogens) are 'consulted'. I have often told what happens at these veladas and for some of my readers this covers ground more or less familiar, but Chapter 2 dealing with the traits of the velada and kindred topics is largely new. Here I begin to present a fresh interpretation of the role of the entheogenic mushrooms in the life of the Mesoamerican Indians before and after the Conquest. I have relied heavily on the detailed studies of specialists, many of which, in the past twenty years, have revealed telling evidence, linguistic, archeological, anthropological. It seems to me that a common denominator unites these studies, a common denominator overlooked by the scholars who have not seen the wood for the trees. But they have supplied the indispensable components for the portrait that I offer of mycolatry in Mesoamerica, and I seize this opportunity to express my boundless gratitude to each of them. They alone have made this book possible.

My argument is many-faceted. I treat one facet in each chapter and each chapter is complete in itself. But this means that occasionally, for the reader's convenience, the same evidence is repeated in the new context. I repeat the evidence and remind the reader that it has appeared before. The ' Consulted Texts ', beginning on p 231, consist of sources actually used and quoted in my book and, to reduce the footnotes, I have added to the entries therein the p ages that I cite without precise source in the text.

The following abbreviations, familiar to all students of Mexico's past, occur from time to time in our text and often in the ' Consulted Texts':

AGN. Archivos Generales de l a Nacion
INAH: Instituto Nacional de Antropologia e Historia
INI: Instituto Nacional Indigenista
UNAM: Universidad Nacional Aut6noma de Mexico

R. GORDON WASSON

Honorary Research Fellow, Botanical Museum,
Harvard University
Honorary Research Associate, New York Botanical-
Garden

CHAPTER 1

A VELADA IN HUAUTLA

My first encounter with Maria Sabina was on Wednesday 29 June 1955, late in the afternoon. Allan Richardson, my friend and photographer, and I had arrived in Huautla the d ay before and Valentina Pavlovna with our daughter, Masha, was expected toward the end of the week. It was my third trip to Mexico in quest of the sacred mushrooms and our second visit to Huautla. Before noon I made my way down the steep, rough alleys,

Fig 1 Huautla de Jimenez as seen from the air in 1956

to the town hall, called in Mexico the municipio. Unsuccessful in finding any first-class shaman who would talk with us, much less celebrate the rite for us, I was increasingly impatient. I was even willing to present myself to the town officials, and if they seemed propitious, to solicit their help. I found only one man in the bare barn-like loft that served as the office of the Presidente: a man about thirty-five years old, athletic, with a genial, outgoing, honest smile. He was the *sindico* of the town, the No 2 man, Cayetano Garda Mendoza, now acting Presidente in the absence of his chief. After we had exchanged greetings, we discussed the outlook for the maize crop, the prices of coffee. Then and there, encouraged by the frankness of this excellent man, I made up my mind to put to him the vital question. (I had been cautioned never to consort with town officials: they are often a bad lot, sly, self-seeking, sometimes downright dishonest or unfriendly.) I leaned over the table and in a low voice said, 'May I take you into my confidence?' At once he was all curiosity, his face suddenly grave. 'Will you help me to learn the secrets of the *'nti'xi'tjo?'* I remember the way he threw his arms back in surprise at the question and at my knowing the Mazatec word for the sacred mushrooms. Without hesitating he said that nothing was easier, and to come to his house at the hour of the siesta. He lived at the other end of town, called *el Plan de la Salida*, about a mile away. Later, when I joined Allan Richardson, he was as excited as I at the possibility that, finally, we were to make a breakthrough.

A little after 4 o'clock Allan and I found Cayetano at home reclining in his hammock and taking his ease. Cayetano's house opens directly on the village thoroughfare running along the mountain side. You enter on the upper level from the road, and then inside the house, by a small trapdoor in one corner, you make your way down a steep and twisting stairway to the floor below, where the events that we are about to relate took place.

Without leaving his hammock, Cayetano asked his younger brothers Genaro and Emilio to take us down into the gully and show us the mushrooms. And so, a little past 4 o'clock on that Wednesday, down we went perhaps a hundred yards below, to the edge of the stream in the gully.

The home of Cayetano Garcia in which the velada took place. Door leading to lower chamber is partly visible. Photo taken in 1955

formality. The proceedings went forward with an easy decorum. Neither on this occasion nor at any other time or place have we ever seen or heard the mushrooms treated as a subject for jocular vulgarity, of the kind that often marks the use of alcohol among 'civilized' peoples. The atmosphere of respectful friendliness was infectious, and we enjoyed reciprocating the welcome extended to us. There is no record that any white men had ever attended a session of the kind that we are going to describe, nor that white men had ever partaken of the sacred mushrooms under any circumstances. For reasons deeply rooted in the mortal cultural conflict of Spaniards and Indians, it is unlikely that any unrecorded event of the kind had ever taken place. By hearsay Sahagun, Ruiz de Alarcon, and other early Spanish writers had reported gatherings of Indians where the hallucinogen was served to many, but we had thought from our previous visits to Mexico that such observances were today unknown. We were now to learn that they still go on, and that they are even today a central experience in the culture of the Mazatec people. The gatherings now are held behind closed doors, but as the 'consultation' with t h e Sacred Mushroom is a private, domestic matter, must not such gatherings always have been private?

Cayetano told us early in the evening that no one on any account should leave the house before break of day, and for the necessities of nature he showed us the rudimentary provision that had been made in one corner of the other room. The contempt of the Spaniards for indigenous rites and the Church's condemnation of them as idolatrous heresies have not killed these assemblies of ancient lineage but have certainly driven them under deeper cover. Our hosts were obviously pleased by our intense and sympathetic interest in all that went on before our eyes. The very fact of our participation must have made the evening memorable for them. They were dressed up for the occasion. Genaro in particular was resplendent in his handsome striped sarape and his freshly washed white cotton trousers or bags, bombachas, which Indian-style were buttonless, being supported by strings tied around the waist. By our respectful behavior we did all we could to make clear that for us the rite we were witnessing possessed full religious stature. We were mindful of the drama of our situation. We were attending as participants a mushroomic Supper of unique anthropological interest, which was being held pursuant to a tradition of unfathomed age.

There were a few home-made wooden chairs in the room, and in the beginning Allan and I used them, my chair in the corner of the room to the left of the altar table. Cayetano's brother Genaro and possibly one other remained seated on chairs the whole night through.

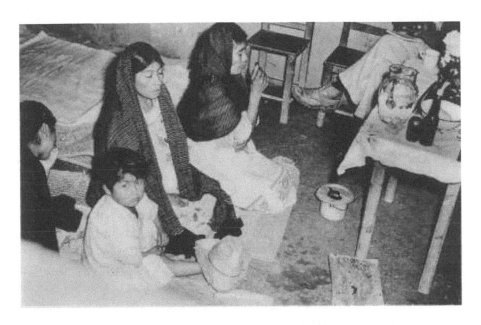

Adoration of the Mushroom. Maria Sabina, sabia, and her daughter Apolonia. Huautla de Jimenez, June 29-30, 1955

The others lay or reclined on mats on the floor, wrapped in sarapes, except of course for the *Senora* and her daughter, who, wearing clean *huipiles* with identical red birds embroidered on them, sat before the altar table on mats. They sat with what seemed a half-studied formality, the daughter a little behind her mother and slightly to her mother's right. Later, in the dark, we could barely discern their triangular shadows as first one and then the other lifted her voice in song. It was then, when the details were erased by darkness and only the geometric mass persisted, that they forcibly reminded me of the pyramids that are the outstanding feature of architecture in pre-Conquest Mexico. Might not the pyramids have been originally a geometric stylization of the worshipping Indian seated on his mat, of the gods that were his magnified projection of himself?

Before we go further we must mention that when we had bespoken the Senora's services in the afternoon, she had asked us what problem was troubling us. Prepared for this, I asked about our son Peter, then in the army. How was he? Alive or dead, or ill, or in good spirits, or in some trouble? This had seemed to her a sufficient justification. We had counted on Cayetano to stay with us through the night as our guide and interpreter. We observed that neither he nor Guadalupe were taking the mushrooms. As we were finishing ours, Cayetano informed us that he and his wife were withdrawing up the stairs and through the trap-door to the room above, where they would guard us against interruptions from the street. He was leaving his brother Emilio to act as our mentor. We sensed that each of the other adults who were taking the mushrooms was consulting Maria Sabina, as we were, about individual problems.

At about 10:30 o'clock the *Senora* and her daughter took their positions before the small table that served for an altar. On it were two holy pictures, on the left the Holy Child of Atocha and on the right the Baptism in Jordan, with a bouquet in front of them, a crucifix hidden in the flowers, three lighted candles of virgin beeswax, and a lighted wick in a glass of wax. There were also two pottery bowls and some cups. The Senora then went through our box of mushrooms, brushing off with her fingers the grosser pieces of dirt and passing them in her hand over copal (incense of resin) that was burning on a metal lid on the floor. Into each of the two bowls she put thirteen pair of mushrooms; one bowl was for her and the other for her daughter. Into each cup she put four pair, or five, or six, and then handed the cups to the grown-ups who were to take them. (The mushrooms are always counted by p airs, in couples.) The children received none. They were profoundly moved by the singing and events taking place in their presence. To me she handed a cup with six pair. Our readers will imagine my j oy at this dramatic culmination to years of pursuit. Then she handed a cup with six pair to poor Allan.

Mary, his wife, had reluctantly consented to his coming with me only on his solemn promise not to let those nasty toadstools cross his lips. He faced a behavior dilemma, but to have refused might have disappointed our friendly Indian companions, and so he coped with the immediate problem first and took the cup. (Later, with him safely back in New York, Mary gave him ready absolution.) By now all lights in the room were out except the wick in the glass. Following the *Senora's* example, we began to chew and swallow our mushrooms.

Our *curandera* ate cap and stem and we did likewise. She ate them one by one, with utmost gravity, chewing each one for a long time. She did not pick them up by pairs, as Aurelio Carreras had done in 1953. She picked them up one by one, although in apportioning them she had counted them by pairs. The flavor of the mushrooms is acrid and unpleasant. The distinctive flavor would repeat itself, as a gaseous beverage does, and pervade the nasal passage. I have since discovered that the Indians, by contrast with us, find the taste delectable. (Long afterwards Robert Weitlaner likened the taste to rancid grease, a taste unfamiliar to us. At the time this narrative is being written, in 1977, I have eaten many species of the divinatory mushrooms used in Mesoamerica, and they are all marked by this singular and unforgettable taste and aftertaste, which seem to be the veritable signature of the divine species.)

We all ate our mushrooms facing the wall where the small altar table stood. We ate them in silence, except for Cayetano's father, don Emilio, who was consulting the mushrooms about his infected left forearm. He would jerk his head violently with each mushroom that he swallowed, and utter a smacking noise, as though in acknowledgement of their divine potency. As I said before, I had been seated in the corner of the room on the left of the altar, a vantage point from which I could observe everything that was happening. Through Cayetano, the Senora asked me to move because the Word would come down there. Twenty years later, in telling the story of her life to Alvaro Estrada, the *Senora* explained her conception of 'the Word': in a notable passage she says:

. . . veo que el Lenguaj e cae, viene de arriba, como si fuesen p equeiios obj etos luminosos que caen del cielo. El Lenguaj e cae sobre la mesa sagrada, cae sobre mi cuerpo. Entonces atrapo con mis manos palabra por palabra.

[*La Vida de Maria Sabina, p 58, 1 26*]

. . . I see the Word fall, come down from above, as though they were little luminous objects falling from heaven. The Word falls on the Holy Table, on my body: with my hand I catch them, Word by Word.

The Senora conceives a mystical opening ('*boquete*') in the roof or high up in the wall. In her mind she adds another dimension to the matters that we discuss further in Chapter 7.

I joined Allan on m y chair immediately behind the *Senora*. We took about a half hour to eat our six pair of mushrooms. By eleven o'clock we had all finished our respective portions, the Senora crossing herself with the last swallow. Then we waited in silence. After about twenty minutes the *Senora* plucked a flower from the bouquet and with it inverted as an extinguisher put out the last of the velas. We should have been in stygian darkness, but by good fortune the night was clear and a gibbous moon, by the transom above the door, gave us just enough light to make our darkness visible. At about 11:20 o'clock Allan leaned from his chair and whispered to me that he was having a chill. We wrapped him in a blanket. A little later he leaned over again and said, 'Gordon, I am beginning to see things', to which I gave him the comforting reply that I was too. Allan l ay down along the wall on the large petate that had been spread for us, and shortly

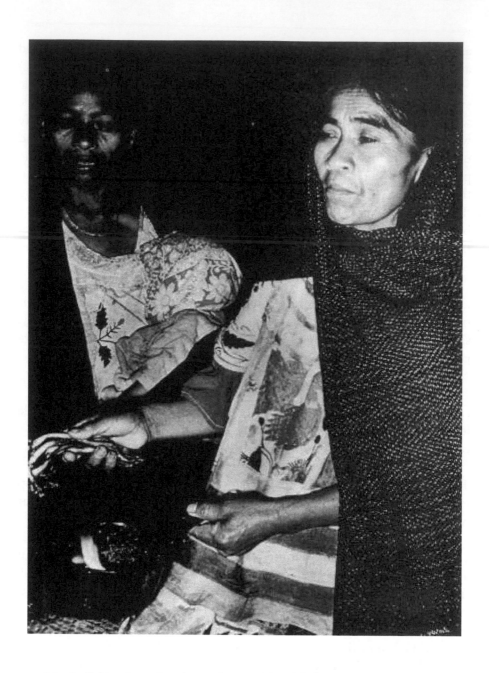

Maria Sabina incensing the mushroom, 12- 13 July 1958, with Apolonia

afterwards I joined him.

Except for the children who had eaten no mushrooms, no one slept that night until about 4 o'clock in the morning. (The last entry in my notebook carries the hour 3:50.) There was no inclination to sleep. At all times we were alert both to our subjective experiences and to the goings-on around us in the dark. I took imperfect notes intermittently and kept track of the hours. But Allan and I were both alive to the fact that we were not ourselves. I was of two minds about the mushrooms, on the one hand I wished to experience them to the full, to know what the Indians were experiencing, and on the other hand I wished to fight off any effects and remain the detached observer. But the mushrooms gave me no choice. They took full and sweeping possession of me. There is no better way to describe the sensation than to say that it was as though my very soul had been scooped out of my body and translated to a point floating in space, leaving behind the husk of clay, my body. Our bodies l ay there while our souls soared. We both felt nauseated; twice I made my way to the other room to vomit, Allan three times. One or two others, not identified in the darkness, did likewise. (I remember how disappointed I was at throwing up: I feared I would not feel the full effect!) But these episodes seemed of no moment. For we were both seeing visions, similar but not identical visions, and we were comparing notes in whispered interchanges. At first, we saw geometric patterns, angular not circular, in richest colors, such as might adorn textiles or carpets. Then the patterns grew into architectural structures, with colonnades and architraves, patios of regal splendor, the stone work all in brilliant colors, gold and onyx and ebony, all most harmoniously and ingeniously contrived, in richest magnificence extending beyond the reach of sight. For some reason these architectural visions seemed oriental, though at every stage I pointed out to myself that they could not be identified with any specific oriental country. They were neither Japanese nor Chinese nor Indian nor Moslem. They seemed to belong rather to the imaginary architecture described by the visionaries of the Bible. In the aesthetics of this discovered world Attic simplicity had no place: everything was resplendently rich.

At one point in the faint moonlight the bouquet on the table assumed the dimensions and shape of an imperial conveyance, a triumphal car, drawn by zoological creatures conceivable only in an imaginary mythology, bearing a woman clothed in regal splendor. With our eyes wide open, the visions came in endless succession, each growing out of the preceding one. We had the sensation that the walls of our humble house had vanished, that our untrammeled souls were floating in the empyrean, stroked by divine breezes, possessed of a divine mobility that

31

would transport us anywhere on the wings of a thought. Now it was clear why *don Aurelio* in 1953 and others too had told us that the mushrooms *le llevan ahi donde Dias estd* - would take you there where God is. Only when by an act of conscious effort, I touched the wall of Cayetano's house would I be brought back to the confines of the room where we all were, and this touch with reality seemed to be what precipitated nausea in me.

On that night of 29-30 June, we saw no human beings in our visions. (The woman in regal attire was certainly not human.) On the night of 2-3 July, I again took mushrooms in the same room, with the Senora again serving as votary. If we may anticipate our story, on that second occasion my visions were different. There were no geometrical patterns, no edifices of oriental splendor. The patterns were replaced by artistic motifs of the Elizabethan and Jacobean periods in England - armor worn for fashionable display, family escutcheons, the carvings of choir stalls and cathedral chairs. No patina of age hung on them. They were all fresh from God's workshop, pristine in their finish. The beholder could only sigh after the skill that might have fixed those beauteous shapes on paper or in metal or wood, that they might not be lost in a vision. They too grew one out of the other, the new one emerging from the center of its predecessor. Here as in the first night the visions seemed freighted with significance. They seemed the very archetypes of beautiful form and color. We felt ourselves in the presence of the Ideas that Plato had talked about. In saying this let not the reader think that we are indulging in rhetoric, straining to command his attention by an extravagant figure of speech. For the world our visions were and must remain 'hallucinations ' . But for us at that moment they were not false or shadowy suggestions of real things, figments of an unhinged imagination. What we were seeing was, we knew, the only reality, of which the counterparts of every day are mere imperfect adumbrations. At the time we ourselves were alive to the novelty of this our discovery, and astonished by it. by it. Whatever their provenience, the blunt and startling fact is that our visions were sensed more clearly, were superior in all their attributes, were more authoritative, for us who were experiencing them, than what passes for mundane reality.

Following the visions that we have already described, on both occasions I saw landscapes. On Wednesday they were of a vast desert seen from afar, with lofty mountains beyond, terrace above terrace. Camel caravans were making their way across the mountain slopes. On Saturday the landscapes were of the estuaries of immense rivers brimming over with pellucid water, broad sheets of water overflowing into the reeds that stretched equally far from the shore line. Here the colors were in pastel shades. The light was good but soft as from a horizontal sun. On both nights the landscapes responded to the command of the beholder: when a detail interested him, the landscape approached with the speed of light and the detail was made manifest. When I was seeing the camel caravans in the distance, an impulse seized me: right away I was upon them, listening to the sounds of their heavy breathing, to the camel bells, to their lurching with their loads, smelling their stench. On Saturday there seemed to be no birds and no human life in the river estuary, until a rude cabin suddenly appeared with a motionless woman nearby, seated on a block of stone. She was a woman by her figure and face and costume, and of course the vision was in color. I could see her breathing. But she was a statue in that she sat there without expression, doing nothing, staring into the distance. She might be compared to those archaic Greek sculptures where the woman gazes into space, or, better yet, the departing woman on the Greek funerary stele who looks into eternity, except that our vision was of a living woman whereas the Greek sculptures, marble white, are mere imitations in stone of what we were seeing. Elsewhere I once wrote that the bemushroomed person is poised in space, a disembodied eye, invisible, incorporeal, seeing not seen. In truth he is the five senses disembodied, all of them keyed to the height of sensitivity and awareness, all of them blending into one another most strangely, until the person, utterly passive, becomes a pure receptor, infinitely delicate, of sensations. What you are seeing and what you are hearing appear as one: singing and percussive beat assume harmonious shapes, giving visual form to their harmonies, and what you are seeing takes on the modalities of music - the music of the spheres. Likewise, with your sense of touch, of taste, of odor: all your senses seem to function as one. My olfactory sense has always been weak, but now for the first time I entered into the world of odors, delicate iridescent harmonies in which other creatures spend their lives.

On both nights I stood up for a long time in Cayetano's room, at the foot of the stairway, holding on to the rail, transfixed in ecstasy by the visions that I was seeing in the darkness with open eyes. For the first time that word 'ecstasy' took on subjective meaning for me. 'Ecstasy' was not someone else's state of mind.

It was no longer a trite superlative cheapened by overuse and abuse. It signified something different and superior in kind, about which I could now testify as a competent witness. There came one moment on Saturday when it seemed as though the visions themselves were about to be transcended, and dark gates reaching upward beyond sight were about to part, and I was to find myself in the presence of the Ultimate. I seemed to be flying toward those august gates as a swallow at a dazzling lighthouse, and the gates were to part and admit me. But they did not open, and with a thud I fell back breathless and gasping. I felt disappointed, but also frightened and half relieved, that I had not entered into the presence of the Ineffable, whence, it seemed to me at the time, I might not have returned, for I had sensed that a willing extinction in the divine radiance had been awaiting me.

(Later in the Zapotec country, the shaman Aristeo Matias told us in a stirring parable the four stages that one must go through from the initial surprise and mental disorder until one finally arrives at the mastery of the mushroom. Here was fatherly advice from an old hand to us who had told him that we aspired to enter upon his vocation. He was telling us that there is or at least can be a growth, an evolution, in the entheogenic experiences induced by the mushrooms. After many experiences with the mushrooms I do not doubt what don Aristeo said. At first the beginner is confused and lost in wonder, but with repeated experience he comes to deal with the mushrooms on equal terms. His initial disorientation contrasts sharply with the discipline that the shaman shows, who has taken an immense dose and whose performance is timed to a nicety, even syncopated.)

Throughout that night in June we were split in the very core of our being. On one level, space was annihilated for us and we were traveling as fast as thought to our visionary worlds. On another level we were lying there on our *petates,* trying to take notes, Allan and I exchanging whispered comments, alive to every twitch and twinge in our heavy (oh so heavy!) earth-bound bodies of clay. At the same time, we were both held in thrall by what was going on in the room around us. For the Senora and her daughter were engaged all night in a religious performance that we had not expected and that no one had ever described to us. After the Senora had put out the last vela, a silence of perhaps twenty minutes followed. The moon was shining brightly outside, and its orbit was such that the shaft of moonlight entering above the door fell squarely on the altar table, but it did little to relieve the general darkness in the room. Suddenly the Senora began to moan, low at first, then louder. There were silent pauses, and then renewed humming. Then the humming stopped and she began to articulate isolated syllables, each syllable consisting of a consonant followed by a vowel, sharply pronounced. The syllables came snapping out in rapid succession, cutting the darkness like a knife, spoken, not sung. After a time, the syllables coalesced into what we took for words, and the Senora began to chant. The chanting continued intermittently all night, first by the Senora and then by her daughter, and afterwards alternately by one or the other. The chanting was in Mazatec, only occasionally in

Maria Sabina invoking the Sacred Mushrooms

Latin or Spanish learned by rote, and there was no one to translate the words for us. I have since learned that most of the music was native in provenience. Both women chanted in that distinctive way which seems always to mark the intoning of age-old chants; much of the singing seemed to me soaked in weary melancholy. Our Senora's voice was not loud, probably not loud enough to be heard in the village thoroughfare. But there was a confidence and resonance in her utterance that imposed itself. There came a moment late in the night when the Senora made her way to the door on the terrace and went outside, holding her hand on the door. (She was free of the prohibition l aid on the rest of us not to leave the house.) When she re-entered, she left the door slightly ajar, and we saw her advance on her knees across the open space in the room, and then turn to the right toward the altar table. Her hands were uplifted to shoulder level, palms exposed. As she slowly progressed, she sang a canticle that seemed like an introit, indescribably tender and plaintive in its musical phrases. Her daughter sang well too, but lacked her authority. From time to time, as they sang, the men who had taken the mushrooms, notably Genaro and young Emilio, ejaculated words, groans, short sentences, and vocal noises. We know not what they said, but they seemed to intervene with their voices to suit the singing, in such a way as to produce a strange harmony.

The singing was not continuous. For stretches the Senora would talk, as though invoking the Spirits or as though the Holy Ghost was speaking through the mushrooms. We heard the names of Christ (which she pronounced with an intrusive 'r', Khristros), of St Peter and St Paul. We heard her cry out 'Pedro' repeatedly in an imploring tone, and knew that the mushrooms were wrestling with the problem of Peter. Emilio made his way to us and whispered that Peter was alive and well, and contrite for not having let us hear from him. We asked for further details, but Emilio said that since we ourselves had eaten the mushrooms, we could expect them to speak to us directly. Our interpreter Emilio then vanished into the darkness for the rest of the night.

Unlike the chants, the spoken utterances were fresh a n d vibrant and rich in expressiveness. The mushrooms were talking to the point. We had never suspected how sensitive and poetic an instrument the Mazatec language could be. The intermittent snatches of the Senora's monologue seemed quick with subtle feeling, laden with dramatic import. In our very presence a priestess of the old religion was pronouncing oracular dictates in spurts, hot and firm with authority. How we regretted that we had no means to record her voice! (At the time we asked ourselves whether our critical faculties were deranged by the effects of the mushrooms, so that we overrated the quality of the Senora's performance. Later when we taped the singing, we found this was certainly so. But here is an aberration typical of the syndrome of mushroomic ecstasy, and our account at least serves to document it for the record, and to establish that our hallucinations were of all the senses, not merely visual.)

The chanting and the oracular utterances turned out to be only a part of what we were to witness. At an early stage we sensed that the Senora was either kneeling or standing before the altar table gesticulating with her arms. We detected this by ear and confirmed it uncertainly with the aid of the meagre moonlight. Then, much later in the night when her daughter took over the chanting, the Senora made her way to the open space between us and the door, and she embarked on a kind of dance that must have lasted for two hours or more. This is the only occasion when I have seen her dancing: in retrospect, clearly, she was putting on for us a very special performance. We do not know precisely what she did, because of the darkness, bur she was between us and the aperture above the door, and we could just make our that she was turning clock-wise, facing in succession each of the four compass points, at the same time raising and lowering her arms. Her daughter was singing, bur she was not silent. She was engaged in a lengthy rhythmic percussive utterance of a kind unfamiliar to us. There was a differentiation in the pitch of the beats and at times the pattern or phrases seemed to us complex. We cannot say for sure how she made her sounds, but we surmised that she clapped her hands, slapped her knees, smacked her forehead, and whammed her chest. We were impressed by the cleanness of the utterance.

1.*We published a partial recording of a velada held in 1956, Folkways Record and Service Corporation FR 8975. The translation and commentary were done by Eunice V. Pike and Sarah C. Gudschinsky. This was followed by a full-dress edition of a complete velada that took place in 1958: Maria Sabina and her Mazatec Mushroom Velada, Harcourt Brace Jovanovich, Inc., New York, 1974. George and Florence Cowan served as our linguists, Willard Rhodes as our ethnomusicologist. The translation of the 1956 velada was done afresh, into Spanish, by Alvaro Estrada with the cooperation of Marfa Sabina and certain senior Huautecos, and published in 1977 in La Vida de Maria Sabina, pp 133-160.*

Every clap or slap or smack or wham was resonant. The percussive effect varied sharply in timing and in volume, and was frequently syncopated. Remembering the role played by pitch in the Mazatec language, we asked ourselves whether the Senora was speaking percussively. On each of our two nights with her, she rinsed her mouth once with water, and the gargling was also rhythmic, and perhaps tonally differentiated. Then she would spit out the water on the ground unrhythmically. On Saturday night, in a moment of illumination by flashlight, we saw and heard her twicking her long finger nails rhythmically.

Maria Sabina invoking the Sacred Mushroom (Aurelio in background)

A remarkable feature of her percussive utterance on Wednesday night was its ventriloquistic property. For a long stretch we were in the blackest darkness while the daughter sang and the Senora was performing her strange dance with percussive accompaniment. As she would snap out her resonant claps and smacks, we seemed to catch them out of the night from various directions. Let the reader remember that all the while we were seeing our visions and attending to the auditory sensations served to us by these two women. There we were, visually suspended in space before the vast panorama of, say, the Gobi Desert, with a singing accompaniment and with percussive cracks assailing us, now from above, now here, now there, exactly like Hamlet's ghost *hic et ubique*, hitting us with a cutting crispness from unpredictable quarters, from underneath us in a whisper, beyond our feet on the petate, out of the night, as though an air borne choir of invisible creatures was peopling the dark void around us, perplexing us with their assorted and shifting cries. Possibly this ventriloquistic effect was caused by the Senora's turning in different directions as she performed, so that the sound caromed to us from the ceiling or walls.' And all the while there was the irregular chorus, subdued in volume, of ecstatic exclamations from the Indians reclining on the ground. Confined though we were in a room without windows or open door, at one point we felt a swish of air, just as though we were really suspended in the great outdoors. Was this too an hallucination? If so, all shared it, for when the wind blew on us, there was general excitement, flashlights were switched on, and our Indian friends were sitting up, amazed at being stroked by the Divine Afflatus.

Suddenly in the night I made a discovery. In the light of a cigarette that someone was inhaling, I saw the Senora, who was performing her dance, lift a small bottle to her lips. From her posture the bottle seemed almost empty. A few minutes later she began to thump the butt end of the bottle on the petate. She did this with a fast, uniform, perfect beat, perhaps a hundred to the minute, and she kept at it for an eternity, minutes on end, until Allan and I could hardly stand it and groaned in agony. The iterated thump, somewhat resonant, became excruciatingly painful, a torture such as Poe might have described. After the night had passed and we were all getting up, I made it a point to find the bottle and smell it. There could be no doubt: it was the familiar six-ounce bottle of *aguardiente,* a distillate of cane. Presumably the *Senora* had shared it with her daughter, but of this we cannot be sure. We asked Cayetano about it. Yes, invariably the person who retains the *Senora* is expected to present her in advance with a *cuarto* (fourth of a liter) of this strong drink. We in our ignorance had neglected our duty, but Cayetano had come to our rescue. Recalling as we did how Aurelio and also our friends in the Mixe country had all said that alcohol was tabu before, during, and after the consumption of the mushrooms, we are still at a loss how to reconcile the conflicting evidence. But of course, the *Senora's* performance from first to last had differed from what Aurelio had shown us in 1953. We had now attended two all-night vigils, both using the sacred mushrooms, but otherwise utterly different from each other. Aurelio's divinatory liturgy, with the elaborate role in it of accessories, could conceivably go on without mushrooms, but in Cayetano's house the mushrooms were everything. We spoke to Cayetano about that other performance that we had seen in the Mazatec country in 1953. He knew all about that kind too, and he told us that the Senora was equally proficient in both ceremonies. We failed to learn, however, when one method is used in preference to the other.

At intervals throughout the night, perhaps every forty minutes or so, there would be what we can only describe as intermissions. After working up to a powerful climax in utterance, the Senora and her daughter would subside into silence. (We recall one such climax when the Senora, half singing, half declaiming, spat forth in endless repetition and with wild violence the syllable *chjon*. Afterwards we learned that this chjon meant ' Woman', and she was listing her own credentials as a shaman in addressing her supplications to the mushroom.) During such intermissions our two votaries and our reclining Indian friends would light cigarettes (ordinary ones) and smoke and engage in the most animated conversation. Clearly, they were discussing what was happening but we had no interpreter. They would flash on electric torches. We took advantage of these moments to study the Senora. She was not in a trance. That is to say, she was one of us, talking and smoking. But she was in a state of excitement, her eyes flashing, her smile no longer that grave smile which we had observed before, but now quick with animation and, if we may use the word, caritas. For there is another major aspect to the mushrooms that we must mention. The spirit of an agape of which we have already spoken was a prelude to an upsurge of generous or tender feelings that the mushrooms aroused in everyone. To illustrate this, we recall how, when nausea first sent me into the adjoining room to vomit, the *Senora*, who had been in full song, immediately stopped the performance, and she and the others manifested the most embarrassing (for me) solicitude about the unhappy episode, which after all was trivial. On the two nights that we passed in Cayetano's house, we were aware of no erotic stimulation among those present. But those who were present felt that we had entered into a warm bond together, by reason of the momentous night that we had spent in each other's company, and this bond I still feel. Twice in the course of that first night the Senora reached out her right hand to me and sought contact with my fingers in friendly greeting, across the chasm of the language and culture barrier. The Indians of Mesoamerica are known for their reticence in the display of affection, even within the family circle. It was now clear that the mushrooms emancipate them from inhibitions of this kind, and what we witnessed on Wednesday night was abundantly confirmed during our second session on Saturday, 2 July.

After the first performance Allan and I, quite stunned and even numbed by what we had witnessed, were disposed to say, 'Never again '. But by Saturday morning there were many questions that we needed to clarify, and so through Cayetano we asked the *Senora* if she would give us a repetition. This she agreed to do. We pled with her to let us take a few photographs by strobe flash while the power was on her. She said yes, and in the course of that night from Saturday to Sunday, Allan took perhaps

41

twenty pictures in the darkness, guessing of necessity as to the distance and direction. (It was raining in torrents all that night, so there was no moon.) But the *Senora's* behavior differed much from what we had seen the first time. Everything was reduced in scale. There was no dancing and virtually no percussive utterances. Only three or four other Indians were with us, and the *Senora* brought with her, not her daughter, but her son Aurelio, a youth in his late teens who seemed to us in some way ill or defective. He was now the object of her attention, not I. All night long her singing and her words were directed to this poor boy. Her performance was the dramatic expression of a mother's love for her child, an anguished threnody to mother love, and interpreted in this way it was profoundly moving. The tenderness in her voice as she sang and spoke, and in her gestures as she leaned over Aurelio to caress him, moved us profoundly. As strangers we should have been embarrassed, had we not seen in this shaman possessed by the mushrooms a symbol of eternal motherhood, rather than the cry of an individual parent. But by any interpretation this untrammeled and beautiful outpouring, incited by the sacred mushrooms, was behavior of a kind that few Middle American anthropologists would ever see.

On this second occasion Allan ingested no mushrooms, for the sake of his photography. The *Senora* asked me how many pair I would take, which I interpreted as a compliment to my status as one already initiated, and I said five pair. The effect seemed as strong as I had experienced from the larger dose on Wednesday, but this time there was no nausea.

Our two nights with the *Senora* drew to a close in the same way. On the night of Wednesday-Thursday, our last notes seem to have been scribbled a few minutes before 4 a m, and soon afterwards we slipped off imperceptibly into a dreamless slumber. Apparently, everyone else did likewise. At any rate, at about 6 o'clock we woke up, our heads clear. Some of the others were already stirring, and in a few minutes, everyone was on his feet. I changed the roll in my camera and resumed with my fingers i n friendly greeting, across the chasm of the language and culture barrier. The Indians of Mesoamerica are known for their reticence in the display of affection, even within the family circle. It was now clear that the mushrooms emancipate them from inhibitions of this kind, and what we witnessed on Wednesday night was abundantly confirmed during our second session on Saturday, 2 July.

After the first performance Allan and I, quite stunned and even numbed by what we had witnessed, were disposed to say, 'Never again '. But by Saturday morning there were many questions that we needed to clarify, and so through Cayetano we asked the *Senora* if she would give us a repetition. This she agreed to do. We pled with her to let us take a few photographs by strobe flash while the power was on her. She said yes, and in the course of that night from Saturday to Sunday Allan took perhaps twenty pictures in the darkness, guessing of necessity as to the distance and direction. (It was raining in torrents all that night, so there was no moon.) But the *Senora's* behavior differed much from what we had seen the first time. Everything was reduced in scale. There was no dancing and virtually no percussive utterances. Only three or four other Indians were with us, and the Senora brought with her, not her daughter, but her son Aurelio, a youth in his late teens who seemed to us in some way ill or defective. He was now the object of her attention, not I. All night long her singing and her words were directed to this poor boy. Her performance was the dramatic expression of a mother's love for her child, an anguished threnody to mother love, and interpreted in this way it was profoundly moving. The tenderness in her voice as she sang and spoke, and in her gestures as she leaned over Aurelio to caress him, moved us profoundly. As strangers we should have been embarrassed, had we not seen in this shaman possessed by the mushrooms a symbol of eternal motherhood, rather than the cry of an individual parent. But by any interpretation this untrammeled and beautiful outpouring, incited by the sacred mushrooms, was behavior of a kind that few Middle American anthropologists would ever see. On this second occasion Allan ingested no mushrooms, for the sake of his photography. The Senora asked me how many pair I would take, which I interpreted as a compliment to my status as one already initiated, and I said five pair. The effect seemed as strong as I had experienced from the larger dose on Wednesday, but this time there was no nausea.

Our two nights with the *Senora* drew to a close in the same way. On the night of Wednesday-Thursday, our last notes seem to have been scribbled a few minutes before 4 a m, and soon afterwards we slipped off imperceptibly into a dreamless slumber. Apparently, everyone else did likewise. At any rate, at about 6 o'clock we woke up, our heads clear. Some of the others were already stirring, and in a few minutes, everyone was on his feet. I changed the roll in my camera and resumed picture-taking, as did Allan. Cayetano and Guadalupe asked after our welfare but were discreet in their inquiries about the night's doings. They served us coffee and bread. By 7 o'clock we were ready to sally forth into the world. We felt no untoward sleepiness that day.

Perhaps in some respects we can define better than we have done the psychic disturbance -caused by the sacred mushrooms. On the one hand, they unhinge one's sense of time. Visions that seem to last an <£on run their course in a minute or so. Only by reference to a time-piece does one keep track of the passing hours. On the other hand, the faculty of memory is heightened by the mushrooms. All the impressions, visual and auditory, are graved as with a burin in the tablet of my memory. My narrative of what took pl ace has been checked with the notes that I jotted down at the time, but my memory is far richer and fuller than those notes.

What can we say about the source of the visions? Did they bubble up out of my own past? I have no conscious memory of having viewed' previously the scenes that I saw. There was nothing in them that repeated themes familiar to me in my adult experience, no modern highways, cars, cities, no faces of friends or acquaintances. Yet all that I saw could be related to themes latent in my imagination, not necessarily things seen, nor even things seen in graphic representation, but those things transmuted afterwards in the imagination, imagined from reading, seen in the mind's eye. ' All of the visions had that pristine quality which we associate most often with the magic of supreme literary expression, especially great poetry.

In the lives of us all, even those who are most earthbound, there are moments when the world stops, when the most humdrum things suddenly and unaccountably clothe themselves with beauty, haunting and ravishing beauty. It now seems to me that such flashes must emerge from the subconscious well where our visions have all this time been stored, for the mushroomic visions are an endless sequence of those flashes. There are those like Blake who have possessed the power to see such visions in abundance without the mushroomic stimulus. Could the mushrooms have done better by Blake than he did without them? What would they have shown him that he did not see? What precisely do our Indian friends see, with their different background? Clearly the visions come from within the beholder, either from his own subconscious or, as some will surely think, from an inherited fund of memories of the race. What an amazing thing that we should all be carrying this inventory of wonders around with us, ready to be tripped into our conscious world by mushrooms! Are the Indians far wrong in calling these divine?

1. *This interpretation was confirmed later by the highly significant testimony of a Mixe Indian in the Mixe country: when we asked him what he saw after taking the mushrooms, he replied that he saw Zempoaltepetl (the sacred mountain of the Mixe) open up, and on entering it he there saw paved streets lined with great houses and cars were plying back and forth on the streets. This Indian had never left the mountains where he lived, far away from highways and towns, but he had heard tell of these modern marvels.*

We suspect that, in its fullest sense, the creative faculty, whether in the humanities or science or industry, that most precious of man's distinctive possessions and the one most clearly partaking of the divine, is linked in some way with the area of the mind that the mushrooms unlock.

I have mentioned William Blake. Many years after the events here narrated I came upon a quotation from Blake that is directly relevant to this discussion:

The Prophets describe what they saw in Vision as real and existing men, whom they saw with their imaginative and immortal organs; the Apostles the same; the clearer the organ the more distinct the object. A Spirit and a Vision are not, as the modern philosophy supposes, a cloudy vapor, or a nothing: they are organized and minutely articulated beyond all that the mortal and perishing nature can produce. *He who does not imagine in stronger and better lineaments, and in stronger and better light than his perishing eye can see, does not imagine at all.*

[Italics mine. From the Writings of William Blake, edited by Geoffrey Keynes, vol 3, p 108]

This must sound cryptic to one who does not share Blake's vision or who has not taken the mushroom. The advantage of the mushroom is that it puts many, if not everyone, within reach of this state without having to suffer the mortifications of Blake. It permits you to see, more clearly than our perishing mortal eye can see, vistas beyond the horizons of this life, to travel backwards and forwards in time, to enter other planes of existence, even, as the Indians say, to go there where God is.

I will anticipate my story by telling here of an episode that took place in 1956, when Professor Roger Heim on my invitation had joined us. The velada in this case took place in a neighboring house. The effect of the mushrooms was at their peak. The *Senora* was singing with magisterial authority and we were all lying awake, keyed up (so it seemed to us) to the highest possible point of ecstasy. Suddenly, I do not know why, someone on one side on the room felt called upon to light a match. There was not the slightest interruption in the *Senora's* performance: she continued singing, clapping, gesticulating as though there was no light. But on the whitewashed wall beyond there appeared her shadow-profile, magnified perhaps by four, her triangular shape angled precisely like a Mexican pyramid, the temple on the top being the projection of her head, her gesticulations keeping slow, measured time with her singing. In the brief light of that match I was living through centuries, millennia, even decades of millennia. Maria Sabina was *The Shaman*, the focus for the woes and longings of mankind back, back through the Stone Age to Siberia. She

45

was Religion Incarnate. She was the hierophant, the thaumaturge, the psychopompos, in whom the troubles and aspirations of countless generations of the family of mankind had found, were still finding, their relief. All this I saw in the light of that one match, in the shadow performance of Maria Sabina. The light of that match seemed to last an aeon of time, and then, suddenly, it was out.

The mushrooms are not habit forming. They differ in this respect, not only from alcohol and tobacco, but from the drugs such as opium that are narcotics stimulating beatific dreams. In the course of our many expeditions to Mexico covering seven cultural areas, we have never heard of a mushroom addict. We believe that use of the mushrooms does not affect the threshold of tolerance for them; that is to say, one does not raise the dose on successive occasions to obtain the same effect, either for the short run as when we used them twice in four days, or over the long term. Our Senora and her daughter took more than twice the dose of the others, but that quota goes with their vocation. Everyone's dose seems to remain constant throughout life, though the dose varies somewhat from person to person. We have seen no evidence that the mushrooms can cause harmful psychic effects. Are persons with neurotic or psychotic inclinations endangered by the mushrooms? After a lifetime of use do mushroom-eating shamans show mental deterioration? May there be individuals whose mushroomic visions are horrifying and who are stimulated to violence by them? We do not know, but think not. The reports to the contrary in the writings of the early friars were prompted by their odium theologicum, by their own ignorance, and by their need to divert the faithful from the 'devil's food'. In considering the clinical effects of the mushrooms, let us not overlook the extraordinary performance of the *Senora* and her daughter. They had each eaten thirteen pair of mushrooms, as compared with five or six pair for the rest of us, and they not only kept hold of themselves: they staged a liturgy that called for disciplined virtuosity of a high order. In the mushroom season they may be called upon to perform every night.

On Friday, 1 July, Valentina Pavlovna and our thirteen-year-old daughter Masha joined us in our village. We had all planned to leave on horseback immediately after the Saturday night experience at break-of-day on Sunday, but the rains came and we found ourselves marooned among our Mazatec friends for most of the following week. On Tuesday the 5th VPW and Masha, having nothing else to do, took the mushrooms in the afternoon, VPW five pair and Masha four, and then they lay down in their sleeping bags, the doors and windows of the room closed. This was the first occasion on which white people were eating the mushrooms experimentally, without the setting of a native ceremony. They too saw visions, for hours on end, all pleasant, mostly of a nostalgic kind. VPW at one point thought she was looking down into the mouth of a vase, and there she saw and heard a stately dance, a minuet, as though in a regal court of the seventeenth century. The dancers were in miniature and the music was oh! so remote, but. also, so clearly heard. VPW smoked a cigarette: she exclaimed that never before had a cigarette smelled so good. It was beyond earthly experience. She drank water, and it was superior to Mumm's champagne - incomparably superior. S h e and Masha felt little or no nausea. Their pupils dilated and failed to respond to our flashlights. The pulse showed a tendency to slow down. But six weeks later, when I in New York took the mushrooms for the third time on 12 August, my visions were accompanied by an insistent beat with variation of pitch, perhaps an evocation of the Senora's percussive performance. The beat was not unpleasant. It seemed freighted with meaning, as though it was the rhythmic pulse of the universe. When the Senora had performed for us, we had passed most of the night in virtual darkness - an environment adapted to dilated eyes. My experience in New York took place in a room illuminated by lights from the street, and moreover on that night of the 12th, a hurricane known at the time as Connie was brushing by the city. I found that the mushrooms retained their full potency in a dried state if indeed their power had not increased. I made another discovery. As I stood at the window and watched the gale tossing the trees and the water of the East River, with the rain driven in squalls before the wind, the whole scene was further quickened to life by the abnormal intensity of the colors that I saw. I had always thought that El Greco's apocalyptic skies over Toledo were a figment of the painter's imagination. But on this night, I saw El Greco's skies, nothing dimmed, whirling over New York.

Now we come to the end of our initial Mazatec experience. We had agreed from the beginning to pay the Senora her usual fee for her services. We p aid her fifty pesos for each night, which was somewhat more than she expected. In dollars this meant $4.00 a night, but in her world the fee meant much more, perhaps subjectively as much as $50.00 in New York. Before we left his house, we asked Cayetano what we could pay him for his contribution to the success of our visit. He turned to his wife and let her speak. *'No hicimos esto por dinero'*, she said, which is to say, ' We did not do this for money', and they would accept none. (For those who know the Mazatec need and appetite for money this remark of Guadalupe's will indeed, be amazing.) We were especially grateful to the *Senora* for having allowed us to take photographs by strobe flash while the power of the mushrooms was on her, during that second night. It had not been easy for her to consent to the rude, and for her, novel interruption of the flashlight. On the morning after, a messenger came to us from her. We were welcome to the pictures, she said, but would we please refrain from showing those particular ones to any except our most trusted friends, for if we showed them to all and sundry, *seria una traicion*, it would be a betrayal.

CHAPTER 2

THE TRAITS OF THE MESOAMERICAN VELADA AND KINDRED TOPICS

In the preceding chapter I have given a largely subjective account of veladas that I have attended. There are at least two manners of night-time divination with hallucinogens in Mesoamerica. In one the shaman casts corn kernels and by the way they fall on the cloth spread before him he learns the answers to the questions put to him. He smokes a strong cigar and to reinforce his divinatory strength he may consume mushrooms or other hallucinogens. His answers come forth after long periods of silence and as he concentrates on the questions he sweats profusely. Valentina Pavlovna and I attended this style of velada in Huautla on the night of Saturday, 15 July 1953, the shaman being Aurelio Carreras Robert Weitlaner was with us, and our account of it in Mushrooms Russia & History, pp 255 ff, was made up from his notes and drawings.

The other manner of velada is sung by the shaman as we have described it in the preceding chapter. The shaman ingests the mushrooms and decides who among those present will take the mushrooms and how many pair cach. There are a number of prescriptions, proscriptions, and attributes of the velada that I will list and discuss here.

ALLOCATION OF MUSHROOMS

Maria Sabina and her daughter Maria Apolonia each take thirteen pair of the *derrumbe* mushrooms (Psilocybe caerulescens Murrill var mazatecorum Heim), thirteen being a favorable number in Mesoamerica. As for her allocations to the other participants, this is based, as a rule of thumb, on their weight and their resistance to alcohol. Naturally the allocation depends on the species of mushroom. The 'landslide' (derrumbe) mushroom is large. The 'nti'xi'tho' 'nti'ni'se' (pajaritos, 'dear little birdies') are tiny and the dosage correspondingly bigger, perhaps twenty pair for an adult suppliant of normal weight.

'EATING' OR 'DRINKING' THE MUSHROOMS

I n every *velada* that I have attended except one _the mushrooms have been eaten fresh and with only the grossest dirt brushed off. They are always ingested raw. On 5-6 July 1960 in Juxtlahuaca, in the Mixteca, the *curandera* (aunt of our host Guadalupe Gonzalez) had had the little girl Juventina, youngest daughter of the house, clearly a *doncella* ('maiden'), grind the mushrooms on a *metate* (grinding stone) and catch the juice with the mushroom pulp i n glasses. My companion Robert Ravicz and I drank the potion. We were told that in former times it was the custom for the *doncella* to gather the mushrooms before sunrise, when the pre-dawn breezes swept the mountain sides and dew lay heavy on the slopes. This practice seems to have died out in *Juxtlahuaca*, but (who knows?) it may still survive in remote rancherias. We were told in *Tenango del Valle*, in 1957, that the mushrooms could be ground on a metate, or (perhaps if dried) pulverized by hand, or torn to little pieces, and then drunk in pulque or *aguardiente* ('fire water'). In *Tenango* the mushrooms are also rubbed on an injured place in the body. In *Amatlan de los Reyes*, far away in the State of *Veracruz* but also *Nahuatl country*, our story teller *Rufina de Jesus*, on the weekend of 4-6 June 1960, told us in *Nahuatl* a story involving the sacred mushrooms, which we taped and filed. Later the *Nahuatlato* (specialist in *Nahuatl*) *Luis Reyes*, a native of that town, transcribed and translated for us her narrative and we came upon the following interchange, speaking of the mushrooms:

'Y 'como, acaso los vas a moler' 'And perhaps you will grind them'.

'No, asi nada mas me comere 'No, I'll eat four dozen. But first I
Cuatro docenas. Pero ahora will go to mass. I'll carry them there.
Primero me voy a misa, los
Llevare.

I find also i n my files a memorandum dated 2 6 June 1962 written by one of our informants for the Chinantla, himself a Chinantec, in which he quotes a curandero in the Chinantla as saying that 'four or five mushrooms well ground are taken in water'. I do not know how common this practice was or is among the Chinantecs. Afterwards I came upon the pre-Conquest Nahuatl poem that starts off:

'I have drunk [sic] the inebriating liquor of mushrooms. '

In aristocratic circles of pre-Conquest times the mushrooms were often taken with the cold chocolate drink and mixed with maize and with flowers of Quararibea funebris called poyomatli but never with alcoholic beverages. The drinking of the crushed mushrooms seems to have been more common formerly; I am inclined to think it was the normal practice. This crushing on a metate supplies us with crucial evidence in favor of our obvious interpretation of the famous ' mushroom stones', as will be explained later.

PURPOSE OF THE VELADA

A Velada is held in response t o a request by someone who wishes to consult the mushrooms about a grave family worry. A husband may be lying sick or injured on a *petate* ('mat'): will he live or die? If he will live, what must he do to recover? What herbs must be rubbed on the injured spot, or should he eat them? What saints must be invoked? Or perhaps he must make a solemn *promesa* to g o on pilgrimage (always on foot) to a specific shrine, when he recovers.

Or again the donkey has disappeared. Did he fall into a ravine and break his leg? Or was he stolen and toward which market is he being hied for sale?

Or again money hidden in the thatch of the roof has disappeared. Who took it and where is he now?

Or again a son has gone out into the world, perhaps as a wetback to the States. Neither he nor anyone else in the family can write and naturally there is no news of him. His mother worries. Is he alive or dead? If alive, is he in jail? (This question is always asked.) Is he married? Has he children? Is he well or sick? The mushroom will tell. If the question is put with a pure heart by a believer, the mushroom will not lie: so, say the Indians. Only after I came to know the Indian country was it driven home to me how every Chicano falling foul of the l aw has a family somewhere in Mexico who cares for him and worries about him.

A *velada* must be held for a worthy reason. It will be of no help in frivolous matters or for selfish ends. Trippers who engage a shaman to hold a velada out of curiosity miss the point completely.

VELADA ESSENTIALS: 1. DARKNESS AND ISSOLATION

One invariable rule governing veladas is that they should take place at night, in the dark, in a house removed from other dwellings, where quiet will reign. Noise and light severely cripple, may render useless a velada. The house of the shaman is usually situated somewhat apart from the village, secluded from town folk, so that the mushrooms work free of untoward interruptions. Some natural noises are not regarded as interruptions: a dog baying at the moon, the braying of an ass in the pasture, even torrential rains and terrifying thunder and lightning are not objectionable interruptions: on the contrary, these forces of nature accentuate the spell of the *velada*.

VELADA ESSENTIALS: 2. THE MONITORS

At every *velada* there must be one or two persons who do not take the inebriant, whether mushroom or other, but who serve as monitors, listening to what is said, handling interruptions and intruders, seeing that no mischance overtakes anyone during the night hours in the dark. These monitors are an invariable post in the *velada* tradition. The doors are securely fastened at the outset of the velada and no one (except the shaman) may sally forth into the night or until the cock crows before dawn. (Once in *San Andres Hidalgo* there was an exception to this rule: the door was left wide open.)

VELADA ESSENTIALS: 3. PROHIBITIONS

Participating in a *velada* requires abstinence of certain kinds. From breakfast on you must fast until the night and until preparations for the *velada* are under way. Then you may drink chocolate, or nowadays coffee, a post-Conquest innovation. For four days before the velada you must abstain from alcohol of all kinds, from eggs, from sexual intercourse; and after the velada for four days more. (These four days seem to have been a basic pre-Conquest ritual pattern of Mesoamerica. I can think of no reason why eggs are banned.) A pregnant woman must never take the entheogen. If you are a novice, the shaman or your sponsor will inform you of these requirements. To drive home the various injunctions your sponsor will always have ready an admonitory tale to tell you, showing you the penalty paid once by a violator. But it is left to you whether you comply: no questions are asked. The practice reported to us from Tenango del Valle of mixing the entheogen with pulque or distilled alcohol is, so far as my experience goes, unique: it may be a legacy from the Matlatzinca (closely related to the Otomi) who once peopled this area.

The liturgy should never be sung facing the west; east is the preferred direction. Outsiders attending the rite should be as inconspicuous as possible, and silent. They should be outnumbered by natives familiar with what is going on.

THE SHAMANS VENTRILOQUISM

A strange feature of the successful *velada* (and one mentioned also in the Siberian accounts of their shamanic *vigils*) is the ventriloquistic effects. Lying there relaxed in the dark, the utterance of the shaman for long intervals being the only sound, you are surprised by the changes in the direction and volume of the rhythmic song and the percussive beats. They jump, not continually, but as it were in quantum leaps, now from beyond your feet, then from above your head, from outside the hut, even accompanying you on your flight through space, again from beneath your head, whispering in your ear so close that you feel the singer's breath on your lobes buried in the softness of your sleeping bag; or again it reaches you from the depths of the earth, faint from distance. I had never before noticed the difference in the quality of sounds of equal volume - a whisper in the ear and the same voice diminished by distance from the bowels of the earth: the two sounds seem worlds apart.

Gonzalo Aguirre Beltran in his invaluable *Medicina y Magia* has combed the manuscript sources in the *Archivo General d e la Nacion* for documentary evidence of practices in the seventeenth century revealed in the *Proceedings of the Inquisition* bearing directly on our subject. (His work is indispensable as a point of departure for anyone exploring this field.) Concerning the ventriloquism, he suggests that it was introduced by the post- Conquest Negro immigration from Africa. But he is mistaken. The hallucinogens contain within themselves the agent that, working in the inner ear, produces this startling effect. Here is the perfect example of the weakness of research done in the study to the exclusion of field experience. Had Aguirre Beltran attended veladas in the Indian country surrounding

Mexico City and had he ingested the entheogens, his observations on ventriloquism would have been utterly different:

In my first velada with Maria Sabina I had been puzzled by the ventriloquistic effects and had gradually come to tentative conclusions, but the darkness made it difficult to be certain. Later an opportunity presented itself. On Monday June 12, 1960 we found ourselves in *Huautla* when word reached us from Herminia Figueroa of *San Andres Hidalgo* that his neighbor the *curandero* Crescencio Martinez would serve us that very night. *Irmgard Weitlaner Johnson, Herlinda Martinez Cid,* and I forthwith set out walking, our sleeping bags and other impedimenta being carried by two young boys. Herminia was the nephew of Herlinda, and his grandfather, the Shaman Manuel Figueroa, had taught don Crescencio his art. We found Crescencio waiting for us in his house somewhat removed from the village. Of middle age, he spoke not a word of Spanish. We passed the night with him, he reciting (not chanting) prayers in a low, clear voice. The night was clear, the stars and Milky Way were brilliant. Whether there was a moon I do not remember. The light shone through the open door and one could make out the people and objects in the room. Here then was my opportunity. Irmgard and I, after ingesting the mushrooms and after they had taken effect, both observed a powerful ventriloquistic result. (They were ' *derrumbes*', my quota being six pair, Irmgard's four, and the Shaman's nine. Irmgard did not find the mushrooms disagreeable or nauseating.) I was in a relaxed trance, the voice, distinct and crisp, coming at me from different directions in succession, in different volume. I had only to open my eyes to see the Shaman on his little stool before the dead or dying fire. To shake off my trance, I would seize some wooden struts that lay to hand and reach for the wall: there was a touch of nausea and then I was in full possession of my faculties, my eyes open and all ventriloquism gone, and I would see and hear don Crescencio saying his *oraciones* in his natural voice. Again, I would let myself sink b ack into trance. The voice once again would flit from pl ace to place. I did this several times: don Crescencio was unaware of my surveillance.

Irmgard later told me what had happened to her: she had suddenly felt with a start that the singing was close by, the singer bending over her. She quickly and quietly turned, her eyes now wide open, only to discover that he was seated on his stool by the fire some seven feet away, paying no attention to her.

THE DESIGNATION OF THE SHAMAN

Mesoamerica is a complex of related and unrelated languages, but through them all the same metaphorical meanings seem to prevail. Thus 'shaman' in classical Nahuatl is '*tlamatini* ', in Mazatec '*cho'ta'chi'ne*', and in the Zapotec of the *Sierra Costera menjak*. All of them mean 'one-who knows'. These terms are broader than 'shaman': they include the herbalists and formerly the priests of the native religion. It would be important to learn how far this 'one-who-knows' extends, and whether it may not reach beyond Mesoamerica, possibly everywhere in the Americas of the Indian, perhaps in Siberia too. The Mazatec and Zapotec terms have another thing in common: they are not nouns like 'shaman'. They are verbal phrases and they conjugate and decline depending on the meaning to be conveyed. In Zapotec for example sanjak is 'that man knows' = 'that man is a shaman '. These terms of respect in the linguistic subcultures of Mesoamerica correspond to 'Wiseman' or 'Soothsayer' used long ago among our own remote cultural ancestors for the elite of their unlettered world. 'Witchdoctor' is a contemptuous name for the wiseman invented by the white man.

In Maria Sabina's mind those who follow her calling are sharply divided into three categories. She is a '*cho'ta'chi'ne*', 'one-who-knows', a *sabia* ('wisewoman') in Spanish, and belongs in the highest class. She says she cures by the mushroom alone, the mushroom serving for diagnosis and guidance in treatment. She has never used her power for evil In the second class is the 'healer', '*cho'ta' xi' v' e'nta*', which means 'one-who builds'; he is the *curandero*. He uses massage with *pisiete* (*Nicotiana rustica*), also, potions with incantations, invoking the spirits of well-known mountains, neighboring springs, and other holy places. The third class is the *tji'e'*, in Spanish *brujo, hechicero*, or *zahori*, in English the sorcerer or witch. In Maria Sabina's mentality this is a class of practitioners who use their magical powers only to work evil. Whether such a tripartite grouping is exclusively Maria Sabina's or whether it is held by Mazatec *sabios* generally, or whether it is even more widespread having until now escaped detection by anthropologists, we do not know. There must be elasticity in these categories. We know for example that in Mesoamerica there is a technique for curing by 'sucking out the evil: which is practiced by the second category. Some *curanderos* apply their lips directly to the spot on the body where they think the sickness or injury lies and suck audibly. Some interpose between their lips and the place on the body a *carrizo* or tube made of a reed, and then suck. Others suck audibly without moving from their position and Maria Sabina is one of these. This sucking is the act of a *chupador,* and from our own tape recordings we know that Maria Sabina is a *chupadora.* Many *chupadores* are prepared to show those in attendance the object(s), whether animate or inanimate, that they have sucked from the body. Belief in the *chupador* is old and widespread: it has been traced across much of Eurasia. Someone has asked whether this could have been the ancestor of 'cupping'.

Now we come to the individual names of shamans. There was a famous shaman in *Santa Maria Huitepec* in the *Mixeria,* whom the *Mixe* called *Pe:t Munt* in speaking with us. In Spanish this would be plain 'Peter World'. But in Mixe his cognomen was *Na:swin,* meaning ' World' or 'Universe' and for the *Mixe* carrying a potent mystical idea. It seems to me unlikely that he was given this name in babyhood. It must have been assumed when in his career he reached a point where his quality justified the new name, just as do the actors in Japan when they assume the name of a great predecessor on attaining his stature in the profession. In San Pedro Nexapa, we made the acquaintance of Marina Rosas, a Nahuatl shaman. In sixteenth century Spanish *rosa* was a synonym for 'flower' and thus 'Rosas' means 'flowers', translating *xochitl* in Nahuatl, a word weighted with all the magic of the entheogens, as will be demonstrated in the next chapter. In Mexico City I have met those who assert with assurance that 'Sabina' is borne by Maria Sabina because she is a *Sabia,* a 'Wisewoman', but this turns out to be impossible because Alvaro Estrada has found her baptismal record in the parish register of Huautla and there she is entered as having been baptized ' Maria Sabina' in infancy. Maria Sabina's maternal grandfather and great grandfather, and a granduncle and a grandaunt, were famous shamans, and the only possibility is that she (as well perhaps as Marina Rosas) was dedicated to her calling by her parents and then grew into the shaman that they were hoping for.

THE SACRED MUSHROOM: THE 'SMALL FRY' OR 'LITTLE TYKES'

Across linguistic lines throughout Mesoamerica the sacred mushrooms are called 'little children' by names that are always both affectionate and respectful. Marina Rosas of *San Pedro Nexapa,* a village in the direction of the *Paso de Cortes* and near the great volcanoes, in the heart of the classical Nahuatl country, spoke of the mushrooms as *a-pipil-tz.in,* the 'little children of the waters'. She is a sabia. In *Tlanixco,* a village near *Tenango del Valle,* in a *Nahuatl*-speaking district, the divine mushrooms known to the villagers are called *mujercitas* (= 'little women') or *señoritas* (= 'young ladies') or *niñas* (= 'little girls') when they use the Spanish words, and when speaking of the sacred mushrooms in general, they say *niños* (= 'children'). The sacred mushrooms are always paired off with *Cordyceps capitata* growing on another fungus, *Elaphomyces granulatus*, and this *Cordyceps* is the masculine element: it has no hallucinogenic potency whatever but is strikingly phallic in appearance. In *Nahuatl* the townsfolk of *Tlanixco* call these mushrooms *nanacatzintzintli*, a word that is pronounced hesitatingly and only in a whisper, and that simply means the 'dear and venerated little mushrooms'. In *Amatlan de los Reyes*, a village in *Veracruz* where *Nahuatl* is also spoken, the sacred mushrooms are spoken of by either of two names:

> *tlacatzitzen*, or = little men
> *chocotzitzen*   = little children

Maria Sabina in Mazatec sings of the *'nti'xtï'*, the *ninitos*, 'dear little children'; and also, of the *sa'se'*, the *payasos* or 'clowns', the *'nti' t'so'jmi'*, the *cositas* or 'little things'; also, of the 'little nuns', uttered with caressing love and reverence, little creatures (they tell us) the size of mushrooms and up to all sorts of tricks. The names for the mushrooms are all evasive. Maria Sabina never uses in her chanting the most holy name of all, *'nti'xitho'*, 'the dear little ones that spring up', and when in conversation she does so, she lowers her voice as though it were too holy to utter, although this is obviously an evasive term for a prior name now forgotten.

In the Zapotec country we learn from Thomas MacDougall that the entheogenic morning-glory seeds, ololiuhqui, are ground on the metate, the resulting flour then poured into water, the solid particles strained out, and the cold liquid drunk. A little girl, *una doncella*, serves the drink to the patient. The seeds number either seven or fourteen or twenty-one. A *curandero* or a friend is present to watch over the proceedings and note what is said. Solitude and silence are essential, and without them the *baduwin*, two little girls dressed in white, will not appear. The seeds of *Turbina corymbosa* (formerly *Rivea corymbosa*) are called *badoh*, and the alternative stronger seeds of *Ipomœa violacea*, ' either *badoh-negro* or by their full rendering in Zapotec, *badungás*. (We visited the Zapotec country early in our Mesoamerican peregrinations and did not know enough to ask about the tiny folk evoked by the entheogens but we did learn that the morning-glory seeds are called by the same name as the sacred mushrooms, *mbeydo'*.) The two little girls are evoked by the accepted entheogen, whether mushroomic or other. In the *Chinantla* Arthur J. Rubel reports that when the mushrooms take effect, children, boys and

57

girls, appear. In Rubel's *velada* only the shaman ate the mushrooms. Professor Rubel sent me samples of the mushrooms and Roger Heim's laboratory identified them as *Psilocybe Hoogshagenii.*

The *Matlatzinca,* once a numerous people living to the west of Mexico City, are now reduced to about 2,500 in a single village, *San Francisco Oxtotilpan.* They still speak their own language belonging to the *Otomi* linguistic stock. In Spanish the sacred mushrooms are called by them the 'little saints', *santitos.* To one who has eaten them the santitos appear as tiny beings the size of playing card kings. This we learn from the study of Roberto Escalante of the mushroom vocabulary in the language of the *Matlatzinca.* The old name in the *Matlatzincan* language is *netoc'hutata,* ne- being the plural, -to- a reverential diminutive, -chu- the root for sacred, and - tata being lord: 'the most holy little Lords'.

In the *Mixe* country Searle Hoogshagen reports that the sacred mushrooms, when consumed under the proper circumstances and in the right number (all as we have said), put one in a trance whereupon little men known as *los Senores* emerge and deal with the problems that concern you.

1.In Medicina y Magia Aguirre Beltran calls attention (p 136) to the use of the adjective moreno with ololiuhqui, 'black morning-glory seeds', and thinks that the seed grows black with age. But they do not change in color with time. When he worked on his excellent book we were just learning of Ipomrea violacea whose seeds are black and more powerful than those of Turbina corymbosa. Both are morning-glories.

THE MUSHROOM 'SPEAKS', NOT THE SHAMAN

A feature of the Mesoamerican *velada* is that the mushroom is thought to speak through the voice of the shaman who is merely the conduit for the utterances of the mushroom. We recall the words of Aurelio Carreras: the mushroom *eshabla,* 'is the Word'. Verses ending with *tso'* in the Mazatec velada are not the shaman's, they are the mushroom's: *tso'* means '[he] says'. From Siberia we learn that this is the way with the mushroom there: it speaks, it utters the Word. The first impression of Westerners with the mushrooms seems generally to be different: they are struck, often stunned, by the kaleidoscopic shapes that they see in the darkness, eyes open or closed. The voice is secondary to the visions. But the testimony of the Indians, including the shamans, on this is conclusive: The *Word* is the thing, just as in Sanskrit it is the *Vac* and in Greek the *Logos.*

ANTIQUITY OF MYCOLATRY IN MESOAMERICA

The records of the past in Mexico are uneven, areas of brilliant illumination alternating with others that run all the way to darkest night. The widespread use of inebriating mushrooms in Mesoamerica, rediscovered and for the first time explored in our own day, is cursorily documented in the sixteenth and seventeenth centuries in the writings of the friars and parish priests of that time, and also in the somber Proceedings of the Holy Office of the Inquisition. Before then for the shamanic use of-mushrooms there is nothing. True, such evidence might compel alert scholars to postulate a widespread ancient use of entheogenic mushrooms. But this evidence, strong though it may be, is immeasurably broadened and strengthened by the shamanic performances that still survive throughout the highlands of southern Mexico. These survivals permit us to gain a perspective on the antiquity of the use of the mushrooms. Maria Sabina's chants in the Mazatec country and Aristeo Matias' far away in the Sierra Costera in Zapotec country, linguistically far removed from each other, seemed to me (as I wrote down at the time and we suggested in *Mushrooms Russia & History*) musically the same. I taped Maria Sabina's singing but did not tape Aristeo Matias'.

Aristeo Matias with bowl of sacred mushrooms. San Agustin Loxicha, 22 July 1955.

Aurelio Carreras

Moreover, Maria Sabina's Mazatec liturgy and the liturgy that we discern in the writings of Ruiz de Alarcon in the early seventeenth century for the Nahuatl world are unmistakably founded on the same oral traditions. I have documented these parallels in Maria Sabina and Her Mazatec Mushroom *Velada* and will not repeat the demonstration here. With these benchmarks we may legitimately triangulate deep into Mesoamerican prehistory to arrive at the age of the divinatory mushroom rite. (We must always keep in mind how slowly cultural changes took pl ace in proto- and prehistory.) When words and music are so wedded that the words cannot be divorced from the melody, nor the melody from the words, as with the RgVeda hymns and the chants of the Mesoamerican velada, we possess in these verbalized musical expressions probably the most ancient of surviving anthropological evidence. It takes only a modicum of historical imagination to perceive a shamanic tradition invoking the mushrooms reaching back for millennia, probably back to Siberia and the cult that survived there until only a few years ago. And this tradition is buttressed on either hand by the same little tykes and clowns and tricksters tumbling around and then, on request, coming and speaking with the voice of authority to us through the shaman, precisely as in Siberia.

A QUESTION OF GRAMMAR

But for the antiquity of the entheogenic mushroom use, we are not confined to the living chants and *Ruiz de Alarcon's* writings: the very grammar and usages of the native languages through fossilized forms testify to it. In Nahuatl, the language of the Aztecs and all other Nahua, nouns representing inanimate things are invariable as to number. There are seeming exceptions of which here are three:

	Singular	*Plural*
Sky	*il huicatl*	*ilhuicame*
Mountain	*tepetl*	*tetepe*
Star	*citlalin*	*citlaltin*

These exceptions are apparent rather than real, for the Nahua personified the sky, mountains, and stars, and the plural form simply expresses the way of feeling that attributed to these cosmic beings a soul. Other exceptions are similarly suggestive.

For example, *tetl*, 'stone', becomes *teme* in the plural, but only when it refers to graven images.

For the Nahua the whole vegetable kingdom is construed as inanimate and therefore all herbs, shrubs, and trees are invariable as to number. Grammarians say that there may be one exception: 'mushroom' is *nandcatl* and this could be the plural form for *nacatl*, 'flesh'. Grammarians concede this much but their discipline does not permit them to go further. I am prepared to advance ethnomycological background supplementing the data of the grammarians and converting what they say is, grammatically, a possibility into virtual certain ty. The sacred mushrooms, possessing a soul, are responsible for the plural shape of *nandcatl*.

In many languages the mushroom vocabulary includes a generic word for that which is eaten - 'meat', 'bread', 'cheese', 'flesh', and 'food' itself. Thus, in dialectal English we find ' toadsmeat' and 'toadscheese'; in Norman French, *pain de crapaud*, 'toad's bread'; in Dutch, *duyvelsbroot*, 'devil's bread', which in classic Latin becomes *cibus deorum* and in Greek *broma theon*, 'food of the gods'. (As the Greeks were mycophobes, the 'food of the gods' gave the mushroom an exalted tabu status that served to exclude men from eating it.) In Pashto, a major Indo-European language of Afghanistan, *pocakai* is the name of an important edible mushroom and that name means 'flesh', the same meaning that appears in Nahuatl nandcatl. Of course, we are not suggesting a genetic kinship of these words with Nahuatl but when we come upon a simple figure of speech in a mushroom vocabulary and find a parallel association of ideas in other languages, a pattern of human thinking begins to emerge. Nandcatl is built on *nacatl*, the word in Nahuatl for 'flesh', a generic metaphor like 'food', 'victuals', 'bread', 'meat'; and by doubling the initial syllable it assumes a pluralized form that gives to the mushroom a soul, a status unique in the vegetable world. All mushrooms - *nandcatl* - are endowed with a soul, a unique status granted to the non-hallucinogenic species by reason of their kinship to the divine kinds, the divine kinds dominating by their overwhelming importance the whole fungal world. The root meaning, 'flesh', is emotionally colorless, neutral (like e.g. 'meat', 'bread', 'cheese' as given above), but it becomes exalted when the plural form - nandcatl - is preceded by tea- or *xochi-*, the designation of the entheogenic kinds.

There is a striking parallel in the Santa! language, a non-Indo-European tongue spoken by a tribe scattered in villages in *Orissa, Bihar,* and *West Bengal.* In *Santal* as in *Nahuatl,* the whole of the vegetable kingdom is viewed as inanimate, but in *Santal* there is a startling exception:

a single species of mushroom, the *putka*, which is animate and being animate possesses a soul. I made a preliminary visit to what are called the *Santal Parganas* in 1965 to inquire about the putka. Again in 1968 Roger Heim from Paris and I from New York, journeyed to *Orissa* and *Bihar* for the express purpose of studying this mushroom, which Professor Heim identified, but no one could remember why it alone of the mushroom tribe was animate! It is not entheogenic and in the season when it abounds is much eaten with rice. Professor Stella Kramrisch in a paper resulting from our inquiry arrived at the etymology of *putka*: not of *Santal* origin, it is a loan word from the Sanskrit *putika*, the first surrogate for the Soma of the Vedic hymns, a loan word that survives to this day only in Santal and possibly other tongues of the Munda family. (Mayrhofer, compiler of the recent Concise Etymological Sanskrit Dictionary, has referred to the Kramrisch explanation in the addenda to his lexicon.) Thus, the parallel with *Nahuatl* is close: the divinity that glows in a mushroom, in each case, gives to the mushroom a soul; in one instance (*Santal*) the specific kind, in the other (*Nahuatl*) the whole tribe of mushrooms embracing perhaps a score of entheogenic species.

An arresting grammatical status for mushrooms exists also in certain Slavic languages. At an early stage in the evolution of the Slavs there developed a tendency to substitute the genitive case for the accusative when a masculine noun representing an animate creature was the goal of the verb. In folk Russian this genitive is used not only for nouns denoting animate beings, but also for the names of various mushrooms and for the oak, when the mushroom or tree is individualized, i.e. is a single entity. ' This use is widespread in Russian dialects, and occurs also in Ukrainian and White Russian. One hears *nashol griba*, 'he found the mushroom', with *griba* in the genitive case; *nashol grusdja, ryzhika, borovika*. Among the trees the oak is especially favored by similar treatment, e.g.: *srubil duba*, 'he chopped down the oak'. The oak used to be worshipped in pagan times by the eastern Slavs as the thunder tree dedicated to the god Perun. Thus, in the folk language certain mushrooms attract a grammatical expression of the animism that survives from prehistory. It is possible to offer yet another example in Russian. In the standard language the mushroom known as the *masljenik* has a special plural form, *masljata*, and the plural of another mushroom name is *opjata* in certain uneducated circles. The plural suffix here used is normal only with certain nouns designating young animals, birds, and children!

Clearly this personification of the divine mushrooms is a fading survival from the time in prehistory when the northern Slavs knew the virtues of entheogenic mushrooms. Professor Marija Gimbutas, the renowned Lithuanian prehistorian, has reported to us on the use down to our own day of Amanita muscaria (i.e. 'Soma') in the remoter parts of Lithuania at wedding feasts and the like when the mushrooms were mixed with vodka, and also how the Lithuanians used to export quantities of A. muscaria to the Lapps in the Far North for use in their shamanic practices. Here in the Lithuanian festivities is the only report that I have so far received of the ingestion of the fly-agaric in Eastern Europe for jollification ends.

Early Man survived longer in Lithuania than almost anywhere else in Europe. These parallels in unrelated languages and cultures reinforce each other and drive home the powerful spell (sometimes reaching to divinity) that the entheogenic mushrooms cast over diverse peoples in prehistory.

'GODS FLESH'

Motolinia in the sixteenth century said that *teonandcatl* meant 'god's flesh' and this has been widely accepted ever since as its meaning. But Thelma Sullivan in a closely reasoned personal communication (13 May 1975) has demonstrated to me that that translation is wrong. The *teo-* of *teonandcatl* means divine or wondrous or awesome, and so teonandcatl means the divine or wondrous or awesome mushroom, nothing more and nothing less. This adjective tea- cannot be construed as the genitive - whether objective or subjective – of 'god'. Motolinia was overreacting: he gave the word a meaning with a direct bearing on the Elements in the Mass, a theological meaning that sacrilegiously and blasphemously (as he saw it) set the mushrooms up in competition with the body and blood of Christ, in competition with the bread and wine of our Christian sacrament. The sixteenth century Spanish friars arrived in the New World encumbered with the theological baggage of their place and time and they saw *nacatl* as an appalling simulacrum of the Eucharistic sacrament rather than a colorless word for the texture of the fungal flesh. That innocent word suddenly became charged with the high voltage of sixteenth century *odium theologicum*. Motolinia's mistake was shared by the clergy of his time: given the doctrines prevailing in the Catholic world, their mistake was natural. In 1537 it finds expression in the Proceedings of the Inquisition, and in the mid-seventeenth century in the writings of Jacinto de la Serna. The leading *Nahua*, not grasping the theological affront that this innocent term, misinterpreted, carried to the Christian hierarchy, must have quailed at the fury of the friars over their *teonandcatl*. ' No theologian seems to have challenged this meaning and we have had to wait four centuries until a grammarian and an *ethnomycologist* have clarified the confusion. The *Nahua* from their position of weakness would not have dared to argue their case and the friars with the passing generations have thrust their erroneous interpretation on the Christianized Indians. But though the friars were wrong in saying that *teonandcatl* meant 'god's flesh' (*carne de dios*), they did indeed find the Mesoamerican Indians adoring mushrooms that could lift them to a superior world where, for the nonce, they were on a level (as they thought) with the gods; where the *Greeks* were when they drank the potion at *Eleusis*, and where the *Aryans* were after ingesting their *amrita*. What a strange confrontation, the sixteenth century friars facing the Wisemen of a culture of Early Man who possessed a secret far older than theirs, neither group understanding the other but the Spaniards backed up by the grim secular arm of the Inquisition.

1.*In sixteenth century Mexican writings I have found the word teonandcatl only twice, in Motolinia and Sahagun. But it still survives: priority goes to Gaston Guzman Huerta, Mexican mycologist, for having rediscovered it. In August 1958 in Necaxa, Puebla, he heard Nahuatl speakers using teotlaquilnandcatl for the entheogenic mushrooms. (Ciancia, Mexico, 20: 3-4; pp 85-88; 10 June 1960) Thelma Sullivan suggests as a possible translation the ' divine sunset mushroom'. On 19 Sept. '72, Irmgard Weirlaner Johnson, Guy Stresser-Pean, and I learned in Xolotla, Puebla, from a shaman of prestige, Bernardo de la Cruz Tecalco, that the sacred mushrooms are known there as tenanacatzitzi. The te- is the eroded tea- and the suffix - tzitzi is a diminutive of reverence and endearment.*

THE MAZATEC MUSHROOM WORLD

In the Mazatec world the sacred mushrooms also enjoy a unique status but it is verbal and not grammatical. The word for 'mushroom' in Mazatec is *thain'*, in which the t is aspirated, the vowels are nasalized, and the word is pronounced in the third tone. The word covers the whole of the mushroom world - edible, inedible, poisonous, whether growing in the earth or on vegetation. It includes the whole mushroom world except the sacred mushrooms. The sacred mushrooms are *'nti'xi'tho'*, an arresting expression. The initial syllable is a p article expressing endearment and respect. The rest of the word means 'what leaps forth'. I have already rendered the whole: 'the dear little tykes that leap forth'. In her first letter to me, 9 March 1953, Eunice V. Pike gave me this Mazatec term and added that she could not explain it. But Early Man, as I well knew, always perceives that mushrooms do not grow from seed, and it seemed to me that the miracle (as Early Man construed it) of their birth found expression in this term. Some months later, when we entered the Sierra Mazateca for the first time we found that our *muleteer* Victor Hernandez had travelled the mountain trails all his life and spoke Spanish though he could neither read nor write nor even tell time by the clock's face. As we were making our way out of the mountains after our visit, we asked him why the mushrooms were called 'what springs forth'. His answer, breathtaking in its spontaneity, its sincerity, was filled with the poetry of religion, and I wrote down what he said word for word as he uttered it:

> El honguillo viene por si mismo, no se sabe de do'nde,
> como el viento que viene sin saber de do'nde ni por que.

> The little mushroom comes of itself, no one knows whence,
> like the wind that comes we know not whence nor why.

My interpretation had found confirmation in Victor's words. Almost a quarter of a century later Marfa Sabina, in her story of her life, dictated in Mazatec to Alvaro Estrada and translated by him into Spanish, disclosed in an extraordinary passage how always present in her mind was the wonder of the birth of the sacred mushrooms. In reading her words we must remember that in the Mazatec mind the sacred mushrooms have sprung, not from seed (which of course they do n o t possess), but from the falling drops of Christ's blood or spittle. In what she says she is impersonating the sacred mushrooms.

Las cositas son las que hablan. Si digo ' Soy muj er que sola cai, soy muj er que sola naci', son las cositas quienes hablan. Y dicen asi porque brotan por si solas. Nadie las siembra. Brotan porque asi lo quiere Dios. Por eso digo: soy l a muj er que puede ser arrancada, porque las cositas pueden ser arrancadas . . . y ser tomadas . . . Deben ser tomadas tal y como son arrancadas . . . No deben ser hervidas ni nada. No se les necesita hacer nada. Como son arrancadas asi deben ser tomadas . . . con todo y tierra. Deben ser comidas por completo, porque si se tira un pedazo, los honguitos pregunran en la velada, ' Don de estan mis pies' Porque no me comiste por completo?' Y ordenan, 'Busca el resto de mi cuerpo y t6mame . . . 'Deb en obedecerse las palabras de las cositas. Habra que buscar y tomar enronces los pedacitos que no fueron comidos antes d e comenzar la velada.

[Estrada: La Vida de Maria Sabina, pp 82-3]

The little things [sacred mushrooms] are the ones that speak. If I say, 'I am the woman who alone came down, who alone was born', it is the little things that speak. And they say so because they sprout by themselves. No one sows them. They sprout because God so wills. That is why I say: I am the woman who can be pulled up, because the little things can be pulled up . . . and be taken . . . They should be taken just as they are. pulled up . . . They should not be b oiled nor anything. There is no need to do anything. As they are pulled up, so should they be taken . . . with dirt and everything. They must be completely eaten, because if a piece is thrown away, the little things ask in the *velada*, 'Where are my feet? Why did you not eat all of me?' And they command, ' Find the rest of my body and take me . . .' The words of the little things must be obeyed. Then you must look and find the pieces that were not eaten before the *velada* began.

THE ART OF THE MUSHROOM VELADA

A salient fact about the sacred mushrooms has almost escaped remark up to now: the beginner gives the appearance of one drunk and this m ay easily outlast several trials. But then by dint of practice he takes hold of himself and discovers that he is able to time his movements, his thoughts, his impressions, under the guidance of the shaman. Finally, he achieves complete self-control. He learns until he and the mushroom perform in harmony. María Sabina, after taking thirteen pair of the big *derrumbe* mushroom, goes through a four- or five-hour performance as taut as a violin string, every note, every motion, timed to a nicety. She neither stammers nor stumbles. Listen now to what the Zapotec shaman (=menjak) Aristeo Matias told us when we asked him what we should do to learn the secrets of the shaman and become one. His answer was a disquieting parable, telescoping the apprenticeship into four stages:

On taking the mushroom for the first time the mushroom introduces himself to the novice: Asime llamo yo ('thus am I called'). Then terrible things happen but be not afraid. You rush to the sea, you plunge in, you go up to heaven, there where Jesus Christ is, and then to hell where the malefactors are. You see the whole world lying in the middle of the sea. On the second try you are thrown into the sea, but be not afraid. Then you see two women and two men who are gathering up the blood where Christ was born [sic]. On the third try everything changes, and now you are strong and the voices begin to come. Then, on the fourth try you arrive there where the Virgin Mary is, and the Lord Jesus Christ, and then they explain good things. Then all the Spirits come, all the Virgins, all the Saints. Then you know and are a menjak. From that moment the mushroom teaches you all things.

Aristeo was voicing a mystical picture. He was describing the confusion – even panic - felt by the novice on first taking the mushroom, and how after many tries and after weathering many storms (divided into the four stages) the aspirant might finally reach his goal, become one-who-knows. The shaman, as also his tiny flock of tried participants, has weathered the initial chaotic and troubling effects. They and the mushrooms consider themselves a brotherhood. Henry Munn describes the effect in his unpublished essay on Maria Sabina, laying stress on the powerful, all-possessing rhythmic beat that sweeps over not only the shaman but the whole gathering. His description, which he permits me to quote, is utterly different from mine and equally valid:

Throughout the 1958 velada [of the shaman Maria Sabina] the image of an old eagle always occurs in association with a watch. 'Woman-watch am I, Primordial Eagle am I'. I submit that the watch is an image for the clockworks of consciousness, the minute wheels and springs of the cerebral machinery, which under the mushroom influence can even become acoustic in the ticking heard in the inner ear. The image of the watch, recurring throughout her chants, introduced by Maria Sabina from the world of technology, expresses by metaphor the neural, cellular, biochemical processes revealed by psilocybin, which not only manifest the mind but the dynamic, rhythmical functioning of the whole body. ' Womanwatch am I', says she. The microscopic machinery, the clockwork of the cells with its fine timing, is what she means, the complex, infinitely mysterious, marvelous workings of the human cerebrum and nervous system. Images such as these do not come from knowledge but from the phenomena themselves. It is as though the mind senses by intuition its own nature by metaphor, in advance of science . . . These are transcendental themes, in which one has a sense of flight through the air. This is what she means by the ancient eagle, the celestial bird . . . [Under the influence of entheogens,] many feel as though they are rushing through the air, riding a great bird with wide wings, whirling high in the sky in wide gyres, looking down on the earth far below.

In Munn's words we catch the voice of proto-history, of prehistory: the shaman and his flock, having taken the mushrooms, lifted to skies of ecstasy, translated from our world to the pure empyrean, throbbing with the beat of the universe.

1.Note the parallel with Exodus 3: 1 4: 'And God said unto Moses, I AM THAT I AM; and he said, thus shalt thou say unto the children of Israel, I AM hath sent me unto you.' It is incredible that Aristeo was familiar with this Bible passage.

Since that night of 29-3 0 June 1955 in Huautla many Westerners have attended a Mesoamerican velada and many of them have ingested the mushrooms or morning glory seeds. Many others without attending a shamanic session have tried the entheogens. Even artists have sometimes tried the mushrooms to see whether their creative faculties would be heightened. These are all mere novices. We must remember the words of Aristeo Matias and know that to cope with the mushrooms one must survive one's astonishment and take them repeatedly to work in beat with them under the shaman's guidance. Thrill-mongers debase the mushrooms and themselves. In Maria Sabina's velada we are permitted to sense one aspect of religion as it irradiated the lives of our remote ancestors during millennia in our own prehistory. The Indian believes in the mushrooms, believes that in the. Course of these veladas he is granted what we call extrasensory perception, what he views as divine guidance. Can we be sure he is wholly wrong? I do not profess to know. But to dismiss these beliefs out of hand is, clearly, a sign of intellectual arrogance born of ignorance.

When Alberto Ongaro inquired of Maria Sabina how she became a shaman, she gave an answer in equally poetic language but subjective and personal:

The secrets that the mushrooms revealed to me are enclosed in a big Book that [the mushrooms] showed to me . . My sister Ana Maria [years before] fell ill . . . I loved my sister and I took many, many more [mushrooms] than I had ever taken before. My soul was entering the world of the mushrooms _ and I was seeing landscapes in the deepest depths of their world . . . At one point a sprite came toward -me. He asked a strange question, 'But what do you wish to become, you, Maria Sabina?' I answered him without thinking that I wished to become a Saint. Then the spirit smiled and immediately he had in his hands something that was not there before, a big Book with many written pages. 'Here', he said, 'I am giving you this Book so that you can work better and help the people who need help and know the secrets of the world where everything is known'. I thumbed through the leaves of the Book, many and many written pages, and alas I thought I did not know how to read . . . And suddenly I realized I was reading, and understanding all that was written on [sic] the Book, and it was as though I had become richer, wiser, and in a moment, I learned millions of things.

These quotations lead us to a major aspect of the mushroom velada, both in Mesoamerica and Siberia. Almost all the accounts published so far have

69

been written by witnesses new to the experience, whether they ingested the mushrooms or watched those who did. Aristeo Matias told us that the novel effects on the initiate are overwhelming, sometimes terrifying. Nausea is the least of these distressing effects. Double vision has often been noted, and the non-participating stranger is apt to mistake the external symptoms for a drunken stagger. Voices come in sequence from near and far, from all directions. Aristeo warns the beginner that he may see *'visions of hell'*. Most of those of our White race who have entered the magic world of the mushrooms are still in the beginners' class: they little suspect what they have yet to learn.

There is no 'catechism' class in the religion of the sacred mushroom. Children seem always to be present at the *velada*. I am astonished, as I look over my slides, to see how children, small and big, are present during the *velada*. Maria Apolonia carried an infant in her rebozo (shawl) throughout the *velada* that she and her mother sang on the night of 13-1 4 July 1958: the sleeping babe, close held against its mother's body, must have felt her singing throughout. In my photo's tots are there, and small children also, their faces filled with wonder as they stay close to Maria Sabina. They do not take the mushroom but go to sleep with the chanting in their ears.

We know that the performance of the *voladores* in pre-Conquest times (as well as now where it still survives) was steeped in religious feeling. The performers would swing down and around a pole some sixty feet high. The head of this troop would stand on a tiny platform on top of the pole and there he would perform a dance to music. Here we find precisely what I think an accomplished shaman, under the influence of the mushrooms, would aspire to do. We know that the ball game of the Mesoamericans was played by youths under powerful religious influence: was their skill enhanced by taking mushrooms? There seems reason to think that the now famous 'mushroom stones' were in some way connected with the ball court, and this then would be the link. (Infra pp 195 ff) We know the glow of religious feeling that follows the ingestion of the entheogens. We know how marvelously disciplined the mushroom adept becomes. The ball court player, the *volador* performer, were both saturated with religious feeling. The Conquest of course put an end to the public use of the entheogens and the informants of the friars were often tongue-tied where these plants played a role. I do not say mushrooms were used in these events. But the possibilities of the entheogens in these situations make inevitable the question, and I think the mushrooms may well have been so used.

Wherever they are known among the Indians the sacred mushrooms inspire awe and wonder. They are *muy delicados*, a word semantically akin to 'dangerous', and the mushrooms call for utmost care in handling. The mushroom *es habla*, is the Word: *Se ve todo, se ve donde Dios está. También*: 'You see everything, you see where God is also'. Among the *Mixe* and as we have seen among the Mazatecs, and undoubtedly among other Mesoamerican people, the sacred mushroom *nace por sí mismo*, 'is born of itself'. In San Juan Mazatlán of the Mixeria, after the mushrooms are gathered, they are taken straight in a covered *jícara* (gourd) to the village church, where there is no incumbent, only a local sacristan (sexton) who has the keys, and with a lighted candle of virgin beeswax they are left on the altar until they are used. In the *Nahuatl* country of *Veracruz, Rufina de* Jesus told us the story of a young man who said he was taking the mushrooms to Mass before ingesting them. I report only the instances that I have witnessed: there must be hundreds of village churches where similar practices are customary. In Huautla, Maria Sabina, though her calling is universally known, has been a church member in the best of standing all her life. The mushrooms have come full circle since the friars stormed against them in the sixteenth century: the fury of Motolinia and his colleagues against them could scarcely find words to express itself. Today, in the Indian villages, the mushrooms share the same altar with the Host.

WORK TO BE DONE

On 13 May 1957 we published our account of Maria Sabina's mushroom *velada* in Life and, expanded, in *Mushrooms Russia & History*. Later the Life article appeared in Spanish and yet later Roger Heim and I told the story once more in *Les Champignons hallucinogenes du Mexique*. These brought favorable reviews not only in the lay press but in scholarly journals, and they drew worldwide attention. In the outside world untold thousands down the years have ingested the sacred mushrooms or psilocybin their active agent. Mycologists, chemists, pharmacologists, and psychiatrists have worked on and with them. There have been a number of valuable contributions to our own work:

a) Fernando Benitez, professional writer, in Vol. 3 of *Los Indios de Mexico*, devoted a long essay to Maria Sabina, accurate and rich in fresh insights; also, in *Los Hongos A lucinantes* published in 1974 in the *Bibliografia Era;*

b) Alberto Ongaro, an Italian journalist with *L'Europeo,* came expressly from Milan to *Huautla de Jimenez* to interview Maria

Sabina, to whom through an interpreter he put a number of cogent questions: her answers of high value carry the ring of poetic and dramatic truth;

c) Alvaro Estrada, a *Mazatec* who has taken down from her mouth and translated into Spanish, in simple words catching the very flavor of her *Mazatec* tongue, the story of her life and her conception of the sacred 'little things';

d) Henry Munn from whose unpublished manuscript with his generous permission I have already quoted;

e) I recorded on tape the entire velada sung by Maria Sabina on the night of 12-13 July 1958; it was translated by the Mazatec specialists George and Florence Cowan; the Mazatec text, and the Spanish and English translations, in three parallel columns, were printed in full, the music transcribed by Willard Rhodes the renowned ethnomusicologist, the photographs of the velada by Allan Richardson illustrating the text; with every aspect of the performance duly commented on by us and by Robert J Weitlaner. Harcourt Brace Jovanovich Inc published the production, with either tapes or recordings, in 1974.

Alberto Ongaro and Fernando Benitez showed what first-class writers can do in treating shamanism, but as journalists theirs were one-shot affairs and we can hardly expect anything further from them. After the reviews no word has reached me of any further response from academia, i.e. anthropologists, archaeologists, linguists, Mesoamerican historians, faculties of religion.

In recent decades shamanism has evoked much discussion from academic circles and far beyond. Yet our knowledge of shamanism has suffered from a vital, a fatal defect: the absence of familiarity with the provenience of the singing and with the content of the verses in the remote tongues that the singers use. Moreover, the difficulties do not stop there: in the liturgical verses of the shaman there often occur obsolete or obsolescent turns of phrase that the shaman himself may be at a loss to understand. The help of the elders in the community is needed in trying to render them. In the Mazatec world with *Estrad a's* and *Muon's* help there is more than a possibility that we. shall soon have unprecedented access to the full meaning of the Mazatec singers' chants. Strangely, the response in the universities to our 1974 publication dealing with the heart of shamanism, itself a product of sixteen years of labor by a team of recognized specialists, has apparently been zero. It was a windfall that Alvaro Estrada, himself a Mazatec, should have offered to us on his own initiative a book on Maria Sabina, and a double windfall that it should be as perfect as it is, capturing in Spanish her way of speaking and thinking, without a trace of vulgarization. Henry Munn's approach is different but no less valid, as we have seen in his paragraph of lyrical prose that I have quoted, and these two men, close friends, constitute an admirable team to do serious work in the Mazatec area.

There is left a whole world of field studies crying to be done before rapidly developing mankind blots out the Old Order, field studies not primarily in the mycological and chemical fields, where Professor Heim and Dr Hofmann and their teams have arrived at the major discoveries, but in the linguistic area and the world of the Indian mind. We know virtually nothing about the mushroom vocabulary in the languages of the highland Maya: this is a big desideratum. Here is an area to be explored until we arrive at the answers as well as we now know the Mazatec. The same holds true with the seven mutually unintelligible Zapotec dialects: a good anthropologist with a passion for linguistics should master this complex, bring back tape recordings of shamanic sessions, take charge of translating them into Spanish and perhaps English as well, and compare the usages with the Mazatec. We know nothing about the role of mushrooms among the Otomi, who played an important part in pre-Conquest times, little about the Totonacs, nothing about the Tarascans. These peoples all once used the mushrooms and perhaps they all do to this day. And how about the Zoque? As the mushrooms are sacred and hedged about with profound tabus, no novices in linguistics a n d anthropology should enter this field: they only muddy the waters. What is needed are accomplished scholars, young, hardy, dedicated, who are capable of a sympathetic approach to religious beliefs that they cannot share.

SIBERIAN AND EURASIAN PARALLELS

As we have seen, the Sacred Mushroom complex of Mesoamerica seems to be linked with the Siberian, suggesting forcibly, perhaps ineluctably, that they have a common origin.

73

a) Throughout Mesoamerica the Sacred Mushrooms evoke an imaginary world of little people, girls and boys, more or less the size of mushrooms, given to pranks when not engaged in their serious business. They are the spirits of the mushrooms. The same holds true in Siberia.

b) The mushroom speaks through the voice of the shaman in Mesoamerica and also in Siberia.

c) In several of the Uralic languages a person inebriated on mushrooms is said to be 'bemushroomed': the tribes speaking those languages before the arrival of the Russians seem to have not known alcoholic inebriation. (In this they are like most North American Indians and Eskimos before the White Man arrived.) In Nahuatl, though the Nahua made fermented drinks from of old, they also have had recourse to a similar word for mushroom inebriation:

In mopoanj, in atlamatink in cuecuenotl: ipan mj toa monanacavia. Of one who is haughty, presumptuous, vain, of him it is said: 'he is bemushroomed'.

(Flor. Codex, Dibble & Anderson, Bk 11 'Earthly Things', p 132)

Unfortunately, we do not know whether the Palaeosiberian tribes Ket, Yukagir, Gil yak, Chukchi, etc - using the mushroom made a verb of it. If Russian linguists have explored this area in the languages of those peoples, their findings have not reached me.

d) In Nahuatl there is linguistic evidence for the special status of entheogenic mushrooms in the very grammar of the language. This corresponds to our similar discoveries in the Santal languages spoken by a tribe in India and in the languages of the East Slavic group - Russian, Belorussian, and Ukrainian. The unique status of mushrooms in Nahuatl must carry us b ack far indeed, perhaps to the migrations from Siberia. It speaks for the religious awe felt for the Sacred Mushroom among these peoples far removed from each other.

e) In Mesoamerica we have developed and published evidence that the music of the chants sung in the velada, and also many of the verses, are of ancient indigenous origin, a n d that evidence i s further supported (as we shall see) by the murals of Teotihuacan. This points to an origin lying deep in prehistory. We need for comparison the recordings of the chants sung in Siberia by the shamans who formerly used the mushrooms.

f) In 1956 in my first paper dealing with ethnomycology I developed evidence that linked mushrooms with the lightning bolt. I will return to this subject in my next book, which will be a sequel to my SOMA: Divine Mushroom of Immortality. For the present I will only say that in Mesoamerica the tie that binds the lightning bolt to the hallucinogenic mushrooms is strong: I find it among the Nahua, the Mazatecs, and the Zapotecs. Here is a powerful folk belief that survives in many places in the Northern Hemisphere, in the Old World and the New. It must go back far into prehistory.

We must not forget the slowness of change in proto- and prehistory. There were perhaps, even probably, other plants to which supernal powers were attributed, but the Wondrous Mushroom seems to have enlisted virtually universal adoration in the Northern Hemisphere. This mushroom may have been a Psilocybe, or the pongo (Amanita muscaria) of the Siberians, the miskwedo of the Algonkians, or a Claviceps, or yet others still unknown to us. Here was the Secret of Secrets of the Ancients, of our own remote forebears, a Secret discovered perhaps sporadically in Eurasia and again later in Mesoamerica. The Secret was a powerful motive force in the religion of the earliest times. By refraction and reflection, the Secret crops out in fossil meanings, fossil sayings, fossilized folkloric bits of our various languages.

One question confronts us: our folkloric world, appealing nowadays chiefly to children, of fairies, elves, gnomes, of Queen Mab and the goblins, of leprechauns and trolls, of duendes and trasgos in the Spanish world, etc, are they descended directly from the world to which the Wondrous Mushroom introduced our remote forebears, the Little People, sometimes endearing, sometimes infuriating, of a Magical Eden?

75

Figure 1. Full-face view of Xochipilli

CHAPTER 3

XOCHIPILLI, 'PRINCE OF FLOWERS' A NEW INTERPRETATION

In the *Museo Nacional de Antropologia of Mexico* there stands a remarkable piece of statuary known as *Xochipilli, the 'Prince of Flowers'*. So far as I know, only in Mesoamerica does the pantheon of Early Man include a divinity dedicated exclusively to *'flowers'*. '*Xochi-*' is from *Nahuatl xochitl*, *'flower'*; '*pilli'* means either 'Prince' or 'child', and parallels our former use in English of 'child' as a high-born youth (eg Byron's Childe Harold), and also the use of Infante in Spanish. No one disputes the meaning of *Xochipilli*. But do the 'flowers' of which *Xochipilli* is Prince mean flowers?

The statue and what we call its base were unearthed at *Tlalmanalco* on the approaches to the volcano *Popocatepetl* in the middle of the last century. The 'base' in reality is an integral part of the statuary, being a reproduction in miniature of the lower part of an Aztec temple on which *Xochipilli*, life-size, is seated. ' On the strength of stylistic features, it is believed that the statue was carved a generation or so before the arrival of the Spaniards. The overall expression of this Prince of Flowers is breathtaking. The skyward tilt of the head and eyes, tense half-open mouth, jutting jaw, hands poised at different levels, crossed legs with feet almost wholly off the ground, the strain expressed by the retraction of the right big toe - they are all of a piece. (Margaret Seeler, who has done almost all my black-and-white drawings, went expressly to Mexico City to study the statue of *Xochipilli*.

Figure 2 a) Retracted big toe of Xochipilli.

77

Figure 2 *b) normal foot*

It was she who discovered the retracted big toe: The Pre-Conquest sculptor spoke alone to her, the artist, across a chasm of half a millennium.) They are far from conveying the quiet joy of a flower buff. The eyes then would be turned earthwards and a feeling of repose should suffuse the whole figure.

One key to the enigma of this figure lies in the mask that the man is wearing. It can be seen in the eye-sockets and better still under the chin. (fig 3) In the cultures of the West, masks are no longer important: they are relegated to children or to light-hearted merry-making as in masked balls and frivolous festivities that welcome in the New Year. But in antiquity and virtually all the other cultures of the world the mask takes on grave import. It shows the salient trait of character that the wearer portrays, being the personification of that trait. In our statue the mask portrays a god living in ecstasy and does so with the power of genius. Here is one who is not seeing, not living as ordinary mortals see and live, who is seeing
direct with the eyes of the soul. This being is not with us, is in a far-off world. He is absorbed by *temicxoch,* 'dream flowers' as the *Nahua* say describing the awesome experience that follows the ingestion of an entheogen. I can think of nothing like it in the long and rich history of European art: *Xochipilli* absorbed in *temicxoch.*

The late Justino Fernandez has given us a detailed description and explanation of this statue in ' *Una Aproximacio'n a Xochipilli'* in Vol 1 of *Estudios de Cultura* Nahuatl. His study is a first-class professional dissection of the statue following conventional standards of the past. I have learned much from it, as anyone familiar with it will discover from my text, b u t I disagree with his overall interpretation. It becomes clear that Fernandez had never enjoyed the experience of the entheogens, had never even given the role of entheogens in Mesoamerican culture serious thought.

Figure 3. Detail of Xochipilli showing mask

Fernandez could not help seeing the 'ecstasy' (this is his word) in the expression on the man's face, but for his explanation ecstasy is superfluous, even out of place, and he would minimize the trance-like pose for the viewers by suggesting that if the eye-sockets were filled with turquoises or other gems, as he is compelled to think they once were, this impression would be reduced or even eliminated. For me it would be surprising if gems had ever filled the eye-sockets. The figure indeed wears a mask, but in this style of mask the sockets are normally empty to allow the wearer to see.

The ecstasy in this figure is of the essence. Here is the work of a master, a supreme carving of a man in the midst of an unearthly experience, the formal hieratic effigy of the God of Rapture, the God of 'Flowers' (as the Aztecs put it) : the god of youth, of light, of the dance and music and games, of poetry and art ; The Child God, the god of the rising sun, of summer and warmth, of flowers and butterflies, of the 'Tree-in-Flower' (*Xochicuahuitl* or *Arbol Florido*) that the *Nahuatl* poets frequently invoke, of the inebriating mushrooms (las Flores que *embriagan*), the miraculous plants that transport one to a heavenly Paradise.

The exposed parts of the body as well as the 'base' are covered with carvings of flowers. Strange that no one, from *Seier* and *Gamio* to Justino

79

Fernandez, no archeologist, no botanist, no art historian, has stopped to identify them! The carved flowers are the unique feature of this statue, but no scholar, no scientist, has entered into this unique feature! From earliest times Mexico has abounded in excellent botanists, Spanish and Mexican and later from the whole world. (An imperative though unconscious inhibition seems to grip scholars when their natural instincts would lead them into the Paradise - the *Tlalocan* - of the entheogens.) Those flowers carved on the body of *Xochipilli* hold the key to the meaning of the statue and moreover to the metaphorical meaning of 'flowers' in *Nahuatl* and Mesoamerican culture.

Since I first fixed my gaze on this statue of Xochipilli in the late 1950's, the emblem adorning all four sides of the base, obviously a plant motif, caught my attention. (fig) 4 Many have referred to it as a 'flower', but what flower? From the beginning I felt the five convex devices with inturned margins arranged in a circle were mushrooms. They represent the mushrooms in profile. A sixth is hidden by the carving of a mythic butterfly. The caps of mushrooms offer us an infinite variety of shapes, in the wide variety of species and the different stages of the life cycle of each species.

Figure 4. Mushroom emblem on base of statue.

Figure 5

Figure 6

Even among the entheogenic species of Psilocybe, Stropharia, and Conocybe there is endless diversity. Let us remember that the statue comes from the slopes of *Popocatepetl*. In the beliefs of the Mesoamericans, Paradise – their *Tlalocan* - was situated on the slopes of a verdant mountain to the East and for the Aztecs the towering massif topped by the volcano Popocatepetl was their *Tlalocan*, their Garden of Eden. Here is where our statue was found, in the heart of the sacred mushroom country. Here in this precise vicinity was where Professor Roger Heim discovered, thanks to the indispensable help of descendants of *Nahua* Indians, *Psilocybe aztecorum Heim*, a species then new to science, illustrated in color in Les *Champignons hallucinogenes du Mexique*. The mushrooms in the refractory stone medium catch admirably the precise convex shape of the actual pileus of the living plant. Henry B. Nicholson in his photograph brings out not only the profile that had caught my eye: his lens gives body to the stipe and flesh of the cap. The inturned margins (*la marge . . . incurvee,* as Professor Heim says) are one of the specific characteristics distinguishing this species of Psilocybe. The left-hand Fig. 9a reproduces what we find on the statue and the right-hand Fig. 9b the illustration in *Les Champignons hallucinogenes:*

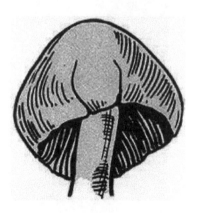

Figure 9A   Figure 9B

Fig 9 Profile of a) design on 'base' of Xochipilli and b) Psilocybe aztecorum

Figure 7

Figure 8

Mushrooms also appear on the body of our man in rapture - on both his knees, on his right forearm, on the top of his head. (Fig 13) There are three in each case, instead of six, and just as on the tablero we see the caps of another row of mushrooms behind and between the mushrooms in the foreground. But on the body the carving is not done with such care. We cannot hazard a specific designation as we did for the one in Fig 9a. I think the mushroom designs on the body of *Xochipilli* express rather a glyph for any of the many species of entheogenic mushrooms, a glyph that we might expect to find elsewhere. (Fig 10)

Figure 10. Glyph of The Mushrooms

On the base of our *Xochipilli* we find what everyone familiar with Mesoamerican art will recognize as a highly stylized butterfly, perched among the mushrooms and concealing the sixth. one, apparently feeding on them. Why the butterfly? In our world of nature mushrooms seldom or never draw butterflies, but in Mesoamerican iconography butterflies play an important mythic role, as we see in the butterflies of the famous mural of *Tepantitla* in *Teotihuacan*, showing us (according to Alfonso Caso) *Tlalocan*, the paradise of the Nahua for certain selected individuals.

Butterflies are associated with the land of fortunate departed spirits. They embody the spirits of the dead. George Cowan in Yan (1953 No 2) has told us that in some parts of the contemporary Mazatec world butterflies are still considered to be the souls of the departed revisiting their native haunts. On the base of the statue of *Xochipilli* the butterfly is feasting on teonandcatl, which may have been considered the food of the gods, to whose world the mushrooms transport for a brief spell the people of this sad workaday world. Mrs. Seeler has reproduced our mythic butterfly, the symbol that ratifies our identification of the sacred mushrooms.

Figure 11 Butterfly on 'base'.

There survives a poem from Chalco, close by to Tlalmanalco where our Xochipilli statue was found, and the carving might have been inspired by these lines:

The flowery butterfly passes and repasses.	Xochin papalotl tepanahuia
May it suck honey from our flowers	Ma in tlachichina Aya toxochiu
Twisting in and out of our bouquets!	O tomac xochiuh in!

(As we shall see, 'flowers' in pre-Conquest Nahuatl poetry is a metaphor meaning the entheogens. When so used I italicize it.)

Figure 12. Xochipilli headdress

Figure 13. Detail of headdress

On three of the four sides of the base, flanking what are the sacred mushrooms, we find two groups of four concentric circles or balls. *Xochipilli's* formal headdress (and what a lordly headdress it is, his chief article of apparel!), viewed from behind, carries six such sets of four circles or balls. This is the Nahuatl *tonallo*, the symbol that connotes the summer season, solar warmth, light, butterflies, and *xochitl* (marvelous word!) in its several senses. On his headdress there are no fewer than five balancing symbols - quadrilateral fields divided into four stripes, which probably were once in diverse colors (the whole statue having been painted) — the symbol called *tlapapalli* - a symbol reinforcing the tonallo and meaning supreme joy, bliss incomparable. Are not the tonallo and tlapapalli felicitous for my reading of this statue of *Xochipilli* as embodying the Aztec esteem for the wondrous entheogen?

Figure 14. Tlapapalli and Tonallo

Above the circles of mushrooms on the sides of the 'base' we see a wavy line all around the four sides. Others have suggested that this meant water - a happy suggestion since mushrooms are always associated with showers, rain, moisture, mountain. Along the top rim of the *tablero* there is an endless sequence of concentric circles. These have been called 'solar symbols' and this would not be an incongruous meaning but I will show later that they can be differently construed in a way to reinforce my mushroom interpretation.

Figure 19. 'Base' of statue.

Let us now look at the '*flowers*' carved on the body of the god. As I am not a botanist, I invoked the help of Richard Evans Schultes, holder of the Paul C. Mangelsdorf chair in Natural Sciences at Harvard and Director of the Botanical Museum there, who with his students, Dr Timothy Plowman and the late Dr Tommie Lockwood, and his colleague the scientific artist Mr. Elmer C. Smith, together with me, have come up with the following identifications.

On the statue's right haunch there is a five-petaled carving, the petals being pointed. Schultes and his associates are confident that this is *Nicotiana Tabacum*, our common tobacco plant, one of the sacred plants of all Amerindian cultures not only in Meosamerica but throughout the Americas. For four centuries observers of the Amerindians have been telling us that they reverence tobacco as a plant en-dowed with mystical powers, what we now call an entheogen. Mrs. Seeler here reproduces the design on the right haunch, Fig 16a, and also when it is repeated on the left forearm, Fig 16b. Fig 16c is *N. Tabacum* as shown in the Britton and Brown Illustrated Flora, edited by Henry A. Gleason, Vol 3, p 205. Let us now turn our attention to *Turbina corymbosa* (L.) Raf., formerly *Rivea corymbosa*, the *ololiuhqui* of the Nahua, the entheogenic morning-glories identified with Mesoamerican cultures.

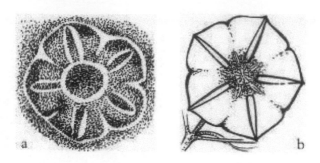

Figure 17. Morning-glory (Turbina corymbosa) a) on statue, b) drawn from life.

On the right thigh near the knee there is a carving of the morning-glory flower as one views it looking into the cup. ' Mrs. Seeler reproduces the carving on the thigh and also copies the illustration of Turbina corymbosa from the same angle as shown in Schultes' classic paper, 'A Contribution to our Knowledge of Rivea corymbosa, the Narcotic *Ololiuqui* of the Aztecs', published by the Botanical Museum of Harvard University in 1941. (Fig 17) On the left leg below the knee, and again just above the knee on the left thigh, there are, we think, carvings of the emerging morning-glory flower that show the plaiting and convolutions characteristic of that stage in the blossom's life cycle. Fig (18) is Mrs. Seeler's design on the left thigh. So much for *Turbina corymbosa* or *ololiuhqui.*

Figure 18 Design on left thigh

Schultes is confident that he has identified the flower carved on the right leg below the knee: *Heimia salicifolia*, the *sinicuichi* of the Mexican highlands. Here is Mrs. Seeler's comparison of the carving and the actual plant:

1.In Archeology, Jan 1973, Vol 26. 1, William D. Sturdevant arrived at the same identification of this flower some months before the first version of my chapter appeared in the Harvard Botanical Museum Leaflets (Vol 23.8). I gladly point out his priority and would have done so in the Leaflet had I known of it. I believe his was the first identification of any flower carved on the Tlalmanalco statue of Xochipilli. But he calls it an 'opiate' which i t is not, either botanically or in psychic effect. One anthropologist insists that this same flower is the toloaclie of Mesoamerica, Datu ra inoxia (= formerly D. meteloides). Impossible: the petals of D. inoxia are pointed whereas our carvings are rounded, a typical morning glory. Nico tiana Tabarnm and D. inoxia are both of the nightshade family, but the carving that we have defined as N. Tabarnm cannot be toloaclte, for the petals of our tobacco carving are acute whereas D. inoxia would be a t tenuate.

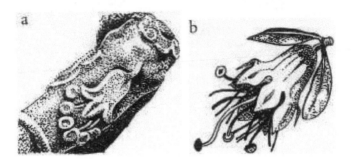

Figure 19. Heimia salicifolia a) on statue, b) drawn from life

Schultes says that the plant has ' mildly intoxicating properties', and adds these details: Sounds seem to come distorted from a great distance. This plant typifies an hallucinogen of which the hallucinogenic characteristics are auditory, not visual. The natives believe that sinicuichi has sacred or supernatural qualities, since they hold that it helps them recall events which took place many years earlier as if they had happened yesterday; others assert that they are able, with sinicuichi, to remember pre-natal events. On contemplating the statue, a new one is tempted to see in the tilt of the head and above all in the open mouth that *Xochipilli* is listening to the far-off voices of *sinicuichi*. Margaret Seeler's drawing is taken from the illustration in the Bulletin on Narcotics, Vol XXII, No 1, Jan-March 1970, p 38, in the article by Professor Schultes.

On the left side of our statue, just where buttock and thigh meet, a well delineated flower holds our attention. Schultes, somewhat uncertain, asks whether it could be a swollen bud of *Heimia salicifolia*, just about to open up. As we have seen, ololiuhqui (the morning-glory: *Turbina corymbosa*) is probably present on the statue at two stages of its growth: why not *sinicuichi* also? The same flower is carved on the inside of the left calf (Fig 20), and apparently on the right torso. (Here the carving seems unfinished.)

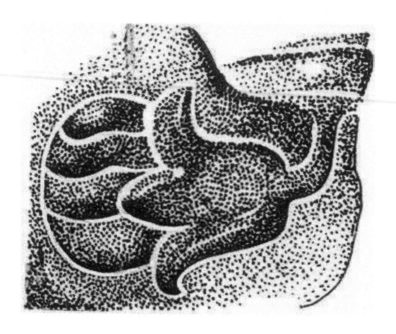

Figure 20. Swollen bud of Heimia salicifolia (?)

On the left torso of our Xochipilli, above the belt, there is the carving of an extraordinary flower. When I suggested to Professor Schultes that it might be the flower of the *cacahuaxochitl*, nowadays known to botanists as Quararibea funebris, and told him my reasoning, I was delighted that he thought it an excellent possibility, the best so far advanced. The cacahuaxochitl occupied a unique place in the culture of the Nahuatl aristocrats. The pre-Conquest poets speak with almost breathless enthusiasm of it in their verses and also of its flower, the poyomatli, ' which at last we can now link with the tree. The sculptor of the Prince of Flowers, having undertaken to carve on Xochipilli's body the flowers that figured large in the cultural life of the Nahua, could not sidestep the poyomatli. It was a must. The artist, unfamiliar with the flower in its native habitat, did the best he could. Here is Mrs. Seeler's drawing of the actual flower, done after the illustration in *Arboles Tropicales de Mexico*, by J. D. Pennington and Jose Sarukhan:

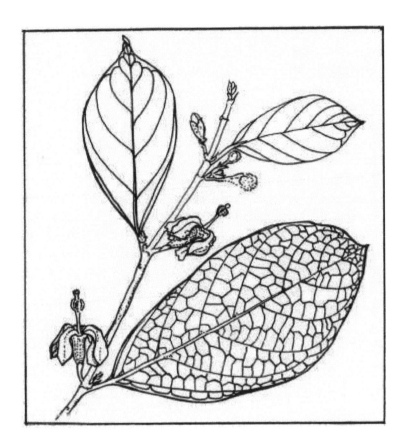

Figure 21. Quararibea funebris in flower

The flower is marked by two features - a bold stamineal tube, and *retrousse's* petals that leave the tube quite naked. The sculptor of Xochipilli just before the Conquest and Sahagun's artist for the Florentine Codex shortly after the Conquest seem to have done their best to do precisely this, though they fell short of the goal they were striving to reach.

1.Though botanists have known the tree for generations, the poyomatli has been identified with it only since 1963, when Dibble & Anderson, plodding ahead in their translation of the Nahuatl text of the Florentine Codex, came across two independent passages that defined it as the flower of the cacaltuaxochitl. Did Sahagun in his paraphrase of the Nahuatl text deliberately omit the identification of this flower that

95

stirred the most intense rapture in Nahuatl circles? See pp 88, 89, 91, also 97 ff for further discussion.

We know that the artist i n the Codex was drawing the cacahuaxochitl because the drawing is so labeled. Admittedly the two artists pictured the flowers wretchedly. But let us remember that this tree grows in *Veracruz* and *Oaxaca,* not in the Valley of Mexico. Unless the artists knew well the flower in situ, they could represent it only by hearsay and by examining the dried pressed blossoms that were carried by porters in bales to the Valley of Mexico. Both artists, after a fashion, managed to catch the distinguishing features - the stamineal tube and the *retrousse's petals* - but neither dared picture these as extreme as they really are. Both showed the stamineal tube and Sahagun's artist catches its blunt end. The Xochipilli carving is slightly better than the artist of the Florentine Codex in presenting us with the *retrousses petals*. We show the flowers as the artists would be familiar with them in dried and pressed condition. With our quick transportation facilities today, we may forget that in pre-Conquest times one had to travel between Mexico-Tenochtitlan and the lands of the *cacahuaxochitl* on foot.

In Fig 22 we show the tree in bloom as represented in Sahagun's illustration, which he gives us without color:

Figure 22. Sahagun's illustration of Q. funebris

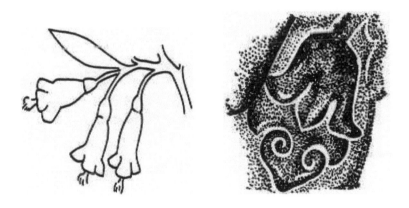

Figure 23. Poyomatli a) in Sahagun and b) as a suggested identification for the flower in Xochipilli statue.

Figure 24. Dried Poyomatli flowers

Finally, we discover on our Xochipilli statue, on the inner calf of the right leg, a four-petaled flower. As to its identity we are at a loss. We hope that our readers will come up with a happy suggestion, a flower probably entheogenic, at least a focus of reverence among the Nahua of the Valley of Mexico. Here is Margaret Seeler's drawing of this carving:

Figure 25. Unidentified carving of flower on Xochipilli

The photograph of this baffling flower was taken especially for us by the *Museo Nacional de Antropologia.*

Figure 26. Photo of enigmatic flower

The reader will have observed that the 'flowers' carved on Xochipilli bear no fixed relation in size to the flower or mushroom that is portrayed: each flower fills suitably the space allotted to it. The reader will also observe that among the flowers carved on Xochipilli no Datura is represented. The statue expressed the culture of the Princes and Nobles of the Nahua, and the Daturas did not rank with the entheogens of the aristocrats. We also observe that no plant linked with alcoholic beverages - neither pulque nor maize beer - is present.

About twenty years have passed since I first saw the mushrooms on the 'base' of our statue, but as time has gone by, the mushrooms and other flowers have taken second place in my thinking: here in this statue is Rapture itself delineated in stone, and the flowers only serve to confirm its meaning. The *flowers* on the tablero and body (among which the mushrooms receive pride of place!) amply ratify, for doubting Thomases, the identification I have given to Xochipilli, the God of Rapture. The elegance of this statue, its subtlety, its nobility, speak for the exalted place accorded to the entheogens by the elite in pre-Conquest Mesoamerica.

They emphasize the surprising ignorance and l ack of respect shown by all Mesoamericanists for this major manifestation of the civilization that is their special field of study. In his paper on our statue of Xochipilli Justino Fernandez begins by denying the ecstasy of this statue and to that end would introduce turquoises into the eye-sockets, but even he finally compromises his position by succumbing to the enchantment of the face:

Por ultimo, el gesto de la mascara tiene tension dramatica y cierta ternura, pues la mirada esta pendiente de algo 'mas alla', que parece mirar fij amente . . .; el gesto de la boca tensa horizontalmente y con los labios un poco entreabiertos sugiere cierto esfuerzo de elevacio'n, . . .

Finally, the mask shows dramatic tension and a certain tenderness, since the look is one of expectancy of something from ' out yonder', where its gaze seems fixed . . .; the expression of the horizontally taut mouth with half open lips suggests a certain effort at elevation, . . .

How close did this able academic art critic come to the esoteric meaning of the statue! Here he seems to have finally abandoned his notion of turquoises in the eye-sockets: he concedes that the 'gaze' is fixed 'out yonder'. If only he had had the entheogenic experience, or alternatively if only he had stopped to examine the botanical specimens carved on this ensemble of noble statuary! Perhaps the reader will have allowed himself to be persuaded by my presentation of Xochipilli without due regard to the consequences: let him be warned. If he accepts my interpretation, he will be committing himself to a reappraisal of preconquest Mesoamerican culture. For going on five centuries those interested in Mesoamerica have ignored the entheogens. The Indian informants of the Spanish chroniclers, knowing well where their bread was buttered, gave accounts of the entheogens that lent themselves to due execration by the ecclesiastical scribes. We must be grateful that the informants tell us as much as they do and that the friars pass on to us, more or less faithfully, what they were told. Xochipilli appears often in the pre-Conquest codices and sculptures of Mesoamerica but the artists naturally felt no need to spell out his meaning. Let me suggest an analogy: the ancient Egyptians used methods of writing that no one could interpret until there was found in 1799 a stone in the delta of the Nile with a text engraved for contemporaries in three modes of writing, in Greek, and in Egyptian hieroglyphics and demotic script. From this bilingual inscription the Frenchman Champollion started us on the road to reading the vast corpus of ancient Egyptian texts. Those who carved the Rosetta stone were not thinking of the use to which it would be put by learned men in distant lands far in the future; neither could the artist carving Xochipilli have imagined, if I am right, what a sensational disclosure his work would be making to strangers from another world half a millennium later. Here Xochipilli discloses the exalted view of the entheogens held by the Mesoamericans in pre-Conquest times: the nobility of this statue speaks loud and clear, with the honesty of all outstanding works of art. Later, some of the friars with distinguished talents and extraordinary zeal leavened with compassion and even admiration for the conquered, wrote down lengthy accounts of life in Mesoamerica before and after the Conquest, but always filtered through the theology of their time and circumstance: inevitably they gave no quarter to the entheogens. Our statue of Xochipilli serves us as a touchstone, as a cultural Rosetta Stone, bypassing the friars encumbered with their theological preconceptions, speaking to us directly with the voice of the pre-Conquest Aztecs.

As an artist's expression of ecstasy in Mesoamerica our Xochipilli is far from unique. He is unique only in that his body bears carvings of the miraculous plants that transport him and us to another reality and that spell out for us his message. In Colima Dr Isabel Kelly has unearthed a number of small stone statues bespeaking rapture with a breathtaking eloquence perhaps unmatched even in our Xochipilli. They date from the end of the seventh century A D. Surely the absence of the plant carvings on their bodies does not negate for us their meaning. Their eyes are open, as is not unnatural in a nocturnal velada held in the dark. Two of them· are on exhibit in the Museo Nacional de Antropologia. (Figs 27, 28)

I think there were two ways of presenting ecstasy in pre-Conquest Mesoamerica. We have seen the grand manner in the Tlalmanalco Xochipilli and the two Colima figurines. This style conveys to the spectator the awesome experience that follows ingestion of the entheogens, but in doing so it translates reality on to a transcendental plane. Those who are experiencing the entheogens actually sit as in a stupor, rapt in their own sensations, their facial expression introverted. In the Museo Nacional there is a Mezcala figurine (Fig 29), eyes closed, carved in hard stone, and dating from the late pre-classic period, B C 600-100. Some may question whether this Mezcala artifact is an embodiment of rapture, so blank and negative is his expression, but I ask what else can it be? For those who have known the mushrooms or the morning-glory seeds, it takes no effort to imagine his state of mind. The artist who carved Xochipilli was giving us reality transfigured, was giving us what the Indian would feel that he was living through, was giving us Rapture petrified.

Figure 27. Stone carving of ecstasy

Figure 28. Another carving of ecstasy.

Figure 29. Another interpretation of ecstasy

The mask tells us what the man in ecstasy felt. The artist of the Mezcala figurine tells us what the same man looked like to others. The late Dudley Easby and his widow Elizabeth, with the prescience that always characterized their work in Mesoamerican archaeology, grouping together a number of small reclining figures, suggested that these particular figures and others like them might well represent ordinary people enjoying the entheogenic experience. Those that they reproduced in the Catalogue of the Before Cortes exhibition in the Metropolitan Museum were in jade (possibly Olmec) or clay. (Figures 30 and 31) They range from 3 1/2 to 8 1/2 inches long and date from the middle or late preclassic period (B C 1 150-100), hailing from Honduras, Central Mexico, and Guerrero. I have no reason to think that the Easbys had ever known a *velada,* had ever taken the entheogens, but they were gifted with rare intuition and their surmise may well have been right.

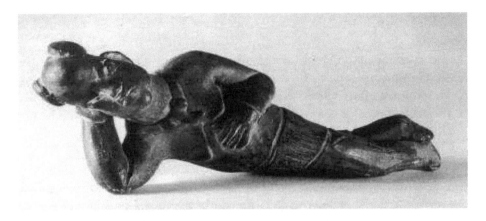

Figures 30 and 31 Figurines expressing ecstasy (?)

How different all these expressions of the ineffable are from the manner of the European religious painters of the late Middle Ages and early Renaissance! For them the Saint is leaning forward on his knees, arms outstretched, his eyes lifted heavenward, perhaps toward a vision in the radiant sky of the Virgin with her supporting heavenly host singing

105

sweetly to the accompaniment of diver's musical instruments and with putti scattered among the clouds. This was the Western conception of beatitude, of bliss, executed often by able artists but artists who had never experienced what they were painting. In Mexico the artists knew what it was they were carving and by the simplicity of their execution they succeeded in conveying to the viewer (who also knew) the sense of the rapture that their opposite numbers in Western Europe could not approach.

The statue of Xochipilli tells us that xochitl could mean in Nahuatl, as a figure of speech, the entheogens and the incomparable wonder-world to which they invite us. The flowers carved on the body of this our exemplar of ecstasy are what the Mesoamerican Indians regarded as sacred entheogens. Miguel Leon-Portilla comes as near to arriving at the truth as one can hope to do who has not known the miraculous plants, has not allowed for their existence: he skirts, but only skirts, in every word of the following eloquent passage, the genuine meaning for the Nahua of xochitl in its metaphorical sense:

La expresio'n idiomatica, in xochitl, in cuicatl, que literalmente significa ' flor y canto', tiene como sentoid metafo'rico el de poema, poesia, expresio'n artistica, y, en una palabra, simbolismo. La poesia y el arte en general, 'flores y cantos', son para los tlamatinime [wisemen, Magi, soothsayers], expresión oculta y velada que con las alas del simbolo y la metafora puede llevar al hombre a balbucir, proyectandolo mas alla de si mismo, lo que en forma misteriosa, lo acerca tal vez a su raiz. Parecen ['flor y canto'] afirmar que la verdadera poesia implica un modo peculiar de conocimiento, fruto de autentica experiencia interior, o si se prefiere, resultado de una intuicio'n.

[*Los Antiguos Mexicanos, Chap 4, p 128 in my reprint; Fondo de Culrura Econ6mica, Mexico, 1961.*]

The idiomatic expression, in *xochitl*, in *cuicatl*, which literally means ' flower and song', has the metaphorical sense of poem, poetry, artistic expression, in a word, symbolism. Poetry and art, 'flowers and songs ', are for ' those-who-know' [wisemen, Magi, soothsayers] an occult and veiled term that may sweep man off on. the wings of symbol and metaphor, stammering, may project him beyond himself, thus perhaps in a mysterious manner bringing him nearer to his origins. *'Flower and song' seem to affirm that true poetry implies a peculiar way of knowledge, the fruit of an authentic interior experience* . . . [Italics mine]

This 'peculiar way of knowledge', this 'fruit of an authentic interior experience'! Leon-Portilla divined the truth. Without knowing it, he was describing a velada with entheogens.

CHAPTER 4

THE FLOWERS IN THE PRE-CONQUEST NAHUATL POETRY

The corpus of pre-Conquest Aztec poetry began to be accessible to the West only a few years ago and almost at once it was remarked that this poetry possessed a feature peculiar to it: on 15 May 1961, The Times (London) in a dispatch from Mexico City observed that the Aztec poets never tired of talking about '*flowers*' but that they seldom distinguished one species from another. Since poets are prone to subtleties in thought and feeling, this lumping together of 'flowers' was odd. No explanation was forthcoming from the Nahuatlatos (as specialists in Nahuatl are called) and none has been advanced since then. But if the Aztec Princes and Nobles, who were the poets that we are speaking about, used 'flowers' as a figure of speech for the entheogens and the entheogenic experience, in short if the poets understood '*flowers*' as the Xochipilli carvings say they were to be understood, all becomes clear. (*I am printing flowers in italic when we deal with a trope for the entheogens.*) The flowers were the breathtaking experience of their lives, supreme and miraculous. The flowers took them to another world where they sang their Aztec poetry to the music of their Aztec instruments, a world that they called their Tlalocan (or sometimes their Tamoanchan), a world of strange and wondrous beauty, where they reveled in sensations beyond imagining. It is not surprising that these Princes and Nobles, able and sophisticated men, composed poetry weighted with flowers.

The Times's correspondent exaggerated: specific flowers are cited in Nahuatl poetry as often as in any other. What is distinctive is the recurrence of flowers. In the four volumes of Nahuatl poetry that I shall discuss flowers are iterated and reiterated times without number. *Flor y canto*, 'flower and song', drew the poets, according to Diego Duran, to their periodical gatherings around their symbolic 'Tree- in-Flower' - *Xochicuahuitl,* Arbol Florido - and to the house of flowers - *xochicalli* - where on the feast of Xochipilli a 'tree' was erected ad hoc and laden with flowers, where children dressed as birds and butterflies gamboled among the flowers, and where everyone sang and danced. This custom had been going on for perhaps a thousand years, for at Tepantitla, in Teotihuacan, the fragments of a mural of this stylized 'tree' were found in the late 1930's, and Villagra Caleti conscientiously restored it for display in the Museo Nacional de Antropologia. Peter T. Furst suggests that this tree represented the morning-glory. He is certainly right in part: the interlacing branches take their inspiration from the twining climber of the Nahuatl *coaxihuitl*, 'snake plant', the morning-glory, whose seeds are known as *ololiuhqui*. But this *'Tree-in-Flower'* is a symbolic tree built for the occasion, a n d t h e Nahua erected it to the glory of all the superior entheogens among which the morning-glory held a most honored place. Diego Duran does not say that at this celebration the participants consumed entheogens but his failure to do so leaves the question open and in the light of our meaning for *Xochipilli*, Prince of Flowers, and of Duran's obvious implication (discussed on p 201) that flowers were present when he does not expressly mention them, it is not an abuse to surmise that flowers were there consumed. Indeed, their presence is compelling.

Figure 1. The Tree-in-Flower, repainted after Tepantitla, Teotihuaciin

We reproduce Villagra's repainting of this 'Tree-in-Flower' in Fig 1. The Mesoamerican conception of such a tree reminds us forcibly of the Maypole in northern Europe, where in Sweden it is still decorated with branches of birch. Those who celebrate the Maypole no longer remember that the birch is the host of choice to the entheogenic Amanita muscaria. All students of Nahuatl culture have become familiar in recent times with the word teonandcatl, the name used for the entheogenic mushrooms that was used by Sahagun and Motolinia. But we ask ourselves why this word is not to be found in Fray Alonso de Molina's big lexicon of the Nahuatl language published in 1571. He gives us another word, *xochinandcatl*, *'flower mushroom'* from *xochitl*, *'flower'*, precisely the word that the statue of *Xochipilli* tells us to expect. *Xochinandcatl* survives to this day in a place name, *'Xochinanacatlan'*, a muncipio of *Tlaola*, District of Huachinango, State of Puebla. 'Nanacamilpa' is a place name near Tlaxcala even now and there is authority for the belief that in Veracruz a village existed in the sixteenth century called *'Nanacatlan'*. One Antonio Xochinanacatl figures in a Tlaxcala law suit that Thelma Sullivan is translating. In the Matricula de Huexotz.inco (a bilingual list of that town's inhabitants in 1560 composed in Nahuatl picture writing and in Spanish) two men bear the name Xochinanacatl. (See p114)

In Mesoamerica we enjoy an inestimable privilege: we have spread out before us the life style of a branch of Early Man possessing an advanced culture, the leader among the cultures round about, where any immediate influence of Eurasia is most unlikely, where earnest and zealous scholars believing in such influences work all their lives to establish threads of ancient contact, where such contacts (and certainly, there may well have been some) do not materially affect the pure strain of what the Spaniards found flourishing in Mesoamerica. They found a people for whom religion was everything, perhaps even more so than for the sixteenth century Spaniards: no human act was performed untinctured by religious beliefs.

Their religion evoked reverence, adoration, awe, but also fear, yes, and terror; as do all religions gripping Early Man. Their 'wars' were often waged solely to take prisoners to sacrifice to their gods. The frenzy, the delirium, of these wars, the dangers that every warrior ran, the courage that the prisoner was expected to show on the sacrifice day, added to life the ultimate in awesome terror. Their cruelty was clean, elegant. When prisoners were being sacrificed with the obsidian knife on a stone slab carved for that purpose, on top of the pyramids, the enemy's leaders would be invited to attend and from behind blinds they would watch the victims climb the long, steep, shallow steps without balustrade to meet their end at the top. (How bitter-sad and proud must their compatriots have been on watching the behavior of their friends and loved ones on this, their last glorious day!) The Nahua were cruel, but who are we to reproach them?

We discover that *'flower'* was also used as a trope for their warfare, just as it was for the entheogens. The Nahua exalted their 'wars' with this their supreme metaphor of enhancement, taken from the metaphor for the entheogens. The entheogenic experience was the supernal event of their lives and it supplied them with a storehouse whence they drew their ultimate in verbal praise, redolent with religious feeling. They believed in the reality of that other world of the entheogens, and anyone who knows the mushrooms and is also imbued with historical imagination will understand why. We must always keep in mind what Early Man did not know: the Nahua did not know they were dealing with a mere 'drug', as we say, a chemical compound with a known molecular structure and a known impact on the human mind. They were dealing with a miraculous, a divine gift. The two tropes - primary and secondary - became interchangeable in a way sometimes difficult for us to follow: there is interplay between them, to the point where we can sometimes only guess at the meaning.

Father Garibay expressly denies to his four volumes of poetry any involvement with the entheogens, even when the inebriating mushrooms (eg *nanacao'ctli*, 'mushroom liquor') are specifically mentioned, saying that here we have to do with poetic metaphor. But how jejune, how flaccid, is this poetry stripped of the divine inebriants! In these verses our Nahua, Princes and Nobles, are treating us to the hot afflatus of poetic passion, courtly poets living in their own proto-history without the alphabet, composing and singing their own verses before they knew that Europe existed, and what preoccupied them? The Mystery of the entheogens. Here lie the bone and sinew, the blood and muscle of their poetry. They were aglow with the rapture of the entheogenic experience, the religious surge that welled up in them. In this corpus of Mesoamerican poetry, we discover Early Man's poetic drive uninfluenced by Eurasian peoples. We surmise a practice and an intellectual legacy from those migrants who came across the Bering Strait, but this takes us back many, many millennia.

If there are any who question my meaning for these poems, I urge them to read the first four poems that I off er in this chapter and then to say whether the poets were singing merely to the fragrance of flowers. They were not only cultivated men but men of power in their world. Effeminacy is not a word that could be linked to them.

The paradise of the Nahua is mysterious alike for them and for us, but the questions it poses for them and for us are radically different. Knowing nothing of this other-world of Mesoamerica, our Mesoamerican scholars are stopped short before its closed portals asking what there is beyond, misunderstanding and baffled by the hints they hear in the verses. The Nahuatl poets, having often penetrated that 'beyond', are on the other hand awestruck by its overwhelming impact on all their senses, on their emotional being, by the certainty they feel that they have here touched base with Truth, by the further question it poses for them about the

111

Absolute and the Ultimate, and by the extraordinary feelings of friendship that it breeds among those who have shared in the common experience. The quality of the singing, the poetry, is enhanced beyond measure by this shared experience, which we in the West have declined to share with them. The poetry, the singing, though they seem to us merely good, take on under the influence of the entheogen the tongues of archangels: both music and verses are of the highest anthropological interest, when understood in the light of the entheogens.

Like almost all of the other top-flight Mesoamerican scholars, Father Garibay was ignorant of the wondrous mushrooms and morning-glory seeds. The Nahuatl poems present obscurities and difficulties aplenty, as he makes clear in his commentary. In addition to all the others there is one fabricated by Mesoamerican scholars: Father Garibay fails to realize that *flores* is the trope for the entheogens. They pervade these volumes of verse with obsessional intensity. Here we are for t h e first time listening in to the aristocrats of pre-Conquest Mesoamerica, without intervention of friars or conquistadores, singing the glories of their own entheogens. It proves to be, for us, an amazing experience. Whatever the obscurities and ambiguities of the poetry, one thing seems to me clear: these Princes and Nobles, men of courage and discernment, find on earth little to live for, other than their vistas of Tlalocan made possible by flowers and the songs that they composed and sang together. Here there is no ambiguity, no obscurity.

In the following poems, which we have selected from the whole published corpus, Father Garibay's version is on the left, my rendering of his Spanish into English is on the right. These poems reflect the thoughts, the feelings, of the elite of the Nahuatl pre-Conquest world. A few words to which I give a different meaning from Father Garibay's are printed in small capitals, and I explain in each case my disagreement. The references in this chapter are to Father Garibay's three volumes of Poesia Nahuatl and to the page number.

1. 'Sacerdotes, yo os pregunro: 'Tell us, o priests, whence come
    De donde vienen las flores que embriagan? The flowers that inebriate?
    De donde vienen las cantos que embriagan? The songs that inebriate?'

    'Los bellos cantos solo vienen   'The lovely songs come solely
    De su casa, de dentro del cielo   From His house, from within the sky
    Solo de su casa vienen las bellas flores.' Solely from His house come the
                                                Lovely flowers.'

Poesia Nahuatl 1 p 77

(I interrupt my argument for a moment to call the attention of the reader to a startling circumstance. Maria Sabina, when repeating the Lord's Prayer in Mazatec, alters the text: 'Our Father Who art in Thy house in heaven,' she says, thus interpolating the phrase used in the above Nahuatl poem, also in the poems 3 and 13 quoted below, and frequently elsewhere. I am told this interpolation is frequent among Mazatec speakers and it supplies us with an apt illustration of the crosslinguistic unity known to the cultural student as 'Mesoamerica', Nahuatl and Mazatec being wholly unrelated languages. It speaks for the high antiquity and strength of that cultural entity.)

2. Pero en verd ad se vive?
   Pereceran las flores que en nuestra
   mano estaban:
   Tambien con ellas se iran embriagando
   nuestros amigos:
   Hemos de perecer en la tierra.

But are we truly alive?
The flowers lately in our hands will
perish.
Our friends with flowers will go on
inebriating themselves Our
destiny is to perish on the earth.

Poesia Nahllatl 1 p 48

3. Ando en el patio florido, en el patio
   florido alzo mi canto.

I stroll in the flowery patio, in the
Flowery patio I raise my song.

***

***

He llegado a su presencia y hago estre
mecer...mis llores embriagadores: es
que alzo mi canto!
Llegaron aca nuestros cantos,
llegaron aca nuestras flares . . .
De dentro del cielo vienen:
alli busco yo mis cantos,
alli busco yo mis flares.

I have arrived in your presence, I
wave my inebriating *flowers*, as I
Raise my voice in song.
Our songs are arrived here...
From within heaven they come;
There is where I seek my songs,
There is where I seek my *flowers*.

***

***

D e la casa del dios vienen las flares,
en su casa ha de buscarse el canto.

From the house of God comes
the flowers.
In his house, song is to be sought.

Poesia Nahuatl 2 p 34-35

4. Deleitaos
   con las embriagadores flares
   que estan en nuestras manos.
   ! Vengan a ponerse en los cuellos

Take delight
   in the inebriating flowers
   that we hold in our hands.
   May they come and encircle our

collares de flares:
nuestras flares de tiempo de lluvia:
esten rescas,   CUEPONIA
                ABRAN SUS CAPULLOS!...
Solo con nuestras flares demonos placer;
Solo con nuestros cantos vaya desapare-
  ciendo nuestra tristeza, principes:
Con ellas huya vuestro hastio.

Las crea el que hace vivir todo,
Las hace nacer el Arbitro Supremo:
Flores placenteras:
Con ellas huya vuestro hastio.

throats.
  the garlands of flowers!
Our *flowers* of the rainy season,
May they be fresh, may they spring
forth!
Only in our *flowers,* let us take delight,
Only with our songs, O Princes, may
Our sadness vanish.
With them (The Flowers) may your
Ennui take flight!

By Him who makes all live are they
created.
The Supreme arbiter gives them birth.
The joyous flowers
With them may your ennui fly away!

Poesia Nahuatl 1 p 50

In these four poems the singers speak to us repeatedly of 'flowers that inebriate'. The flowers are the plant entheogens, the inebriating mushrooms or morning glory seeds. Flowers is a metaphor but 'inebriate' is not. (Father Garibay thought 'inebriate' a metaphor and 'flowers' just flowers.) Support for my thesis lies in the carvings of the statue of Xochipilli, in the iteration without parallel of flowers in the songs of the Nahua, in the word xochinandcatl that Molina gives us for the inebriating mushrooms, and finally in the added muscle and sinew that my interpretation gives to the poems.

Unexpected and telling support for my reading of these poems appeared some years ago in Marino Benzi's book on the role of peyote in the culture of the Huichol. The name for the inebriating cactus in Huichol is *jikuri,* as is well known. But Benzi tells us that in their chants the jikuri is called *toto'* and sometimes *ruturi,* both of these words meaning 'flower'. When the Huichol wish to designate the plant to a stranger, they call it by the Spanish word *rosita,* 'the little flower'. In the sixteenth and seventeenth centuries *flor* and *rosa* were used indifferently for '*flower*'. (See p 337 in Benzi's Les derniers adorateurs du peyotl.)

THE MEANING OF CUEPONI

In line 7 of our Poem 4 we discover the Nahuatl verb *cueponi* which Father Garibay renders by *abran sus capullos*. The word recurs often in the Nahuatl poetry before us and he almost always renders it by this expression, which in English means *'open their corollas'*. I submit that cueponi must be translated differently. In Molina's *lexicon* the first meaning of cueponi is to burst forth as a chick from the egg. The second meaning is to burst open as a chestnut when it is roasted. The chick makes its first sounds on this earth as it cracks its shell; the chestnut pops its cuticle as it roasts. This audible effect seems basic to the meaning of *cueponi*. Only the third rendering covers the flowers that emerge from their buds. If my reading of the statue of Xochipilli is right, if xochinandcatl means what Molina says it means, if my meaning for 'flowers' is right, then the meaning in the poetry of the Nahua of cueponi must often be the bursting forth of the divine mushrooms from the 'egg' that marks their first appearance on earth. And as we all know, at first, they do look like eggs, round and white, and they do burst forth overnight. The spirited crackling of the shell as the vigorous chick thrusts its way into the world, the bursting of the chestnuts in the heat of the fire - are not these fitting poetic analogies of the songs, the drum beats, that the divine mushrooms inspire? *Cueponi* occurs so frequently and *cueponi* fits the mushroom world so nicely that it is as if made to order for my argument.

Note that in this last poem the poet links the growth of flowers with the rainy season. While of course we know that rain is always associated with the growth of plant life, especially is it so with mushrooms: rains must come before we go on foray to look for mushrooms. In Mesoamerica the Indians await the rains eagerly, knowing that they bring forth the divine mushrooms.

In another poem that Father Garibay gives us (No 5), the second verse, speaking of flowers, reads as follows:

Cueponticac xochitl ixpan ipalnemoani

Which he translates;

Flowers open their corollas before the Life-giver

115

But this is obviously a mistake. 'The flowers spring forth [like chicks from the egg] before the Life-giver.' The first verse of this poem reads:

Panhuetz panhuetz xochitl

and Father Garibay translates it:

Brotaron las flares, brotaron las flares,

meaning, 'Flowers spring forth, flowers spring forth.' According to Molina, 'panhuetz' means 'to surmount', and the first two lines of this poem should be rendered:

Surmounting, surmounting all
Flowers spring forth [like chicks from the egg]
before the Life-giver.

The entheogenic mushrooms, in the poet's mind, surmount everything else in this world. The poem that we are discussing draws a brief note from Father Garibay. He says it is undeniably obscure but that none more merits study. I agree with the latter remark but does not my interpretation clarify the sense? Here are the verses of this poem to which I would draw the reader's attention.

I give Father Gari bay's version and then my own:

5. Brotaron las flares, brotaron las flares,
Abren sus corolas ante el que da vida.

Surmounting all, all,
Flowers spring forth like chicks
from the egg before the Life-giver.

***   ***

Ricas olientes flares se van esparciendo,
van al patio enflorado de las mariposas.

Rich fragrant flowers are being strewn,
They go to the patio bedecked with
flowery butterflies.

Todas alla llegan de donde esta La Flor
enhiesta:

They all arrive from there, where the
flower stands high.

Flores que trastornan, flares que pertu
rban,

Flowers that upset, flowers that perturb,

Los humanos corazones de los que se
Afirman

Human hearts of those who command.

Vienen a derramarlas, vienen a esparcirlas,

They come to strew them, come to scatter
them,

Cua! tejido de flares que embriagan.   Even as a web of flowers that inebriate.
Poesia Nahuatl 2 p 113

The coming of the flowers (= entheogens) is analogous to the birth of life. Raising the voice in song is an offering that serves to express our appreciation of them, our feeling for them. The reader will have observed that in this poem the butterfly figures as in our statue of Xochipilli. This song may have been composed to be sung on the Feast of Xochipilli: it harmonizes well with Diego Duran's description of that amazing annual celebration, which seems to have had as its focus a gigantic effigy of a flower raised on high. That effigy could well have been an enormous mushroom made of the stuff of beaten bark, *amate.*

For me, of English ancestry and by deepest cultural inheritance a mycophobe, the divine mushrooms smelled sickening, and on the first occasion I had difficulty in swallowing them. But the Indians, to my surprise, praise smell and taste! Their attitude justifies 'the rich, fragrant flowers' of the poem. (Recently I have found some Westerners who also find the taste not bad.)

6. Llegaron las flores:
   Que sean ellas gala
   Que sean ellas riqueza, Oh principes.
   Bien nos muestran su faz,
   VIENEN CUECUEP ONTIHUITZ
   ABRIR SUS COROLAS
   Solo en primavera alcanzan su perfeccion,
   las innumerables flores,
   Llegaron las flores al borde de la montatana

   The flowers have arrived:
   May they bring joy
   May they be our wealth, o Princes!
   Well do they show their faces [caps],
   They have just burst forth
   Only in spring do they reach perfection,
   The flowers without number,
   Flowers have arrived on the approaches to
   the mountain!

Poesia Nahuatl 2 p 131

FLOWERS FOSTER FRIENDSHIP

7. Solo las flores son nuestra riqueza:
Por medio de ellas nos hacemos amigos
y con el canto nuestra pesadumbre se
disipa,
Y en las flores preciosas se ven sus flores
en la tierra.
Lo sabe el corazon nuestro.
Cantad como lo quiere el corazon de
aquel por quien vivimos en la tierra.

Only flowers are our wealth:
Through them friendship between us grows,
And through song our sadness vanished
And by the Precious Flowers we are permitted
to see your flowers on earth.
We know it in our hearts.
May you sing according to His heart's desire
by Whom we live on earth.

Poesia Nahuatl 1 p 47

The opening lines of this Poem call attention to the effect of the
entheogens on friendship: those who share in the entheogenic experience
feel tied to each other for evermore by the warmest fraternal bonds. They
need never mention to each other the shared experience: each knows it.
In Siberia the fly-agaric had the same effect: its allayed animosities,
encouraged friendship and understanding. Also, in classical sources the
annual Mystery of Eleusis gave rise to a bond of friendship among those
who had passed that momentous night together. Here is a spontaneous
and mighty source for the feeling of compadraz.co, a Spanish word that I
have difficulty in rendering into English.

'Precious Flowers', in the Nahuatl original, is xoclticacahuatl and this
is the name of the tree growing in the state of Oaxaca, in the ancient
towns of Huayapan and Zaachila, known to botanists as Quararibea
funebris, the tree that yields flowers called in Nahuatl poyomatli, a flower
to which marvelous virtues were attributed, in the first instance having a
powerful, lasting fragrance. Its flowers were always mixed with chocolate,
a drink that accompanied the ingestion of the sacred mushrooms. These
flowers ranked in esteem with the entheogens and seem to have been

considered hallucinogenic also. They will be discussed further in the next chapter. The warmth of fraternal feeling generated by flowers is a repeated theme, as illustrated here in this verse:

8. Tambien con flares
   alli entonces hay abrazos de unos a otros
   Con cantos alli se cargan unos a otros.
   Es embelesadora vuestra palabra,
   Oh principes,
   se deleitan unos a otros los principes.

   Also, with flowers they embrace one
   another;
   With songs they there treat one another.
   Your word, o Princes, is enchanting,
   The Princes delight in each other.

   Poesia Nahuatl 1 p 34

Another poem that Father Garibay calls ' The Tree-in-Flower of Friendship starts out thus:

9. *Ya abre sus corolas el Arbol Florido de la
   Amis tad.*

   *Already burst into bloom the Tree-in-Flower
   of friendship.*

   Poesia Nahuatl 2 p 5

119

SIGHTS AND SOUNDS BECOME ONE

In my first veladas with Maria Sabina i n 1955, I observed that melodies seemed to take on shapes and colors, and sights assumed the modalities of music. Imagine then my surprise when I discovered, in the '60's with the publication of Father Garibay's rendering of the pre-Conquest poems, that these poets had recorded the same phenomena.

10. En estera de flares
    pintas tu
    tu canto, tu palabra,
    Oh principe mio, Nezahualco'yotl.
    Se va pintando tu corazo'n
    con fl ores policromas;
    pintas tu
    tu canto, tu palabra,
    Oh principe mio, Nezahualco'yotl.

    On a mat of flowers
    thou paintest
    thy song, thy word,
    o my Prince, Nezahualco'yotl.
    Thy heart is being painted
    with polychrome flowers;
    thou paintest
    thy song, thy word,
    o my Prince, Nezahualco'yotl.

        Poesia Nahuatl 1 p 49

The same theme recurs in this poem:

11. Oh, tu con flores
    pintas las cosas,
    Dador de Li Vida:
    con cantos tu las metes en tinte,
    las matizas de colores . . .
    Solo en tu pintura hemos vivido
    aqui en la tierra.

O, thou with flowers
    paintest things,
    Giver of Life:
    with songs thou tintest things,
    blendest colors . . .
    Solely in thy paintings have we
    lived here on earth!   Poesia Nahuatl 1 p 85

12. Libro d e cantos es tu corazón
    Has venido a h acer oir tu canto.
    Tañiendo estas tu atabal
    eres cantor,
    entre flores de primavera
    deleitas a las personas.
    Ya esras repartiendo
    Flores d e fragancia embriagadora,
    flares preciosas.

    Your heart is a book of songs;
    You have com e to let us hear your song.
    You are sounding your drum.
    You are a singer,
    among flowers. of spring
    you delight people.
    You are apportioning
    Flowers of inebriating fragrance, precious
    flowers.

    Poesia Nahuatl 1 p 93

'Your heart is a Book of Songs', - the 'book' is *amoxtli*, the codices in picture writing some of which have survived. This is the 'Book' of which Maria Sabina sings repeatedly, four centuries later and in a tongue utterly different from Nahuatl. Such was the fame of the 'books' of the Nahua and Mixtecs! Father Garibay gives us evidence that this poem was composed almost certainly by *Nezahualco'yotl*, renowned king of Texcoco . . . .. 'Flowers of inebriating fragrance, precious flowers '. In the Nahuatl text these flowers are the flowers of Quararibea funebris: *poyomatli* and *cacahuaxochitl*.

13. Soy cantor y me deleito
    Cuando miro las flores y cuando alzo mi
    canto.
    Deleitaos con el, Oh principes!
    De la casa de dios vienen las flares, en
    su casa ha de buscarse el canto:
    No lo sabian acaso vuestras corazones,
    Oh principes?

    I am a singer and I take delight
    When I look on flowers and when I raise
    my song.
    Rejoice in my song, O Princes!
    From the House of God come the flowers,
    In His house one must look for song:

Do not your hearts perhaps tell you so,
O Princes?

Poesia Nahuatl 2 p 35

Another Nahuatl poet asks:

14. (Acaso de versa viene
   desde el cielo florida pintura
   en media de las flares?

   Is it indeed true that from Heaven
   comes the flowery painting
   in the midst of flowers?

Poesia Nahuatl 2 p 88

Surely this poet is recalling in tranquility his emotions on experiencing an entheogenic *velada* and asking inevitable questions. And as though answering him another poet sings:

15. De dentro del cielo es de donde vienen
   estos bellos cantos, estas bellas flares,
   Destruyen nuestra amargura, destruyen
   nuestra tristeza.

   From innermost Heaven come these lovely
   songs, these lovely flowers:
   They destroy our bitterness, our sadness.

Poesia Nahuatl 2 p 99

Support for the view that Quararibea funebris was considered an entheogen is to be found in this poem:

16. Bebamos ahora
   Comamos ahora
   Cacahuaxochitli.
   Con el deleitemonos.
   Que ya CUEPUNQUI
        SUS COROLAS ABRIERON
   tus flores.

   Cacahuaxochitla
   embriaga mi corazo'n,
   embriaga mi corazo'n,
   Con el ande yo adornado
   yo d e igual modo tambien
   pueda ir mi corazo'n.
   ! Que no se marchiten las flores!

Now let us drink,
Now let us eat
Quararibea funebris:
Let us revel together.
For already thy flowers have
burst forth.

Quararibea funebris
inebriates my heart,
inebriates my heart.
May I go about adorned with it,
and also, my heart!
May the flowers not wither!

Poesia Nahuatl 1 p 23

In 'A Monologue of Nezahualco'yotl' he exalts the '*flowers* that inebriate':

17. Hay cantos floridos: que se diga yo bebo
     flares que embriagan,
     ya llegaron las flores [poyoma] que
     causan vertigo,
     ven y seras glorificado.

There are songs in flower: let it be said
I drink flowers that inebriate,
Already came flowers causing vertigo.
Come! and you will be in glory.

Poesia Nahuatl 3 p 11

and he continues singing the glory of the blossoms (*poyomatli*) of
Quararibea funebris that 'color his heart'.

ANELHUAYO: WITHOUT ROOTS

I now call attention to a stanza that Father Garibay gives us:

18. Yengo presuroso a entretejer
    al Arbol Florido
    flores rientes.
    In Tamoanchan
    en alfombra florida
    hay flores perfectas
    hay ' flores; ANELHUAYO
    　　　　SIN RAICES

    I come hastening to interweave
    on the Tree-in-Flower
    laughing flowers.
    In Tamoanchan
    on flowered carpets
    there are perfect flowers,
    there are 'flowers without roots'.

    　　　Poesia Nahuatl 1 p 29

Flowers without roots! What does this mean? And again:

19. Diferentes flores yo estoy esparciendo,
    vengo a ofrendar cantos, flores
    embriagantes:
    Soy cara traviesa y vengo de
    alla donde el agua sale;
    vengo a ofrendar cantos, flores
    embriagantes.
    Diferentes flores, aun, aun tu coraz6n
    lo sabe:
    para til as traiga, para ti las venga
    yo cargando.
    Vamos a tu casa, vamos,
    traigo como carga
    flores ANELHUAYO
    　　　　DESARRAIGADAS
    traigo como carga flores perfumadas:
    Esta es tu casa: aqui se yergue
    La Flor Blanca.

    Diverse flowers I scatter,
    I come offering songs, inebriating flowers;

With mischievous face I come from
afar where gushes forth the water,
I come to offer songs, inebriating flowers.
Diverse flowers, already, already,
your heart knows,
May I bring them to you, come loaded
with them.
Let us go to your house, come,
I come loaded with 'flowers without roots',
I come loaded with aromatic flowers,
Here is your home: here stands high the White Flower.

Poesia Nahuatl 3 p 39

Again, we find 'flowers without roots', *anelhuayo* in Nahuatl! And a third citation:

20. Tu estas enlazado al Arbol Florido
    a las flores que rien en Tamoanchan:
    sobre estera d e flores medran
    aquellas flores,
    y ANELHUAYO
      RAIZ NO CONOCEN.

You are enlaced with the Tree-in Flower,
flowers laughing in Tamoanchan:
On a carpet of flowers
those flowers prosper,
and roots they have not!

Garibay, Hist. Nahuatl Lit. 1, p 181

In none of these three instances does Father Garibay add a note of comment on 'flowers without roots', an odd expression. For me there is no doubt: we possess here another instance where Early Man perceived the distinctions that mark the mushroomic world. Fungal growths multiply without seed and are without roots. The Mazatec herbalists stressed the seedlessness: in *'nti'xi'tho'*, the formal way of referring to the divine mushrooms, they are saying, 'the dear-little-ones that leap forth', i.e. come up miraculously, suddenly, without seed. The Nahua, as we see in these poems, emphasized their rootlessness.

Father Garibay explicitly apologizes for the inadequacy of his version of the Nahuatl original of his verses, and now I, a fortiori, for my English rendering of Garibay's Spanish. I trust no reader will think that he has

125

been in contact with the Nahuatl poets. But in this chapter, I am confident that I have caught and revived an old and major meaning for *xochitl* in the language of the Nahuatl aristocrats, perhaps also (thanks to the distinguished Nahuatlata Thelma Sullivan) come closer to the meaning of the word cueponi, and finally given a sense to the word *anelhuayo* in the verses before us. Moreover, when I was first under the influence of the potent mushrooms in veladas in the late 1950's, long before I had access to the poetry that we have been discussing, I reported repeatedly the powerful spirit of the ancient agape that came over us in those gatherings. I also reported how hearing and seeing coalesce. What you are seeing and what you are hearing appear as one: the music assumes harmonious shapes, giving visual form to its harmonies, and what you are seeing takes on the' modalities of music - the music of the spheres, is what I then said and published (Harvard Botanical Museum Leaflet 19: 7 p156). Imagine my surprise on finding the Nahuatl poets so impressed by these same phenomena that they felt impelled to dwell on them in their verses.

CHAPTER 5

THE INHEBRIATING DRINKS OF THE NAHUA

In *Poesia Nahuatl* 2 there is a poem that begins with this verse as rendered by Father Garibay:

He bebido vino de hongos y
Llora mi corazo'n. [page 55]

I have drunk wine of mushrooms
and my heart weeps.

This single verse reveals the need for disentangling the words used in Nahuatl and Spanish for the inebriating drinks of Mesoamerica. In Nahuatl it reads:

Oyanoconic in nanacaoctli, ya noyol in choca.

I have drunk the liquor of mushrooms and my heart weeps.

Here we find the clue to the full meaning of *octli* in Nahuatl: it was applicable to any inebriating drink, whether alcoholic or entheogenic. In the past *octli* has been taken as the Nahuatl word for any fermented drink, especially *pulque*, the fermented drink of the succulent *maguey*, but *nanacaoctli* is also clearly the [inebriating] liquor of [enthcogenic] mushrooms: *nanaca-* from *nandcatl*, 'mushroom', and *-octli*, 'liquor'. For centuries we have simply ignored the entheogens.

When Cortes and his men mingled with the Aztecs in the Valley of Mexico, they found themselves before a complex of strange inebriating drinks for which they had no Spanish names. The common drink was the fermented sap of a succulent (not a cactus) classified by botanists as a species of *Agave*, made according to complicated steps elaborated through millennia of cultivation. The plant today is known in Spanish as *maguey*, a word introduced into Mesoamerica by the Spaniards from Taino, a language of the Antilles. (The specific name in Nahuatl is *metl*.) This drink is familiar to us as pulque but where pulque comes from no one knows for certain. It is not a Nahuatl word. The earliest citation for it is in a letter that Cortes addressed to his Emperor Charles V dated 15 October 1524, a date so early that it precludes a borrowing from any South American

127

Indian language. An ingenious suggestion is that it was a deformation on the rude tongues of the Spanish soldiery of Nahuatl *puliuhki* meaning 'perish', 'gone to waste', a pejorative characterization of the native drink. *Pulque* is fit (and excellent) for human consumption for only a little more than 24 hours, whereupon it does degenerate into a decomposed, rotten, stinking fluid. We may assume that this is probably the origin of pulque until a better explanation presents itself.

The Nahua called *pulque, octli,* but as we have seen this was the name given to inebriating drinks in general, of which there were many, alcoholic and entheogenic. Father Garibay followed the practice of the Spanish friars in translating *nanacaoctli* by *vino de hongos,* ' mushroom wine', a grave mistake for it plants in the mind of the uninformed that the mushrooms were either alcoholic or bore an analogy to fermented grape juice. For the Spanish soldiery wine was the common inebriating drink, beer and brandy hardly being known in Spain in the early 1500's and not known at all in the New World, and naturally the friars with their poor vocabulary for inebriating drinks and their non-existent experience with the mushrooms resorted to 'wine' for the entheogenic mushroom juice. But it is surely time that we do better.

Father Garibay did not enter into the intricacies of Nahuatl drinks, which were alien and confusing for him. It seems to me certain that the flowers (*xochitl*) of the Nahua were used for what we would call today the entheogens, and furthermore limited to those entheogens considered fit for the aristocrats. Father Garibay says that a plebeian who drank chocolate (with flowers?) exposed himself even to the penalty of death.' He does not cite his authority for this and neither I nor my acquaintance among Mesoamerican scholars can supply it. The Nahua paid high honors to *pulque* in certain religious celebrations but by comparison with -*xochi*-potions, it was a vulgar beverage, easily accessible to anyone and a source of much drunkenness. The -*xochi*- beverages were not drunk by the elite at the same time as pulque. Father Garibay says that the flowers were drunk with pulque or alone, but in the four volumes of poems that he has given us only two seem to mix flowers with pulque, and those two serve but to prove my rule, for they are expressly composed (though by Nahuatl poets) in the Huastecan and Chichimecan manner. These peoples were considered barbarians by the Aztecs, possibly admired in some contexts in a condescending way but with a reputation for wild drinking habits. Our two poems, then, even in the Spanish rendering, reflect this change of pace and tone well, especially when a vulgar woman of low degree, a Huasteca, declares herself drunk on a mixture seemingly of *flowers* and *pulque*. (Her part was probably played by a Nahuatl man dressed to fit the role.) The incessant reiteration of *xochitl* and -*xochi*- in this body of poetry astonishes the reader today, mostly in a context of drinks, but in the elegant poetry of the Princes and Nobles there is never an instance where *pulque* is linked to *flowers*.

The anthologies that are represented in Father Garibay's volumes serve us admirably in conveying the poetic voices of the *elite* of the Nahuatl world. The collections were assembled for us by leading survivors of the defeated race and these survivors must have enlisted the cooperation of m any eager to contribute the poems that they had memorized to those who had succeeded in learning our alphabet and who could write them down. What pathos! With their world laid waste, their own exalted position in it destroyed, yet their precious heritage of verse, esteemed by them above all else, was put down on paper for someone, somewhere, sometime, somehow to decipher (and with what labor!) and then for this shadowy audience to enter into their magic world and relive what they had experienced and thought. What likelihood did they think there was that these verses in Nahuatl would be read? Yet today we can listen to the poets of this extinct world in proto-history speaking and singing to each other. What we hear is surprising: awe and wonder at what the flowers disclosed to them, the excitement and delirium of their 'wars', and the somber shadow of human sacrifice against which there is no whiff of opposition though the poets themselves were sometimes destined to be its victims. There i s even a poem composed probably by a captive already awaiting the obsidian knife.'

We have the best of outside evidence that alcohol was not mixed with the entheogens in the festivities of the upper caste of the Aztecs and others in the Valley of Mexico and thereabouts. Diego Duran, the chronicler who relied heavily on the now lost Cro'nica X written in Nahuatl by someone who moved in the highest circles in pre-Conquest times, is giving us a detailed account of the coronation of Ahuitzotl ca AD 1486 and then Duran adds:

In this whole story I have noted one thing: mention is never made that anyone drank wine of any kind to get drunk, but only woodland mushrooms, which they ate raw, on which, says the History (i.e. Cro'nica X), they were happy and rejoiced and went somewhat out of their heads, and of wine no mention is ever made, unless for sacrifices or funerals; mention is only made of the abundance of chocolate that was being drunk in these solemnities.

When Duran here speaks of 'wine', he means alcoholic beverages such as pulque, and the chocolate was taken with flowers. This quotation will be further discussed later.

129

In our own explorations through Mesoamerica we found repeatedly that alcohol was expressly forbidden to those who were ingesting the sacred mushrooms. The duration of this alcoholic abstinence varied: for one day before, or two, or three, or most often four. These were norms; I do not say they were always observed. And Maria Sabina always looked to her host at her *veladas* to supply *un cuartito* of *aguardiente* (a half pint of alcohol) for her to drink when her strenuous night's work was drawing to a close. (This was obviously a post- Conquest innovation.) In Mesoamerica there were two categories of inebriation, divine inebriation from the superior entheogens (i.e. mushrooms or morning-glory seeds) and alcoholic inebriation from *pulque* and the like.

The whole world today knows the cactus *Lophophora Williamsii* as *peyote*, or in standard Nahuatl as *peyotl*, the whole world except the Indian peoples (*Huichol* and *Tarahumara*) in whose religious life it figures large and who have their own names for it. But I raise the question whether the meaning of *peyotl* in Nahuatl was confined to the cactus *Lophophora Williamsii* in pre-Conquest days. This word circulates throughout much of Mesoamerica in regions where the importation of the cactus from the far arid north seems highly improbable. It takes various shapes as it passes from one linguistic area to another. Aguirre Beltran documents it in the Proceedings of the Inquisition in these forms: *peotl, piot, piyolli, peyori, peiot*, and above all *piule*.

There is no reason to think that the meaning of these words is confined to the cactus. In our own day the lexicographer Santamaria says that *piule* is used in *Oaxaca* for the entheogenic morning-glories. Richard Evans Schultes found it thirty years ago applied to entheogenic *Rhynchosia* seeds in the market place of Villa Alta, in Zapotec country, and also in the market of the city of *Oaxaca*. In 1955 Robert J. Weitlaner and I were in San Agustin Loxicha, in the Sierra Castera south of Miahuatlan, and we found that *piule* was applied here by the *sabio* don Aristeo Matias to two species of entheogenic mushrooms and also that it figured in the powerful myth linking the origin of the mushrooms to thunderbolts. May not *piule*, derived as it is from *peyotl* in pre-Conquest times, have been used for any entheogen in the vulgar language, called macehuallatolli, and then have spread far and wide, being deformed on alien tongues as it crossed linguistic frontiers?

But if *peyotl* was any entheogen, why do we never find it in the four volumes of verse that Father Garibay has given us in Nahuatl? Perhaps the answer lies here: the Nahua of the highest social class spoke their language in an elegant manner known as *tecpillatolli*. Was it not this manner of speaking that our poets were giving us? And for them in tecpillatolli the entheogens (or the superior entheogens) were as we have seen flowers. Peyotl or piule was left to the masses, whence they were borrowed by the linguistic groups of Oaxaca and perhaps beyond.

The Nahuatl poetry available to us is filled with entheogenic drinks. One verbal element is common to all of them: -*xochi*-, the various drinks in the -xochicycle having effects on the human psyche that are indistinguishable. The other verbal elements linked to -*xochi*- are *teo*-, 'divine' or 'wondrous', *octli*, any inebriating drink, and the word for water, *atl*, often reduced to at or its root a. To this day on the slopes of Popocatepetl the divine mushrooms are called in Nahuatl the 'little children of the waters', *a-pipil-tzin*, a- for 'water', -*pipil*- for 'children', and - *tzin,* a diminutive of endearment and respect.

Are not the drinks to which water is linked the ones made from the sacred-mushrooms? Only those who, like the Russians, are brought up to love and crave mushrooms, the mycophilic peoples, know the meaning of rain for their adored mushrooms. In Russia there is a special rain, 'mushroom rain', *gribnoi dozhd'*, that everyone knows is especially favorable to mushrooms. And a *fortiori*, raised to the nth power, is the joy in mushroom rain of a folk who know and make use of their own entheogenic mushrooms. A rain peopling the land with the divine mushrooms, the little-children-of-the-waters, is a gift that only a god can give. Here then, in Father Garibay's four volumes in Nahuatl verse are the words for inebriating drinks of which many specifically mention, if we are right, the entheogenic mushroom flowers.

Poesia Nahuatl 3 (No. of poem and line)

13.92,99; 14,21	xochi-octla	entheogenic potion
8. 9; 14.7	xochi-octli	entheogenic potion (not 'pulque' as Father Garibay renders it in 8.9)
2.26; 5 .7; 14.99; 23-I.8	xochi-atl	wondrous mushroom potion
13. 103	xochi-a ihuintimetl	wondrous mushroom potion with Pulque
16. 12, 14	xochi-a ihuintihus	wondrous mushroom potion
13. 30, 36, 117	xochi-a-octli	wondrous mushroom potion
13. 106	i-xochi-cuaxoxome	???
11. 1	xochi-a-tototl	???
14. 71	a-xochi-octli	wondrous mushroom potion
13. 63; 19.24	teo-a-xochitl	ʺ ʺ ʺ
13. 38	teo-a-xochitica	ʺ ʺ ʺ
13. 87	teo-a-xochi-octli	ʺ ʺ ʺ
13. 11	teo-a-xoch-octla	ʺ ʺ ʺ
13. 37	teo-atl	divine water (mushroom potion?)

Poesia Nahuatl 21st sec.

131

But the question remains how it came about that *xochitl* acquired its unique status as the symbol of the divine draught among the Princes and Nobles of the Nahua. The evidence for this status in the carvings on the statue of Xochipilli, in the name xochinandcatl for the sacred mushroom that Molina gives us, in the poetry of the upper caste of Nahua, where the theme of the 'flowers that inebriate' is insistent, is I think conclusive: the flowers enjoyed exalted, even divine status and lent themselves to a further level of metaphorical use when they served for the 'wars' or raids for sacrificial captives, a constant activity of these Indian peoples, for their war gear, and for the captives themselves.

Up to now we have not mentioned *xochitl* in a verbal combination that occurs more frequently than any other: cacahua-xochitl or occasionally *xochitl-cacahuatl*. Cacahuatl is none other than the chocolate or cacao tree, the *Theobroma cacao* L. of botanists. (Linnaeus gave the name '*Theobroma*', the 'food of the gods', to the *cacao* tree allegedly because of the esteem in which it was held by the Indians.) Chocolate was drunk cold and mixed with aromatic *flower* petals of which the overwhelming favorite was *cacahua-xochitl*. Indeed, it seems as though these particular petals were indispensable. Our poets' 'chocolate flowers' had nothing to do botanically with *Theobroma cacao*, but everything to do with the chocolate beverage as drunk by the aristocrats, according to Father Garibay. If he is right, we find here additional underpinning for my belief that the flowers of the Nahuatl poets come from their exclusive privilege for indulging in the flower petals of the *cacahuaxochitl*. Here we are dealing with a tree that grows in Veracruz and Oaxaca, known today to botanists as *Quararibea funebris*. Whether the petals of these flowers were entheogens such as the mushroom and morning-glory seeds, I do not know, but that the lords of Nahua so regarded them seems virtually certain. That these mushrooms or the *ololiuhqui* seeds (ground to fine powder on the *metate*) were often or perhaps always drunk with the *cacao* potion is also certain: when they are not mentioned, the poets may well have taken them for granted. After all, the poets were writing for each other, certainly not to inform us. Sometimes we read that the mushrooms were eaten but then mention is usually made of the chocolate-flower beverage accompanying the mushrooms. In glowing terms, the poets speak of this chocolate drink as an excitant, an aphrodisiac, possibly an entheogen. It inspired them to compose their poetry and music, to dance, to sing. So far as the evidence goes, we should not think of these celebrations as riotous drinking parties:

they were suffused throughout with religious feeling and with the melancholy that, soon or late, attends man's thinking here below. The poems bear witness to this.

There comes down to us in the writings of the friars the name of a mysterious vegetable product, poyomatli, but they never identify it. Everything concerning *poyomatli* written by the friars is enigmatic, tantalizing, mysterious. Did they not deliberately conceal its identity, feeling it was best for them to hide from the laity a product of such enticing potency?

Yet already in 1963, its identity was accessible to us: Dibble and Anderson, slowly and carefully progressing in the difficult translation of the Nahuatl text of the celebrated *Florentine Codex*, came at last to the description of the tree called cacahuaxochitl (our *Q. funebris*) and here is our answer:

[This tree] has cup-like [blossoms]; the name of its cup-like [blossoms] is poyomatli; a really pleasing odor is their aroma. The tree, the blossoms, its foliage, all are of pleasing odor, all perfumed, all aromatic. I cut [the blossoms], spread them out, arrange them, cover them with leaves, thread them, make a flower mat of them, make a bed of flowers with them, spread them over the land. [The perfume] spreads over the whole land, swirls, constantly swirls, spreads constantly swirling, spreads billowing.

[Bk 11, Earthly Things, p 202]

And so, to the long list of references to cacahua-xochitl we must now add all *poyomatli* citations!

Ten pages later Sahagun's Nahuatl informant dictated this additional comment on poyoma-xochitl:

This is the cup of *cacahua-xochitl*. They say it makes one falter, it deranges one, provokes one. It makes one falter, it deranges one, it provokes one.

[ibid, p 212]

'They say . . . '! Who are ' they'?

Let us pause a moment and examine that brief, innocent-looking phrase.

On the heels of the Conquest, Bernardino de Sahagun, the Franciscan friar, spent his entire adult life, about half a century, studying the Nahuatl-speaking Indians. He chose his informants carefully for their maturity, their experience, their character and knowledge. *The Florentine Codex* and the priceless manuscripts in Madrid are an invaluable treasury, in Nahuatl and Spanish, concerning the history, the customs and manners, of the Nahua, assembled under Sahagun's editorial supervision. Many other inadequate observation in Bernal Diaz d e Castillo's memoirs. Speaking of Montezuma, he wrote:

Traian en unas como a manera de copas de oro fino con cierta bebida hecha del mismo cacao; d ecian que era para tener acceso con muj eres, y entonces no mirabamos en ello. [Chap xci]

They would bring in to Montezuma something after the style of cups of fine gold with a certain drink made from the same cacao; they would say it was to have access to women, and so we did not inquire further.

Here is the chocolate beverage surely spiked with poyomatli and perhaps other superior hallucinogens. But Bernal Diaz says no more.

The poetry of the Nahua aristocrats supports with overwhelming evidence the hold on their imaginative life of *Quararibea funebris* and its *flower poyomatli*: I suggest that therein lies the origin of the metaphorical use of xochitl (*'flower', flor*) for the hallucinogens and for the dominance of '*flower*' in the poetry of the Nahua. This dazzling yellow flower swirls, constantly swirls, spreads constantly swirling, spreads billowing over the whole land.

Father Garibay was helpless before the inebriants of the Nahua. He called *xochioctli 'pulque'*. (*Poesia Nahuatl* 3 17.9) He described *poyomatli* as a '*stupefier*', again as a root, again as a '*species of peyotl*', all in one breath. (*Poesia Nahuatl* 3, p xxv) He said in 1967 that *ololiuhqui*, the entheogenic morning-glory, was a '*stupefier*' and probably a *Datura* (*Poesia Nahuatl* 1, p 226), though its identity had been established with finality by Richard Evans Schultes as long ago as 1941. He translated *poyomatli* as a '*narcotic of flowers*' (*Poesia Nahuatl* 3, pp 11, 19), as ' *lethargy producing*'
(*Poesia Nahuatl* 1, p 1), as '*enervating*' (*Poesia Nahuatl* 3, p5). He thinks that the poets with all their talk of the entheogens were engaging in metaphorical wordplay! At least he says so in his commentary. He never tells us where they gained their experience of those other worlds of Tamoanchan and Tlalocan.

True, in the past many have called drugs with mental effects by terms such as these without discrimination. But plants that inspired an outpouring of extraordinary poetry, of music, of dancing, are hardly stupefiers, narcosis-producing, enervating, or lethargy-producing. It is time that we learn to characterize our mental states with feeling for the words we use, and also that the Nahuatlatos learn to talk with living botanists, rather than rely on obsolete botanical sources. But let me hasten to add that we all and I in particular owe an immeasurable debt to Father Garibay. He marked an *etape* in Nahuatl studies that will never be forgotten. He has triggered a new interest in pre-Conquest Nahuatl culture that promises to illuminate a field of proto-history of incalculable cultural importance. These chapters of my book obviously could not have been written had he not provided the Nahuatl text of the poems I discuss.

Furthermore, Father Garibay's unfamiliarity with the inebriants of the Mesoamerican Indians in no way differentiates him from scholars past or present in this field of inquiry. If he shows up worse than others, it is only because he had the courage to confront texts that deal directly with the entheogens.

Now it is urgent that the entire corpus of Nahuatl poetry, most of it pre-Conquest, be transcribed and published, and that it be rendered into a modern language, presumably Spanish, not in verse but in a scholarly translation. Father Garibay has whetted our appetite: we wish to listen to the pre-Conquest Aztecs speaking freely with each other, without the intervention of even the best of the friars. The number of our Nahuatlatos is slowly increasing, and the ideal would be to find the one who combines in himself (or herself) the severe discipline of an exegete and the afflatus of the poet.

In the earlier chapters I have given a picture of the shamanic use of the entheogenic mushrooms in Mesoamerica as it survives into our own times. How widespread was this shamanic use? In Mazatlán de los Mixes, we discovered that a shaman was not needed for consulting the mushrooms: there was a l ay use of them. Anyone facing a grave problem would consult them, or perhaps a friend on his behalf and in his presence, also with a monitor, and then the mushroom would converse audibly with the eater and the monitor would make mental note of what was said. This might be regarded as a degeneration of an earlier shamanic practice, but Mazatlan de los Mixes is secluded, far from the beaten track, and may not their ways be rather an archaic survival in the Indian world?

An essential of shamanism is conformity, in the flow of words from the shaman's lips, in the music of his chants, in the percussive beats that accompany the singing. In each performance the shaman is limited in the deviations that he may introduce by the circumstances of the particular consultation that he is giving. He invokes a ritual whose authority lies in its antiquity and its universality, and the vocation of a shaman is essentially anonymous. True, in a given generation such-and-such a shaman is said to be of *primera categoria*, 'top category', but this is simply because he performs better than others a fairly rigid procedural canon, not because of innovations in that procedure, and when he is gone his memory lingers only for a few years among those who were his contemporaries.

Now let us contrast our shamanic veladas with the Nahuatl poems that Father Garibay has enabled us to examine. These are as far removed as can be from the chants of Maria Sabina, the unlettered shaman of the Sierra Mazateca. They are poems written in the decades that preceded the Conquest by the Princes and Nobles in the cities in and around the lakes of the Valley of Mexico. Each poem is an individual's studied composition. In some cases, the poets are known: their names, when they lived, and some of the circumstances of their lives. Their poems are sophisticated literary productions of individual poets, and the *elite* of the Nahuatl world were immensely proud of them. Many, perhaps all, of them were recited or sung at gatherings of the poets around the *Xochicuahuitl*, the *Arbol Florido*, the Tree-in-Flower. This was an idealized tree, set up ad hoc for such festivities. If Peter Furst is right, it was an ancient institution and we find it represented in a painting at Teotihuacan, which Villagra Caleti has reproduced for all to see in the *Museo Nacional de Antropologia*. Furst goes further: he argues that it is a highly stylized morning-glory (*ololiuhqui*) 'tree' and as I have said I think he is partly right.

The question is how to reconcile, on the one hand, the veladas held by shamans throughout Mesoamerica for millennia, in the dead of night, to help all kinds of humble suppliants facing life's problems, and on the other the festive open-air performances with music, dancing, singing, and poetry readings by the self-assured princes and aristocrats around the Tree-in-Flower and on other grand occasions, these performances going back, back beyond memory, if our interpretation of the *Tepantitla* 'Tree-in-Flower' is right. Both were inspired by flowers. In sophistication they were at opposite ends of the spectrum: would not the teeth of the aristocrats have been set on edge by the shamanic chants, so self-conscious were their highly spontaneous verses? Individual poets achieved fame for their excellence but in a culture where there was no way other than human memory to preserve the words of a poem, the fame of even the best poets was not likely to endure for more than a few decades. Is there any reason why the Tree-in-Flower could not have been celebrated every year, perhaps in every important community, from the days of Teotihuacan and long before, down to the Conquest? Social institutions and customs evolved slowly before easy writing came to mankind.

Maria Sabina and the poets of the two sixteenth century Nahuatl anthologies express the same profound reverence for the '*Book*', *amoxtli*, by which the poets meant the superbly painted picture-writing codices, kept beyond the reach of the masses in the *Amoxcalli*, the House of the Books, the Holy of Holies. And what that reverence must have been! It survived in Maria Sabina's chants into the late twentieth century, though for her it is become a purely mystical book, as it may well have been for her predecessors. For when a provincial shaman, even one of exceptional quality, visited Tenochtitlan, what access had that shaman to see and examine the Treasures of the *Amoxcalli?*

CHAPTER 6

CODICES, LIENZOS, MAPAS

CODEX VINDOBONENSIS

The documentary sources for the pre-Conquest history of Mesoamerica include a considerable number of what are called in Spanish codices, texts painted in picture writing that are being progressively deciphered by scholars dedicated to that task: they do not lend themselves to easy and assured reading. They were painted by priests of the Old Religion and were originally accessible only to the priesthood, but their renown was breathtaking. It seems to have run far and wide throughout Mesoamerica and we find the shaman Maria Sabina even today singing (and in Mazatec!) of the Libra with its numinous message, by which scholars seem agreed that she means, transmuted through more than four centuries of oral tradition, what were called by the Nahua amoxtli and by us in English. the painted codices of pre-Conquest times. The memory lingers on, severed from its roots, having had no contact for almost half a millennium with the documentary sources that originally inspired it.

We had refrained from tackling these codices in our quest of mushrooms partly because our hands were full with other sources easily accessible to us but chiefly from a feeling of inadequacy. What then was our surprise and delight when Dr Alfonso Caso, dean of Mesoamerican scholars, published a paper in the 1963 number of *Estudios de Cultura Nahuatl*, Vol IV, revealing our entheogenic mushrooms on a page of the celebrated *Codex Vindobonensis*, the 'Vienna Codex'. This Codex was painted, not in a Nahuatl but in a Mixtec scriptorium, and it gives the mythological Origin of Things. (Fig 1) Our interest is in the origin of the entheogenic mushrooms. The reader enters p 24 at the lower right hand and reads upwards in the right-hand column until, reaching the top, the mushroom agape of the gods fills both columns.

Abbreviating the story, we find near the bottom the god Quetzalcoatl in full panoply and wearing a mask with a bird's beak. He is listening respectfully to an aged god who is, it seems, giving him instructions. On the next level up and to the right a woman in a mask sits next to two burning incense (*copal*) balls. She is the incarnation of the spirit of the mushrooms and she wears four mushrooms in her hair. To the left we find Quetzalcoatl carrying this woman on his back after the manner of a bridegroom carrying his bride. Her headdress still carries mushrooms. On the level above, Quetzalcoatl, now facing to the right, is singing and beating time on a sinister musical instrument, a skull resting on a corded ring. He faces Piltzintecuhtli, 'Most Noble Prince', securely identified by his calendar sign Seven Flower, and this divinity is now holding aloft a pair of mushrooms. From his eye falls a tear, in response to the song of Quetzalcoatl.

Figure 1. Codex Vindobonensis, p 24

Let the reader note that Piltzintecuhtli is an aspect of Xochipilli, Sun God, the Prince of Flowers. We shall return to Piltzintecuhtli in Chap 7. Above and to the left of this scene we see seven gods and goddesses all bearing in their raised left hands a pair of mushrooms that (presumably) they are about to ingest. (There is one exception: a crone at the extreme left in the second row holds, strangely, only one mushroom. The second divinity on the top level also seems to hold but one: however, in the codex itself the figure is seriously eroded and we cannot s ay what she holds.) I take it this scene is not a banquet but a velada, the religious rite held at night.

141

There can be no question: in this Mesoamerican document we find full dress recognition of the major place occupied by mushrooms in the culture of the Mixtecs; in what we, being alien to that culture, would call their mythology but what the Mixtecs would have regarded as a feature in the story of their origins. W. Lehmann published a commentary in 1929 on this codex and he remarked on the 'objects in the shape of mushrooms', but as he (as well as everyone else at that late date) was living in ignorance of the role of mushrooms in Mesoamerican culture, he did not link this lordly scene with the mushrooms of the friar chroniclers.

(Since I wrote the foregoing paragraphs Mr. Frank Lipp, associated with the New York Botanical Garden, has called my attention to another Mixtec pictogram in the *Lienzo de Zacatepec* No I, which lies today in the *Museo Nacional de Antropologia*. It repeats the message of the woman bearing mushrooms in her hair,

Figure 2. Detail of Lienzo de Zacatepec No I

except that here the head is a man's. The head rests on top of *cerro* (hill). May it not represent a sacred mountain on the summit of which sabios or wisemen were accustomed to celebrate the mushroom agape?)

In the opening paragraph of his paper Dr Caso recognized his indebtedness to Roger Heim and us for calling attention to the entheogenic fungi. He even specifies our repro duction of five Teotihuacan murals and endorses our identification of mushrooms in them. This was a gratifying accolade, all the more so because of his authority. But I would point out that there are in his paper marked traces of the legacy of the sixteenth century Spanish friars. Our writings (Heim's and the Wassons')

. . . han dado a conocer ampliamente este aspecto de la hechiceria que se ha conservado en algunas panes de! pais . . ..

. . . have amply made known this aspect of the witchcraft that has been retained in some parts of the country . . .

'*Amply made known*'! He seems to have though t that we had exhausted our theme in what we had already published. But we had only opened up a vast subject, not merely in the Indian world of Mesoamerica but in the Americas and Eurasia, and perhaps elsewhere. He did not sense the implications of the entheogens in Early Man's life. Dr Caso treats our mushrooms gingerly. With the tips of his fingers, he advances his interpretation of the mushroom scene in the Codex tentatively: it is a 'hypothesis', it 'may be' right, although he has copper-riveted his proofs as we shall see shortly. He echoes the friars when he expresses his antipathy to the realm that he denominates by the pejorative, question-begging epithet 'witchcraft' and when he speaks of the mushrooms as *esta practica magica*, 'this magical practice'. Only in recent decades have scholars made serious inquiries into the peculiar 'witchcraft' phenomena of the l ate Middle Ages and Renaissance, and the panic that they provoked in the Churches, Catholic and in the later stages Protestant. ' There was no witch-hunting in Eastern Orthodoxy.

Let us pause a moment and develop this thought. For some centuries there had been in Western Europe a polarization between the Established Church on the one hand and an amorphous body of 'witches', whose beliefs such as they were had nothing in common with native Mesoamerican beliefs. The Spaniards brought over to the New World the religious beliefs held in Western Europe, including Catholicism and *brujeria*: both were equally strange to the natives and, as coming with the Spanish Conquerors, enjoying equal prestige. By grafting on to the unknowing Indians the old-world *brujeria* and later reproaching the Indians for entertaining it, are we not supplying a supreme example, a textbook case, of *anatopism*, an error in space corresponding to an anachronism in time? What of witchcraft or magic is to be found in entheogenic mushrooms? In psilocybin? (The 'witchcraft' of the time had nothing to do, of course, with the heresies that preoccupied some of the best minds of the age in Western Europe and that culminated in the Reformation.) The clergy treated alcoholic inebriation as a venial sin. It was condemned severely by the Nahua in pre-Conquest times, when pulque was expressly reserved for the oldsters who had passed their period of usefulness and were awaiting their end. (Of course, the official attitude may not have reflected the practice: prohibition was probably a failure with them as with us.) Inebriation from mushrooms and certain other hallucinogens, on the other hand, was confused by the clergy, not with alcoholism, but with brujeria and heresy.

As for the pre- Conquest codices, I looked at them and could not read them, but I was approaching them from a new perspective, the perspective of one who knew the entheogens from m any years back. The variegated colors, the play of angles and curves, the interlacing of planes, the reduced figures, the complicated masks and vestures - these all seemed somehow familiar to me. It came over me gradually: the dancing kaleidoscopic designs of the mushroomic experiences were what inspired the painter of the *amoxtli*. Henri Michaux and many others have attempted to find artistic inspiration in entheogenic drugs, but to discover an art that was saturated with. their influence and at the same time under the disciplined control of masters with a lifetime of entheogenic experience, we must look to pre-Conquest codices. Here is no fumbling of the novice. Many have been awestruck by the haunting beauty of these codices but until now it seems not to have occurred to anyone that they were painted by priests whose lives were constantly illumined by the unearthly glow of the divine *piule*. From childhood the priests were brought up in its ambiance. Whether the codices were painted while the priestly scribes were *bemushroomed* we will never know but I think this may have been possible for the trained *elite*. The *amoxtli* enjoyed a prestige that we sense to this day in Maria Sabina's chants: the gods themselves dictated these picture writings. This is a *cesthetic* judgement and is not open to demonstrable proof. On the other hand, only those who have known the hallucinogens well and under the right circumstances are qualified to assay my view . . . How startled and fascinated would Dr Caso have been at our new perspective on his codices!

CODICE INDIGENA NO 27

Dr Caso began his paper on the Codex Vindobonensis with a discussion of another Codex, post-Conquest, dating from 1549, a legal document written in picture writing on one side and in Spanish on the other. He found here solid grounding for his interpretation of the Vienna Codex. (Fig 3) This second Codex was an extraordinary discovery.

The Indians of Tetla in Morelos were filing a complaint alleging that Cortes in 1532 had taken some lands of theirs to make a road running to Mexico City. (Fig 3) The road is plainly indicated bisecting the land with human footprints marking the trail. On the left is a field apparently sown to sugar cane, on the right a terrain bearing the name 'Nanacatepeque'. The glyph for this name appears inside the land in question. In picture writing 'Nanacatepec' consists of three words: *nandcatl* meaning 'mushroom', *tepetl* meaning 'hill', and c, a locative meaning 'place' 'Mushroom Hill', The farmlands that adjoin Mushroom Hill are identified by other glyphs, all of which Dr Caso explains, his explanation being supported by the Spanish summary. In the glyph for Mushroom Hill the mush rooms are shown by a pair of mushrooms represent ed in cross section emerging from the hill. Dr Caso sees in the pair of mushrooms the identical glyph that we find in the Vienna Codex.

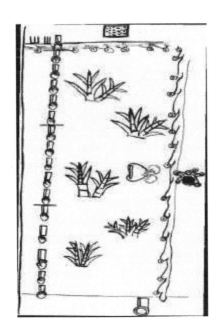

Figure 3. Cadice Indigena No 27

Figure 4. Detail of Cadice Irtdigena No 27

Before we leave this Cadice Indigena No 27, I will call attention to the two glyphs that mean running water, one along the top of the field and the other down its right side. The wavelets along the top are linked to snails alternating with circles, the circles in turn containing tiny concentric circles, reduced occasionally to a mere dot. Down the right side we find similarly flowing water but expressed here by the circle-and-dot. In the pictographic 'shorthand' the snails are dropped and the inner circle is hardly more than a dot. There is no commoner glyph in the picture writing of Mesoamerica than the one of water represented precisely as here. In this same Codex No 27 it occurs again to the right of Mushroom Hill , in the rebus glyph, which means '*Olaque*', the name of the adjoining village . This glyph consists of *Ol-*, taken from *ollin* meaning rubber, *a* for *atl* meaning water, and the locative *que*. The place name '*Olaque*' is thus expressed by a ball of rubber and the symbol for water.

I will revert to these glyphs for water when we come to discuss the Teotihuacan murals.

SAHAGUNS FLORENTINE CODEX

AND THE MAGLIABECHIANO CODEX

From the beginning of our inquiries into the mushrooms of the Nahua we were on the lookout for sixteenth century illustrations of them. The botanist Hernandez in his text said that he was depicting four kinds of mushrooms including the *teyhuinti*, the inebriating one, but the 1790 edition carried no illustrations, and his drawings, which would have been precious for us, must have been consumed in the Escorial fire. However, our quest has not been bootless. In the Florentine Codex of Bernardino de Sahagun's famous chronicle and account of the Mexican world we discovered one picture theretofore unremarked by students, and Robert J. Weitlaner has drawn our attention to a second in the Magliabechiano Codex. We here reproduce both of them, this having been facilitated by a happy chance: the two codices, though lying in different libraries, are both in Florence. The illustrations are singularly significant for us, being complementary, one of them executed by a Spanish artist and the other by a native in the tradition of his people, though he may show traces of Spanish influence. Both illustrations are in the nature of pictographs, vignettes intended to convey a verbal message. Neither tells the mycologist anything about the sacred mushrooms, but both are eloquent and curious expressions of the contrasting attitudes of the two peoples toward them.

Sahagun's writings survive in several depositories, the Florentine Codex in the *Biblioteca Laurenziana* being the best known. Although most of the many illustrations in it were done by native artists, some were by Spaniards, and it was a Spaniard who made the five small pictures representing various mushrooms that Sahagun discussed. A close inspection of the five pictures and Sahagun's text makes it clear that the artist worked from the text and possessed no knowledge outside the text. (Did Fray Bernardino think it safer not to turn to a native of Mesoamerica to depict the dangerous mushroom?) When he came to the inebriating mushroom, the painter undertook to convey his iconographic message in a way natural to a sixteenth century Spaniard: a demon is portrayed rising from a number of nondescript tawny mushrooms and the demon carries those conventional stigmata commonly identified with demons in the Gothic and Spanish worlds. He is clothed cap-a-pie in fur, a huge beak emerging from his fur-enclosed face. For hands he has claws. One foot is unformed or malformed, perhaps a splayfoot. This is the malformed foot that survives in the English 'cloven hoof', that led the French to speak of the Devil as le Bot, the Clubfooted One, the Cripple. ' In le Bot as in this picture we find blended the themes recurring in our writings – Satan portrayed as le Bot, a demonic mushroom, also called le Bot in Old French, and offstage, by metaphoric transfer, the toad again in Old French called le bot. The common toad was a focus of execration in Western Europe at that time, an attitude that runs back far and deep in West European history. In the 'witchcraft' trials of the Middle Ages I have nowhere found reference to mushrooms, but as a common denominator lying behind ordinary words of everyday use, we find Devil, toad, and toadstool. Did the Catholic clergy in Mesoamerica sense this ancient layer of meaning linking these three - Devil, toad, and toadstool - in an unholy trinity?

Malformed and bestial feet characterize several Aztec divinities. Thus, the god Tezcatlipoca was distinguished by a missing or deformed foot. But it would be rash to assume that t h e demon of the Flo ren tine Codex was influenced by Nahuatl artistic conventions. The craftsmanship reveals a European mind. the dubious visual expression corresponding to the verbal denunciations that the clergy were heaping on the 'demonic' mushrooms.

Figure 5. Illustration of Satanic Mushroom. Florentine Codex

Figure 6 Illustration from Magliabechiano Codex

The second illustration, in the Magliabechiano Codex, offers us three elements mushrooms, a m a n eating the mushrooms, a n d behind and over him a supernatural figure. The reader will note that the man holds a mushroom in each hand, i.e. a pair. According to Professor Jimenez Moreno, the spirit is probably Mictlantecuhtli, Lord of the Underworld, who is depicted on other pages of the same Codex. The Codex is painted on European paper, and dates probably from shortly after 1528. How far removed from the Spaniard's conception is the native's! Not only is the craftsmanship of these artists, contemporaries of each other, poles apart: their message is likewise. The Spaniard is reporting prosaically the existence of a demonic mushroom to his European public. The Indian, though undoubtedly a baptized Christian, conveys a sense of the reverence that he still feels in the presence of the awesome *teonandcatl*. That the mushrooms in this miniature are green should not disconcert the mycologist: green, the color of the precious jade, meant in Mexican iconography that the object so depicted was of great worth, was holy.

MATRICULA DE HUEXOTZINCO

In 1560 a census was taken of Huexotzinco, not only of the town but of the whole province. In pre-Conquest times Huexotzinco was a famous city not many miles from the lake, also famous, in which Mexico-Tenochtitlan was built. The census of everyone in Huexotzinco was written in duplicate, the names spelled out in Roman characters and also drawn in the picture writing of the Nahua. Karl Herbert Mayer has drawn my attention to two individuals in the list of names called Xochinandcatl, a word that, as we already know, means 'sacred mushroom'. We do not

149

know why these individuals were so called. Were they specialists in the gathering and use of the mushrooms? Or were these names unrelated to the mushrooms? Here are the pictographs for Luis and Diego *Xochinanacatl,* two of the entries in the Census of Huexotzinco for 1560:

Figure 7. Men named for the Sacred Mushroom. Matrirnla de Huexotzinco

In each case, as well as all other cases in this census record, a line invariably connects the face to the drawing that represents him. It will be noted that one spot on the right distinguishes the pictograph of Diego who is represented by one mushroom, and four spots accompany the pictograph of Luis who seems to be blessed with four mushrooms. What this means we know not, but it certainly meant something to the artist.

LIENZON DE TLACOATZINTEPEC

In April 1952 Robert J. Weitlaner discovered a *mapa* in the Chinantec village of San Juan Tlacoatzintepec, a map drawn in the picture-writing of the Indians dating back perhaps to the late sixteenth century or the early part of the seventeenth. The original, badly dilapidated from age, was drawn on tightly woven cotton cloth. Fortunately, it was copied in March 1892, and a tracing of this copy was made by Carlo Antonio Castro, Weitlaner's colleague. This typical post-Conquest Codex is reproduced in Fig 8. It represents a momentous event in the history of the village, a battle over lands between the village of Tlacoatzintepec and a neighboring town. We will dispense with the reading of the mapa, of interest to specialists, and concentrate on the crossed mushrooms in the upper right-hand corner, of which we supply the detail in Fig 9. Weitlaner was in no doubt that they represented the sacred mushrooms: ordinary mushrooms would never enjoy the prestige to be included in a mapa esteemed and guarded by the villagers as this one was. The same would hold true of the Cadice No 27 previously described. No mountain or hill would be named after ordinary mushrooms edible or inedible. In examining the Lienzo, the reader will smile on noting that the divine mushrooms are next to a Christian cross.

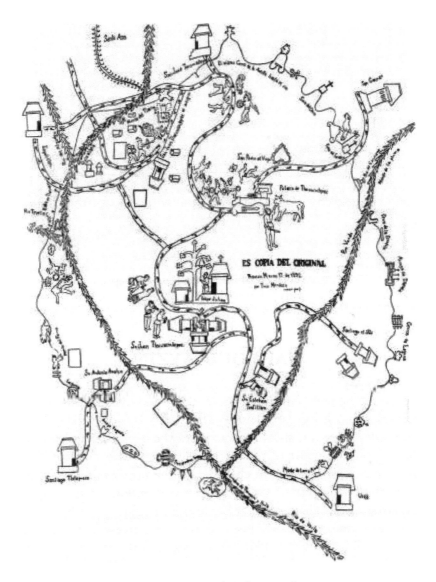

Figure 8. Lienz.o de Tlacoatz.intepec

napo vallatrolli ōcā
2ca... ya. ỹ :x ʠ·h mih
roar-a y mih teʠ
ỹ tinanxin quj ỹ. ꞏ!.
ir h tlatolli ỹ nïl tõ-
ꞏꞌ ꞏ ̃. ʃ ılu.

Figure 12 Further detail of drawing after Mapa Quinatzin

This chart bears explanatory comments and one of them deals with the two individuals seated in the room above our mushrooms. It explains that this is the audience chamber where justice is rendered: an audience in which the rights in certain lands are being adjudicated. The comments are in Nahuatl written in our alphabet. There is agreement on the translation as far as it goes.

Whether the two figures are colleagues discussing the merits of the case, or whether one is a judge (presun1ably the one on the l eft) and the other the plaintiff or the defendant, I would not say. They are both speaking, the one on the left uttering two *virgulas de habla*, 'commas of speech ', the other only one. *Virgulas de habla* is the customary way to designate in Spanish these common glyphs for speech in Mesoamerican writing. And *virgulas de habla* are what the mushrooms are uttering, the divinatory mushrooms, speaking with the voice of the gods. The court is having recourse to xochinandcatl to arrive at the just decision. The mushrooms are playing their proper role.

This Mapa Quinatzin has been described at length by Mesoamerican scholars, the Nahuatl comments translated, but apparently no exegete has ever remarked on these mushrooms uttering their *virgulas de habla*. I shall never forget Aurelio Carrera's arresting characterization of the sacred mushroom: es habla, it is speech, it is the Word.

CHAPTER 7

PILTZINTLI, CHILD GOD OF THE NAHUA, AND HIS CHRISTIAN PROGENY

SANTA MARIA TONANTZINTLA

A reader unfamiliar with the world of the Middle American Indian and acquainted only with the text of our *veladas* might jump to the conclusion that the divine mushrooms are primarily a device for predicting the outcome of a particular illness in a particular individual. True, this was the purpose of the shamanic sessions that we have offered to the public. But the horizons conjured into being by the mushrooms are far wider in time and space, and beyond time and space, than the mere outlook for a stricken patient. They translate one to a prismatic, iridescent, pristine world, a Garden of Eden and a Tlalocan, fields of asphodel, well-watered, clean, where the air and the breezes are good, where birds and butterflies and flowers abound, where men live off nectar and ambrosia. The divine mushrooms step up our drab existence to heights of great poetry and music. Those who commune with them find opening before them the portals to the playing fields of the gods.

And here I will interrupt my exposition to recapitulate certain developments in recent Middle American studies. In 1942 Alfonso Caso brought out a brilliant paper' in which he reported on the uncovering of a mural in the sacred precincts of Teotihuacan, a mural that he called Tepantitla after the solar or villa where it was found. Enough of the mural (painted probably between A D 300 and 600) survived to show that it portrayed Tlaloc the Rain-god, and Tlalocan his heaven. This heaven was a lovely scene of natural beauty where the chosen among the dead disport themselves in various games and pastimes. The Aztecs placed Tlalocan traditionally in the folds of the mountains below Popocatepetl.

In some quarter's doubts have been expressed as to whether Dr Caso was justified in assuming that the ideas and ideology of the Nahua of the fifteenth century could be projected back a thousand years into the Teotihuacan culture. I do not share these doubts. In our days of dizzy and accelerating technological change we must try to picture a stable world of unchanging ways, a world without an alphabet, without even draft animals to help in the performance of manual labor. Though we are not sure what language was native to Teotihuacan, we can be reasonably certain that, whatever the tongue spoken there, the ideas and habits of life were substantially unchanged until the arrival of the Spaniards - figures of Outer Space - erupted on the scene early in the sixteenth century.

In 1951 there was published a collection of papers in honor of Dr Caso and among them was a brief one contributed by Francisco de la Maza in which for the first time the Tlalocan of pre-Columbian days was linked with the Christian church of Santa Maria Tonantzintla near Cholula, a nineteenth century church that is almost in the shadow of the great Cholula pyramid and is within a long day's walk from the upland valleys where lay the Tlalocan of the pre-Columbian beliefs. There lie, over the crest of the mountains, San Pedro Nexapa and Amecameca where the sacred mushrooms are still consumed and consulted. Cholula is only a short distance away in every direction from the teonandcatl and ololiuhqui country. Each year in mid-September when the sacred mushrooms abound the Indians still go on pilgrimage to Cholula and thereabouts. Tonantzintla is also near Puebla, about a third of the way from Mexico City to Huautla. De l a Maza perceived that the remarkable interior of the church of our 'Little Mother' is decorated, not precisely in baroque or Churrigueresque style, but in a folk style consonant with the astonishing display of Churrigueresque extravagances manifesting themselves at that moment in Puebla. Those extravagances - did they not give an opportunity to the parishioners of Tonantzintla to indulge in aberrations of their own that were wholly of pre-Conquest inspiration? Throughout the interior of the church of Tonantzintla, De la Maza saw the *Nahua xochime* (flowers), *piltontli* (children), *ixtli* (faces), their wide-open eyes speaking for their amazement at finding themselves in Paradise, *xayacatl* (masks) covered with *ihuitl* (feathers) feasting on *xochicualli* (fruits). De la Maza's discovery deserves conspicuous honor, associating as he dared to do the pre-Columbian culture of the Indians with an eighteenth to nineteenth century expression of that same culture in a Christian temple. Here, he thought, was the key to what had been an amazing riddle. In retrospect his reading of the decor of this church seems obvious, as all major discoveries seem, once they have been made.

Then, in 1956, there came a little book by Pedro Rojas, Tonantzintla, illustrated with seventy-six of his photographs. It was a spectacular essay on the parish church of Santa Maria. The idea only adumbrated by De la Maza here unfolds, fills out, and takes flight. In words of extraordinary eloquence, interlaced with Father Garibay's translations of Nahuatl poetry, he discourses in minute detail and with authority on the decorations of this famous fane, a supreme expression of the religious belief and aspirations conceived and executed by the humble parishioners of this neighborhood.

157

Caso, De la Maza, Rojas - these men went far in interpreting Tepantitla and Tonantzintla. They omitted only one element, an element that supplies the keystone to the arch - the sacred mushrooms, *teonandcatl* and *xochinandcatl* of the Nahua, *'nti'xi'tho'* of the Mazatecs.

I had visited Tonantzintla before attending a *velada* conducted by Maria Sabina. Here was a simple village church where the folk art of the parishioners ran riot over ceilings, walls, and sanctuary, *hauts-reliefs* of flowers and fruit, of children and faces mostly young, some singing, some with masks, others making music on stringed instruments, many joyfully naked, the whole area of walls and vaults, columns and pilasters, crowded with these figures in a riotous display of vivid colors and bewildering curves. I had already stood, like thousands before me, struck dumb at the spectacle, wondering what genius loci had inspired the farmers and artisans of this neighborhood to let themselves go, decorating their church in so unorthodox, so dazzling, a fashion, with no parallel in Mexico, in the whole world. What a spontaneous outpouring of joy in life!

On returning to Tonantzintla in 1955 after attending two veladas and sharing in the mushrooms (but not understanding what Maria Sabina was singing), it came over me as a revelation, when entering the church, that these were the color values, the phantasmagoria, of the mushroom world. There was not the slightest doubt in my mind. But how could I prove this to people who had never taken the mushrooms, would never do so?

In 1957 Valentina Pavlovna and I brought out our *Mushrooms Russia & History*. In it we presented our reasons for believing that the Tepantitla and Teopancaxco murals, both from roughly the same period perhaps fifteen or sixteen centuries ago, are shot through with unmistakable mushrooms. The mushrooms alternate with marine snails and bivalves, in a manner that we all recognize at a much later date as a glyph for water. In these murals the mushrooms, not yet stylized beyond recognition, are mushrooms, not the 'jade rings' that some have surmised, nor the water lilies that others have suggested, for they lack the deep cleft in the leaves that characterize the water lily. *In Les Champignons hallucinogenes du Mexique* that Roger Heim and I with others published at the end of the following year, I told the story again, now adding to my illustrations a mural from the *solar* of Zacuala, in Teotihuacan, which was called to my attention by Mme Laurette Sejourne. In this mural we find the same symbol representing, as I believe, teonandcatl, a Nahuatl name for the sacred mushrooms, or *xochinandcatl*, that other name supplied in the great sixteenth century lexicon of Nahuatl by Alonso de Molina. But here in Zacuala the symbol stands alone, not with seashells as a glyph for water. Though our book drew wide attention from laity and specialists both, the particular p ages in which we pointed out the teonandcatl in the murals of the sacred precincts of Teotihuacan seem to have drawn comment from no one: no one except Dr Alfonso Caso who, in the opening paragraph of his paper on the mushrooms in the *Codex Vindobonensis*, referred to us (Heim & the Wassons) as having drawn his attention to the fungal representations in the murals of Teotihuacan.

I then went to the Far East and concentrated almost exclusively on the role of mushrooms in the cultures of India, China, Japan, New Guinea, and elsewhere. Toward the end of the '6o's and early '7o's I returned to the Mexican field, re-read Francisco de la Maza's paper and Pedro Rojas's book dealing with the church of Tonantzintla, admired the care with which Fernando Benitez followed in our footsteps and, giving us full credit for our discoveries, reported his talks (through Herlinda Martinez Cid, his and our interpreter) with Maria Sabina. Above all I studied the *veladas* that Henry Munn, Alvaro Estrada, and we have had rendered from the Mazatec tapes. There is no need for further documentation on the strength of these *veladas,* whatever Christian overlay it may show, the parish church of Tonantzintla is a *paean* to the inebriating mushrooms of Middle America, a *paean* almost as inebriating as the mushroom itself, a *paean* that surpasses by far even Tepantitla in its exuberant eloquence.

When asked by Fernando Benitez how she viewed the sacred mushrooms, Maria Sabina had said, as rendered into Spanish by Herlinda Martinez:

Yo veo a las hongos coma ninios, coma payasos. Ninos con violines, ninos con trompetas, ninos payasos que cantan y bailan a mi alrededor. Ninos tienos coma las retonos, coma las botones de las flores: ninos que chupan los malos humores, la sangre mala, el rocio de la manana. El pajaro que chupa la enfermedad, el chupamirto bueno, el chupamirto sabio, la figura que limpia, la figura que sana.

[*Los Indios de Mexico, 3, p243*]

I see the mushrooms as children, as clowns. Children with violins, children with trumpets, child-clowns who sing and dance around me. Children tender as sprouts, as flower buds, children that suck out the evil humors, the bad blood, the morning's dew. The bird that sucks out illness, the good hummingbird, the wise hummingbird, the face that cleans, the face that heals.

Maria Sabina has never visited Santa Maria Tonantzintla but do not her words fit that church's delirious decor? We recall how in the *velada* Maria

Sabina and her daughter Maria Apolonia kept singing of the many 'children', *'nti'xti'*, of the ' clowns', *'sase '*.

Pedro Rojas says of the interior of Santa Maria Tonantzintla words that echo Maria Sabina's conception of her romping children:

Ninitos y flores y mas ninitos aparecen por doquiera . . . Es un espectaculo hecho de jardines de ninios. Y a todo costo, porque acuden tantos actores que donde no se ven angeles y amores es porque aparecen caras y mas caras y hasta mascaras . . . Ahi esta Tonantzintla con tantos ninios y flores que con palabras cantan unos la flor de la vida y otras la vida en flor.

[Pedro Rojas, Tonantzintla, UNAM, 1956, pp 33, 40]

Little children and flowers and more little children appear wherever you will. . .. It is a pageant of gardens of children. And at whatever cost, for so many actors hasten hither that where angels and winged children are not seen it is because faces and more faces and even masks appear. . .. There stands Tonantzintla with so many children and flowers that in words the children sing of the flower of life and the flowers sing of life in flower.

Fig 1 Parish Church of Santa Maria Tonantzintla near Puebla

Fig 2. Children's Orchestra on Ceiling beneath Choir Loft i n Narthex of Church

Fig 3 Archway under Choir Loft

161

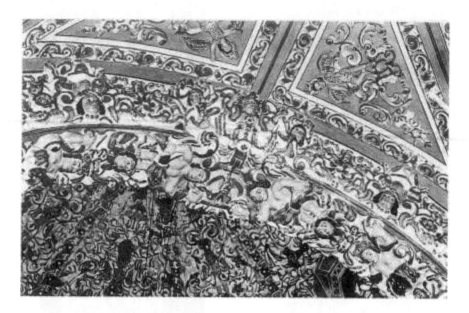

Fig 8 West side of arch leading from Nave into Crossing

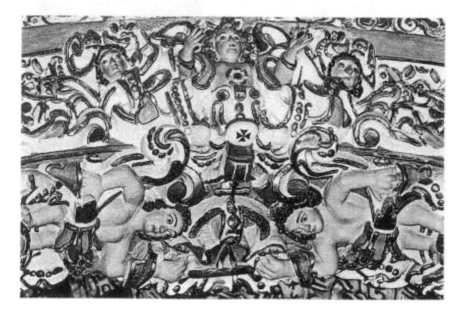

Fig 9 Detail of same: Child Preacher Expostulating

Fig 10 View facing west from Altar steps of ceiling with figure of Plunging Youth

Fig 11 Detail of Same: Plunging Youth

Fig 12 View of Archway and Ceiling, looking North and East from Crossing. St. Mark is Figure in Blue

Fig 13 Detail of above: St. Mark the Evangelist

Fig 14 Six columns supporting north side of Ciborium

Fig 15 View of Cupola and Ceiling of South Transept

*Fig 16 Children carved in arch
(North Half) leading
from Crossing into Sanctuary*

*Fig 17 Detail one of several
carved in arch leading
from nave into crossing*

All these children of Santa Maria Tonantzintla, who are they? Who but
the 'children' of Maria Sabina's chants and the Benitez interview with her?

In her talk with Alberto Ongaro, already cited, she also stressed the 'children' that are the spirits of the mushrooms. Signor Ongaro told me that in Huautla a second shaman (whose name he could not recall) emphasized the same theme. Who are these children but the a-pipil-tzin, the 'little children of the waters', of Marina Rosas, the shaman of Aztec lineage, living on the slopes of Popocatepetl a day's walk from Tonantzintla?

Let us carry our inquiry into the '*children*' of Tonantzintla further. In the Christian tradition angels, seraphs, cherubs, are all male, reflecting the male-oriented culture that is dominant with us. But in Santa Maria Tonantzintla little girls with budding breasts bared to the world are there along with the naked boys. We may assume that among the children who are clothed there are girls and boys. In Tlanixco, a Nahuatl-speaking community on the other side of Mexico City near Tenango del Valle, the entheogenic mushrooms are called *siwatzitzintli*, a word meaning 'little women' and conveying a feeling of affection and respect. In Spanish they are *mujercitas, senoritas, or ninas*, and sometimes the Spanish words are used when the village folk speak in Nahuatl, the hispanicisms nowadays coming natural to the villagers even when they use their native tongue. In June 1960 I taped a discourse in Nahuatl on the sacred mushrooms in Amatlan de los Reyes, Veracruz, by the informant Felipe Reyes F., 60 years old, and when the text was translated by Luis Reyes G., we find the 'young people' answering the questions put to them by the shaman. In a footnote to the translation Luis Reyes, a Nahuatl speaker himself, adds this comment in Spanish on the youths who appear:

These youngsters in other contexts are called *xocoyome* and they dwell in Tlalocan with Tlaloc and his wife. They are children who die unbaptized and for that reason go to Tlalocan and there become blue in color. They hold in their hands snakes that serve as whips to drive the clouds. By another name these children are known as Lightning Bolts.

But these figures of speech are not confined to the Mazatec and Nahuatl worlds. In my early Mesoamerican peregrinations, I did not know enough to inquire of my informants and shamans about the 'children': they are probably present wherever entheogens are used. In the Zapotec country. Thomas MacDougall reported in 1960 that after the inebriating seeds of the morning-glory are taken, and where silence and solitude reign, the *badu-win* (two little girls) appear dressed all in white to reply to the questions that are put to them. Arthur Rubel has said that in the Chinantla in 1971, when he attended his mushroom session, 'little people' answered the questions put to them by the shaman. They are *chamacos*

171

('children') of both sexes but are small, of the height of the mushrooms themselves.

Perhaps a related association with children is found to this day in the Mixtec culture: the sacred mushrooms were formerly gathered just as day was breaking by *doncellas* ('maidens', 'virgins'), and even now the mushrooms are still ground on the *metate* by *doncellas*. We learned all this when we visited the Mixteca in 1960 with Robert Ravicz. In outlying *rancherias* of the Mixteca it seems likely that even now doncellas still gather the mushrooms on the dewy mountain slopes as the sun is about to come up. Maria Sabina's *velada*, sung in the depth of night in the distant mountains of the Mazatec country, turns out to evoke responsive chords from diverse quarters of the Mesoamerican world and far beyond, even to the far reaches of the Siberian forest belt, where the 'fly-agaric girls' respond to the shaman's summons. They answer questions and play all sorts of tricks.

The artisans of the parish of Santa Maria Tonantzintla conceived the design of their church in the second half of the eighteenth century and work on it continued until around 1900. Over this long period the unity l ay not in a plan l aid down by some famous architect but in the continuing conception of their church held by the community. When the work began, all over Mexico the prestige of the style of architecture known as Churrigueresque was at its apogee, and a supreme example of this extravagant variation on the baroque is to be seen in the Capilla del Rosario in the Church of Santo Domingo in Puebla only a few miles away. We may safely assume that the parishioners of Tonantzintla were familiar with what was going on in this famous *capilla*. There also *angelitos*, cherubs and seraphs, are scattered about, their faces peering forth from nooks and crannies, many flying through the air usually with wings. In the Capilla there are differences, however. The figures are less numerous and they look alike, bland, devoid of expression, repetitive. (Perhaps the craftsmen were paid by the piece.) Here indeed we find '*cherubim* and *seraphim*' who 'continually do cry, "Holy, Holy, Holy " ' in a boring Christian heaven. In Tonantzintla every child is bursting with j oy each in his own way, excited, gesticulating, addressing the onlooker wholly absorbed in the astonishing pleasure of living. There are fewer of the figures with the conventional wings of European style. The Churrigueresque of the Capill a del Rosario certainly put ideas into the heads of the Tonantzintla parishioners, but then they stretched those ideas to the limit.

When we took our photographs of Santa Maria Tonantzintla we dealt with the lay officials of the church whose names spoke for their Nahua origin: the *jefe de Iglesia*, Fiscal Amado Moytl, the Mayordomo Onesimo

Teconquey, the SegundoTeniente Crescencio Topia, the portero Cecilio Ixmoyotl. They informed us that the old people thereabouts still spoke mexicano (Nahuatl). Down through the nineteenth century Nahuatl must have been the tongue of everyone.

In that eighteenth-century generation of luxuriant ecclesiastical architecture, the Nahua of Tonantzintla must have felt safe in expressing heretical concepts when decorating their church. But were they even aware of their heresy? As in Maria Sabina's mind, were not the two streams of religious tradition already thoroughly blended and did they not do honor to the Virgin Mother by expressing their reverence
for the Santo Nino plunging headlong into the center of her temple?

We have linked her *velada* with the thinking and feeling of the shamans of the Nahua, as preserved for us in *Ruiz de Al arco'n's* treatise, rendered into Spanish by the distinguished Nahuatlato Alfredo Lopez Austin. Maria Sabina fills out with flesh and blood the interpretation of Santa Maria Tonantzintla that had been adumbrated by Francisco de la Maza and fully developed by Pedro Rojas. Her world of the entheogens, gay with creatures and flowers, is peopled with the same order of little sprites that are equally active in the vast reaches of Siberia, where the 'little girls' evoked by *Amanita muscaria* play the roles that we know are also elicited by the species of Psilocybe of Mexico. Her extraordinary world completes with eloquence what we are already perceiving among the Nahua, the Otomi, the Mixtec, the Zapotec, the Chatino, the Mixe, the Matlatzinca, and the Chinantec. She clothes with rich vesture what were little more than the dry bones of their vocabularies for the entheogens.

Listen now to this: Pedro Rojas is baffled by a theological enigma. Occupying a key position in the church is a figure that has no Christian interpretation. Our Lady is enshrined, and properly so, in a ciborium that rises above and behind the altar. Directly in front and above Our Lady, at the peak of the dome of the crossing, is the Holy Ghost naturally embodied in a dove. This dove turns his head to the entrance of the church, and is regarding the conspicuous figure of a naked youth plunging head down, b ack towards us, over the key to the arch of the crossing that leads to the nave. The head is framed with black curly hair. The large size of this figure and its conspicuous location rule out the possibility that we have here a purely decorative motif. A puzzle in Christian iconography, as Pedro Rojas freely declares.

In the parish church of Tonantzintla the 'little children' are scrambling, scampering, all over amidst the fruits and flowers. These *ninos* are gesticulating to us, those yonder are trying to explain to us and we almost catch their voices, others are climbing the walls, crossing the arches, swimming in space, flying through the air, all over the inside of the cupola or dome, even up the columns that embrace the ciborium high above and behind the altar. The figure plunging head down that baffles Pedro Rojas is surely the leader of this band, this rout, of children. True, he is not to be reconciled with Christian iconography. But need we confine ourselves in this superb church to Christian iconography? Is he not the 'young, well developed man' of Maria Sabina's chant, whom she, by an act of religious syncretism has identified with Jesus Christ? Here is the *Principe Nino* of the Nahuatl world, the Child God of Mesoamerica, the divinity known to the Nahua under various names:

Pilzintecuhtli, or	Teopiltzintli, or
Piltzinteotl, or	Piltzintli,

all of them embodying a different aspect of Xochipilli. But today he is also, surely, the *Santo Nino de Atocha* of Maria Sabina's *velada,* the Sacred Mushroom, and we discover him as captain of the romping children, the world of the 'dear little people' of the entheogens. In Santa Maria Tonantzintla even the Evangelists are young. They are bearded, to be sure, but are not grave and venerable oldsters weighed down with their assignments. Their beards are neatly groomed, their garments clean and tidy. They are in their early thirties. Here then we find the solution to Pedro Rojas' theological enigma: in this Christian Church, dedicated to the Holy Mother of God in our Christian religion, the Holy Child, the Child God, receives equal honor with her. The Holy Child is the Child Piltzintli of the Mesoamerican pantheon, surrounded on all sides by his supporting cast of 400 joyous boys and girls, he himself being the young Sun God, the God of Springtime, of light and warmth and flowers and butterflies and hummingbirds, of music and dancing and song, of the Tree-in-Flower, yes of Ecstasy, the god of the miraculous entheogens, the Master of the Divine Revels of Santa Maria Tonantzintla. The answer to Pedro Rojas' riddle lies in the pre-Conquest pantheon of Mesoamerica.

I have reserved until now evidence of a nature to speak only to those who have experienced and are familiar with the divine inebriation of the mushrooms, of *teonandcatl.* The folk art of Santa Maria Tonantzintla testifies admirably, in an unexpected way, to the truth of my thesis that it was inspired by the entheogens. Most of the children are blonds, obviously not Indians. Those who ingest the mushrooms do not see what they see in everyday life. They see life immeasurably enhanced, transfigured. They enter into a supernal world that is normally on the subliminal fringes of their consciousness. Of course, the Indians would not see Indians. They see (as Henry Munn puts it) important people, high class people, people with power. These people are white, *gente de razo'n*, *gente guera*. (In Mexican Spanish guero has come to mean 'paleface'.) This conception may go back to pre-Conquest times: Quetzalcoatl, the banished god, was to return some d ay from the East and it is said that Montezuma expected him and his fellows to be white. Here is one of the meanings conveyed to this day in Huautla by that extraordinary multifaceted word of exaltation, *'nti'chi'con'*, 'white', the lords and masters of this world, the ultimate in Mazatec terms of enhancement.

Only those who are at home with the mushroom experience are in a position to feel how securely this throng of white children in the Church of our Little Mother of Tonantzintla favors our interpretation.

THE NICHO DE HUEYAPAN

In the vicinity of Tonantzintla, within a radius of ten miles, there are churches innumerable, mostly today in ruins. Cholula was a center of religious devotion in pre-Conquest times, and throughout this rich agricultural valley the same devotion prevails today, though the Indians have changed their religion. Yet of all the churches only one other bears a few carvings that are unmistakably of the same inspiration as Santa Maria Tonantzintla: San Francisco Acatepec, about a mile away on the highway from Mexico and Puebla to Oaxaca.

But Gutierre Tibo'n has lately drawn my attention to another cluster of carvings of children, markedly different from Santa Maria Tonantzintla, though in the same lively and highly individual style. They adorn the Nicho de Hueyapan, executed in 1828 by the anonymous Master of Zacualpan. (The date is consonant with Santa Maria Tonantzintla.) The Nicho was removed from its Church in Hueyapan to the Museo de Cortes in Cuernavaca almost ten years ago. Many of the older inhabitants of Hueyapan still speak Nahuatl and they occasionally go on pilgrimage to Cuernavaca to visit their Nicho. I do not suggest that the Master of Zacualpan was influenced by those who were embodying their conception of Paradise in the children of Tonantzintla. But for his inspiration was he not drawing on the same reserve of winning 'small fry' that we have seen in Tonantzintla and have felt in the words of Maria Sabina?

175

Fig 18

Fig 19

Fig 20

Figures 1 8-24 Nicho de Hueyapan
and details thereof

Figure.21

Figure.22

Figure.23

Figure.24

179

As this Nicho de Hueyapan deserves far more attention than it has received, I offer some views of it in Figures 18 to 24. The artist's conception of St John the Evangelist as a lad in his teens (Fig 19) is perhaps unique. In these children, if I am right, is another instance of the happy synthesis of Christian and pre-Christian feelings.

THE SANTO NINO DE ATOCHA

In his Historia del Nombre y de la Fundacio'n de Mexico, Gutierre Tibo'n cites a tradition preserved for us by Fray Antonio Tello (one of the less read early friar chroniclers) that it was the child god Teopiltzintli who guided the Aztecs, somewhere between the third and sixth centuries, on their migration from their ancestral home of Aztatlan ('Aztlan' in today's spelling) to their new site of Santiago Ixcuintla in what is now Nayarit. Here is Tello's text:

... y el dios que adoraban era una estarua, hecha a manera de un hombre, al cual llamaban Teopiltzintli, que quiere decir nino dios, que es el que guio' a sus antepasados cuando los trajo d e Aztatlan para que poblasen aquellas tierras; a este le ofrecian cuentas, conchas y algodo'n, no le sacrificaban gente, coma en otras partes hacian a otros idolos; so'lo le adoraban e incensaban.

... and the god that they worshipped was a statue, made in the manner of a man, whom they called Teopiltzintli, which means ' child god', who is he who guided their ancestors when he brought them from Aztatlan for them to populate those lands; to him they offered beads, shells and cotton; they did not sacrifice people to him, as was done elsewhere to other idols. Only him they worshipped and to him offered incense.

Knowing as we do that the 'Child God' of the Nahua was the spirit of the entheogens, we find him here exercising his proper role as the divinatory scout selecting the spot for the new home of his followers. I will now suggest that the Holy Child of Atocha embodies in the Christian era the Child God of pre-Conquest times, the Child God known in Nahuatl under various closely related names. We shall call him Piltzintli.

In the Indian country of Mexico everyone knows the Santo Nino de Arocha but in the villages I have never found anyone, whether Indian or mestizo, who could explain what 'Arocha' meant. Often the word is deformed as eg 'Antocha'. In the Spanish of Spain *atocha* is a tough esparto grass from which brooms are made, and 'Atocha' as a place name was an area just outside of Madrid where that grass grew in abundance. (Madrid has long since absorbed this barrio.) Since the Middle Ages and perhaps beyond there has been in Atocha a basilica dedicated to *Nuestra Senora de*

Atocha, 'Our Lady of Atocha', the Virgin bearing the Holy Child on her knees. In 1523, at the very moment of the Conquest, the Dominican Order received charge of this basilica, and Our Lady of Atocha appears to have been a focus of devotion throughout Spain, perhaps second only to Santiago de Compostela. The present effigy in wood of Our Lady with the Holy Child on her left knee is said to have been carved in the thirteenth century, replacing an earlier one that presumably had become dilapidated, where Our Lady was holding the Child seated on both her knees. There is a tangled fragmentary record of various secondary images in the round (*de bulto*), one of them an effigy for pregnant women who would call for her presence as the labor pains began. This effigy would be borne to the prospective mother's bedside. The figure in the Basilica of Our Lady has always been carved from a single block of black wood and the Holy Child is inseparable from Our Lady. It seems that the cult of Nuestra Senora de Atocha is today in decline. This is as much as I have l earned about Our Lady of Atocha in Spain. (Fig 25)

We do not know at what date the Dominicans introduced their cult of Our Lady of Atocha into the New World, nor when Our Lady with the Holy Child ceded her place to the Child alone. The Dominican fathers in Mexico and Spain, though with utmost courtesy, have seemed unable to help us and indifferent to our theme. Somewhere in the archives of the Vatican or of the Dominican Order there must be documentation that will unfold the story. A moment must have come when the Holy Child was wrested from Our Lady's knees (or arms) and elevated to the High Altar in solitary splendor. The deviation clearly responded to a popular need, and the need, I feel sure, was for the Christian Church to supply a Piltzintli incarnate, or rather a Christian surrogate for Piltzintli.

The Dominicans must have formally approved of this substitution, either locally or by an Act of the Order. Did they substitute the Child for the Virgin- and-Child all unknowing? And did they discover the appalling link to the execrated entheogens too late? Was not this discovery behind the queer Spanish costume and accoutrements that the Nino possesses in the stereotyped icon that we all know? The Holy Child is here represented (Fig 26) as wearing a plumed hat, of a style in vogue in Europe in the late seventeenth century, a long gown and cape, sandals on his feet, carrying a shepherd's staff with a basket for flowers in his right hand, and for good measure a sheaf of wheat (rather than an ear of maize) along with a bottle gourd and a *venera*. (A *venera* is the scallop shell that pilgrims to Santiago de Compostela always carried, to eat and drink from and for alms, and as a symbol of their mission.)

Fig 25 Nuestra Senora de Arocha, in Madrid

To this icon there were often added, in the upper corners, tiny insets that illustrate the Holy Child performing the miracles habitual with him, consoling or curing the ill, thwarting crimes of violence, and such like. ('*Santonino*') is the name of the burglar's 'jimmy' in Mexican Spanish, opening as they both do all doors!) The icons in quantity were crudely painted on tin and in recent decades, as racial amalgamation has progressed and religious indifference has spread, they have made their way in countless numbers into the flea markets of Mexico, grimy from the smoke of centuries of tapers burning in the humblest homes. The costume of the Child in the typical icon did not antedate the last quarter of the seventeenth century and this m ay indicate when the worship of the Child, rather than Mother and Child, became definitive.

Fig 26 Santo Nino de Arocha. Traditional icon familiar throughout Mesoamerica

Aguirre Beltran in *Medicina y Magia* gives us a lively account drawn from the Archives of the Inquisition of the various thrusts made by the Indians to find in the new religion of the Conquerors a way to still adore their Piltzintli, although it must be said that the author never suspects the presence of the Child God of the Indians as the motivating force behind their maneuvers. In the early years of the seventeenth century the Holy Office forbade the use of peyote (a word that certainly included all the entheogens), and from then until 1630, and again at intervals later for a century, the Inquisition administered by the Dominicans prosecuted those who resorted to peyote. As early as 1617 the Indians identified peyote with the Nino Jesus, the Child Jesus, in the guise of a lad. Then it is reported that *peyote* became the Holy Trinity, appropriately enough because the Indians, especially the Huichol, linked the cactus with the deer and maize in a mystical triune being. From 1625 to 1665 peyotl became identified with Nuestra Senora [de Atoch a?], Our Lady.

Fig 27 Santo Nino de Nundichi

Fig 28 Santo Nino d e Arocha, bought in the Flea Market in Mexico City

In 1692 we find the entheogen emerging as Santa Rosa Maria: in those days rosa meant 'flower' in Spanish, and '*flower*' was *xochitl* in Nahuatl, which as we have seen was a figure of speech for the superior entheogens. In 1713 it figured in the Proceedings as Santa Maria del Peyote. In 1742 *peyotl* is being called Senor don Pedro, Our Lord St. Peter: who but St Peter holds the keys to Paradise?

There have been reports in recent times of a mission in Durango bearing the name of El Santo Nombre de Jesus Peyotes: this arid region is rich in the famous cactus *Lophophora Williamsii*.

In Mexico the cult of the *Santo Nino* has its center, ostensibly, in Plateros, a mining village near Fresnillo in Zacatecas, a dry region where the cactus *peyotl* abounds. The *Santo Nino* is the patron of miners, but the mines around Plateros have declined in importance. The annual festival takes place on Christmas Eve, *la Noche Buena*, and from 20 December on the faithful gather. Here there are no mushrooms nor *ololiuhqui*. In Plateros the immense popularity of the Child Jesus is not among the indigenas: his appeal today is exclusively to the mestizos and the lower class of Spanish blood, where we do not find the entheogenic plants put to use. Father Miguel Martinez, the incumbent, deprecated to us the 'miracles' attributed to the Child Jesus: *Son creencias populares*, 'They are popular beliefs.' He would have none of them. The Virgin - Nuestra Senora del Refugio - is now high up, standing with her arms outstretched, to the left of the altar as the worshipper looks on her. But we see another Virgin on the same plane as the altar and to the worshipper's right as one faces the altar, standing in a white gown with a long blue cape, her arms placed as though holding a baby towards which she directs her gaze with love and adoration. But the babe is gone. We find him above and behind the altar: he is the infant Jesus and his garments are changed daily, according to Father Martinez, being garbed in clothes donated by the faithful. He does not bear the slightest resemblance to the cheap icon representing the traditional *Santo Nino de A tocha*. Being only an infant, he is incapable of performing the miracles expected of the Spanish child-pilgrim of the familiar icon and still more incapable of the feats of the pagan sprites of the entheogens. He is in short finally and completely dissociated from Piltzintli. Are we not justified in supposing that the Dominican friars were aware from an early date of the ambiguity of their Santo Nino, and that in two stages, first as an exotic Spanish pilgrim, lately as an infant, they were interposing distance between their Santo Nino and the Child God of the Mesoamerican world?

There is one other church in Mexico where the Santo Nino is the primary object of adoration: the church of Nundichi, a village high in the hills above Tlaxiaco northeast of this town in the State of Oaxaca, south of the Pan American Highway and halfway to the Pacific Coast. We are here in the Mixteca. The annual feast of this Nino is on the first Sunday in January. The Nino carries a cross, not a staff, and his head wears a regal resplandor (a variety of halo) instead of the plumed hat.

On our visit to Plateros in January 1972 we were told by Father Martinez that this church draws no indigenas. *Solo la gente adora al Nino*, 'Only people worship the Child', Indians not being people in his mentality. His offhand use of this contemptuous expression is a legacy of Colonial Mexico and is seldom heard now . . .. Two centuries ago, of course, the mining population of Plateros and the Fresnillo area may have included large numbers of monoglot Indians who adored a 'Santo Nino de! *Peyotl'*.

(Fig 27) Innumerable pieces of paper with writing on them are pinned to his garment - expressions of gratitude for miracles that he has effected and that are set down for all to read. (These pieces of paper are themselves known familiarly as *milagros*, 'miracles'.) Here also the appeal today is chiefly to mestizos. In both centers the *Santo Nino*, according to the popular belief dating from the time when the Infant was a lad, sallies forth from his throne at night to succor the faithful who are in trouble, returning to the church before daylight. The proof (so people say) that these stories are true is the mud (in Plateros) or sand (in Nundichi) that sometimes clings to the sandals when he resumes his place on the altar. But Father Martinez in Plateros dismisses these stories with a wave of the hand. The *sacristan* of the church in Nundichi pointed to another church in a village some miles away across the valley, San Antonio Indoajico, where there is, he said, the cult of a Virgin of Arocha.

In San Juan Amatitlan, on the shores of Lake Amatitlan in Guatemala, we find also a famous cult of the Santo Nino in a church founded by the Dominicans. The day of the *Santo Nino* in Amatitlan is May 3.

In Huautl a de Jimenez the parish church displays a *Santo Nino* in traditional style. Nearby, also in Mazatec country, in the village of San Mateo Eloxochitlan, not long ago, well within the memory of those still living, there was a Santo Nino who was an Indian child, barefooted, wearing breeches, a shirt with a check pattern, a sash, and a rosary. But one day, without consulting the parishioners, the priest replaced him with the effigy of the Santo Nino of Prague. The parishioners still speak with nostalgia of their former Santo Nino and express resentment at his kidnapping. In Tlacotepec on the road from Puebla to Tehuacan there is a Holy Child and in Puebla itself, in the Church of San Marcos, 2 January is set aside for the celebration of the Holy Child before his icon. Formerly he was *de bulto* also, but the figure disappeared during the religious persecution under Elias Calles, or so it is said. There must be churches without number in Mesoamerica where the cult of the Holy Child is a focus of devotion: I have cited only those that I know about along my routes in Mexico.

The pagan cult of Piltzintli still survives in the *rancherias* and villages where on altars in the humblest homes of monoglot Indians the traditional icon of the *Santo Nino* has the place of honor, a bouquet of flowers before him, perhaps a *vela* of virgin wax lighted in his honor, and from time to time a velada being sung all night by a hierophant to invoke his aid in the extremities of life. In these Indian homes lies the real focus of the cult of the Santo Nino, a cult of immemorial antiquity that is now fast dying out; here, not in Plateros nor in Amatitlan nor in Nundichi, where the acculturated worshippers have never heard of the Child God of the Mesoamerican Indians. In 1955, when I attended the *velada* sung by Aristeo Matias, in San Agustin Loxicha, a Zapotec village in the Sierra Costera, I was struck by his invocation in Zapotec of the *Santo Nino de A tocha* and in my field notes jotted down that observation. At the time I knew nothing about the *Santo Nino de A tocha* other than his name and did not link him with the entheogens. Today we possess the text translated into Spanish of three *veladas* sung by Maria Sabina in Huautla, one from 1956, another from 1958, and the third from 1970, the first two recorded by me and the third by a Mazatec at a *velada* where no outsider was present. In each of them, toward the end of the velada, she invoked the *Santo Nino de A tocha*. Many saints such as St Peter and St Paul enter into her singing repeatedly, as though she had recourse to them when her verses were running thin. But the *Santo Nino* occurs only once, near the end. For her as for Aristeo Matias, and doubtless for all other Mesoamerican shamans, the invocation is, I think, a structural feature of the pre-Conquest *velada*. Piltzintli - the 'Holy Childe' - was there from the start. He is there to this day, for all to see, as he dives down head first to the High Altar of Santa Maria Tonantzintla.

By divine grace we are given the supreme example in ecclesiastical architecture of the adoration of the *Santo Nino del Peyotl* (in its broadest sense) in the Church of Santa Maria Tonantzintla. In it the Christian and pagan elements achieve a harmonious blend. Here the little sprites, youths and maidens, are peopling the enchanted scene. Here there is no brutality - no Holy Office, no human sacrifice - only a garden that surpasses all dreams where mankind lives off the rich produce of the fields round about and on the entheogens of Mesoamerica, entheogens that the Greeks knew as ambrosia, the Aryans as amrita, the Siberian tribesmen as pongo. The Aryans used another word for their divine inebriant, '*andhas*', cognate with the Greek word for 'flower', 'λουλούδι' and both of them are the equivalent of the Nahuatl metaphor *xochitl*.

The *veladas* of Maria Sabina and the inebriating world of Santa Maria Tonantzintla have led us to see with the eyes of Early Man a major aspect of his life that we did not know before, a vision of another world whose very existence remained almost hidden from us, a world surcharged with the vitality of youth and of incomparable beauty. In the fertile valley of Cholula religion meant much to the Indians before the Conquest and it suffuses their lives to this day. Here we find the answer to the theological enigma that Pedro Rojas put to us with extraordinary acumen: Piltzintli, the Master of Revels, the Holy Child, is plunging down to the altar where his mother the Virgin Mary is enthroned.

But let us go further. Is not this divinity the same as the plunging figure in the Codex Borgia, the nino dios, Piltzintli, that we display in Fig 29? Is he not the same that Maria Sabina had in mind, at an early point in her velada, when she asked me to vacate my seat because I would obstruct the descent of the divine spirit who was to arrive from above by way of the very corner that I occupied? (See p13) There is a possibility that she speaks of the same divine epiphany in Chapter VI of the story of her life that Alvaro Estrada has given us. And what of the Diving God murals of Teotihuacan to which Arthur Miller draws our attention? Nor should we overlook one striking style of mushroom stone, from the Maya Highlands, of which we reproduce two examples on page 192. Are not these Maya effigies siblings to the plunging god of the *Codex Borgia*, of Santa Maria Tonantzintla, of Maria Sabina's world? This *nino dios*, wherever we find him, is the god of the entheogen, is one aspect of Xochipilli.

189

Fig 29 Plunging Piltzintli. Codex Borgia (Folio 8, Fig 50) x 2 1/2

CHAPTER 8

TEOTIHUACAN AND THE WONDROUS MUSHROOM

THE MEANING OF THE MURALS

In Mushrooms Russia & History (1957) Valentina Pavlovna and I set forth our reasons for thinking that certain details of the murals of Teotihuacan represented inebriating mushrooms. With one notable exception no Mesoamerican scholar has publicly commented on our discoveries although twenty years have elapsed and our findings elsewhere in Mexico have not gone unnoticed. The exception is Dr Alfonso Caso, who in his paper on the *Codex Vindobonensis* ratified our identification, specifying the murals that in this Chapter appear as Figures 1, 2, 7, and 12. His endorsement was unequivocal, although (as I have already pointed out) he dropped our mushrooms then and there. Apparently, he felt that this theme, far from calling for further inquiry, was exhausted. Caso was like all other scholars in the Mesoamerican field: inhibited when dealing with the divine inebriants. Archeologists, the clergy, anthropologists, linguists - all touch them gingerly or not at all. They respond to my inquiries most courteously but on their own initiative do nothing. The exceptions are few. It would seem as though there were a subconscious reluctance on the part of our Western society to recognize the role played in prehistory by entheogens.

I will now go further than we did in our 1957 book. Arthur G. Miller's *The Mural Painting of Teotihuacan* appeared in 1973. That ancient city, covering eight square miles in its heyday (ca AD 450-650), counted a population of at least 70,000 and perhaps up to 200,000, according to the careful study of R. Millon. In Miller's book, beautifully laid out, he gives a comprehensive survey of most of what had been discovered in the ruins up to the time of its publication: plans of the structures that had been excavated from the start of archeological inquiry about a century ago, photographs of their famous murals, black-and-white drawings to help the reader see in the photographs what the specialist sees in the murals, floor plans of the various edifices, and finally numerous and skillful repaintings of the murals by Felipe Davalos G. to recapture the full effect on the worshippers of the originals when these were fresh. Anyone endowed with imagination is certain to be profoundly moved and also mystified by a school of sophisticated painting the like of which exists

191

nowhere else in the world. One can see a kinship only with the art of the Maya and the codices of the Nahua and Mixtecs.

Miller plants squarely the basic questions. What was the purpose of the labyrinthine building complexes where the murals have been found? What was the meaning of the strange, the haunting Teotihuacan paintings? He does not hazard so much as a guess. He says no one knows. But in a fecund paragraph Miller draws attention to the often-elaborate borders of the murals, with broad curvilinear and rectilinear bands braided together at intervals in sweeping rhythm (as he says) that is almost musical. And he adds:

> I do not mean to suggest that lines in Teotihuacan murals are recorded music, but I do suggest that they can have values which are music like *and may have been so to the Teotihuacanos.*
>
> [*Italics mine; Miller, p 29 col 1*]

What astonishing perspicacity! Miller lacked only the key to the mystery. Here again in our inquiry we are finding the same missing clue: The Wondrous Mushroom.

The reader will recall how Maria Sabina in her velada intones chants that for the bemushroomed person assume rhythmic shapes, curving in and out of each other, and how the kaleidoscopic play of colors that the bemushroomed see in their visions pulsate with musical rhythm. The artists of Teotihuacan succeeded in conveying this sensation to Miller who knew not the mushrooms! (My impressions are paralleled by Henry Munn's, though he conveys them in utterly different language.) Miller speaks of the 'vibrantly colored shapes' of the murals of Teotihuaca'n, their 'intensity and vivid colors'. He cites Miguel Covarrubias who dwelt on their 'intensely religious' message,' austere and distinguished, gay and graceful'. What a tribute to the ancient artists are these sensitive responses to their murals by acute observers who were ignorant of the entheogens!

Imagine then my astonishment when I found Miller saying that the 'disembodied eyes are important' both in the main composition and the border of a mural in the complex known as Zacuala. Why was I astonished?

In my Life article, 13 May 1957, describing my own experience when I was bemushroomed in my first velada with Maria Sabina two years earlier, I wrote:

There I was, poised in space, a *disembodied* eye, invisible, incorporeal, seeing not seen.

I had myself been the disembodied eye that Miller discovered some dozen years later in the murals of Teotihuacan painted a millennium and a half before!

Miller perceived the ' disembodied eyes' peopling the entire corpus of Teotihuacan painting, not merely in the Zacuala complex. When I wrote my Life article, Zacuala had not been excavated and Miller's book lay some sixteen years ahead. Miller did not remember my text: on the contrary, had he remembered it his text would have been utterly different. But had he even seen it?

In 1957 my knowledge of Teotihuacan was cursory. I had paid one visit to Teopancaxco and to the fragmentary murals of Tepantitla left *in situ*. (I did not see, much less take in, the ' disembodied eyes' in the lower register of the Paradise scene. Fig 12) Miller speaks of the 'disembodied eyes' mainly when he is discussing Zacuala, but, as many of his illustrations show, they permeate the murals of the city sanctuary of Teotihuacan. The 'disembodied eyes' are the mushroom worshipper's eyes, whether open or shut, contemplating the scenes of another world, three dimensional, unearthly yet more real to the bemushroomed viewer than our world of everyday experience.

Miller was on the brink of discovering the answer to both his major questions: the purpose of the labyrinthine building complexes and the meaning of the Teotihuacan paintings. Neither in his text nor in his captions nor in his bibliography does he cite any of our writings, which have been numerous and circulate widely, nor Roger Heim's, equally numerous, nor (somewhat later) Peter T. Furst's and others'. He speaks in a caption of a personal communication from Furst in 1971 identifying certain flowers in the paintings as morning-glories but fails to explain to his readers the meaning here of morning-glories. He is certainly not at home in botanical iconography nor the entheogens.

My thesis is simple. For centuries Teotihuacan was a vast sanctuary dedicated to the two or three hallucinogens that enjoyed superlative prestige. What we have been calling the building complexes were simply groups of *cenacula* where small gatherings of pilgrims would assemble to consult the entheogen under the direction of one or two or more hierophants. The number and elaboration of the building complexes speak for the ritual activity that went on over centuries at Teotihuacan. Pilgrims came from near and far. The permanent population of hierophants and their families, augmented by the host of personnel needed to provide services for the pilgrims, accounts for the 70,000 that R. Millon puts as his minimum figure, and the transitory pilgrims m ay have occasionally pushed that figure as high as 200, 000. There were the

193

rudimentary hostels to house and feed the pilgrims: their needs were simple. There must also have been a mechanism to pay in kind for board and lodging, for the services of the hierophants, for the use of a chamber, and for the consumption of the holy elements of the divine office the mushrooms or morning-glory seeds, copal, cacao for drinking with dried poyomatli flowers, guacamaya feathers, pisiete with lime, perhaps turkey eggs. I should suppose the hierophants were recruited from the various linguistic groups of Mesoamerica and if so, the pilgrims might then choose one from his own country, even his own village, possibly a kinsman. After dark on the appointed night the pilgrims would make their way to the building complex where they were expected: the thoroughfares were narrow, but there was no need for wider passages as there were no horses nor hand-drawn 'rickshaws'. Carrying flares (properly speaking, 'links'), the little comp any of pilgrims, on arriving at their building complex, would be guided through the passageways, sometimes along lengthy corridors, where by their flickering lights they would see murals of hierophants, in their impressive vestments, until finally they would arrive at the *cenaculum* where they were expected.

The chambers were small after the layout of Cayetano Garcia's, suggesting rather a group confessional than a vast church or temple. The murals on the walls were painted in flat two-dimensional colors devoid of perspective, as Miller's book shows us, the hierophants in their vestments more or less as in our Figure 2. Each chamber had its own band of suppliants, perhaps hailing from the same neighborhood. The worshippers, often after days of walking, would finally arrive, keyed to the highest state of expectancy, at the appointed cenaculum. The vast amphitheater of Teotihuacan supplied the noblest of settings and the celebrants were masters of their craft - greeting the worshippers, asking each what problem preoccupied him, administering the mushrooms (or infusion of morning-glory seeds), ushering in the period of silence and darkness while the entheogen took over the company. In Teotihuacan the celebration of the sacrament must have been a model of excellence, the liturgy being elaborated with all sorts of subtleties and refinements: the superb vestments and masks of the celebrants, their bearing and gestures, their voices beautifully trained.

Before the lights were extinguished the murals and the celebrants were the last visual impressions. As the entheogens took effect, the next sights the pilgrims saw, in the dark, eyes open or closed, were the murals springing to three-dimensional life, far more real than what they knew from the workaday world. Then they heard the chants intoned by the celebrants, the percussive beat of the small drum, the sounds being tempered to the small room, subtly played in syncopation, the sights and sounds being bathed in the fragrance of burning copal, of *poyomatli*, of other aromatic herbs, the sounds coming ventriloquistically, from suddenly shifting directions, in suddenly shifting volume, the whole blending inextricably into one harmonious sensation uniting sight, sound, fragrance. At that moment in the night when the entheogens reach their peak effect, then would come the oracular utterances of the hierophant, sweating profusely, perhaps having inhaled draughts of tobacco smoke, in response to the specific problems preoccupying the individual worshippers, each verse ending with 'so says the mushroom', just as I have heard it in Huautla.

All this is gone now: all that is left are what remain of the murals of Teotihuacan rendered by Miller in his noble book and the chanting of shamans like Maria Sabina. We know that her chants are of immense antiquity and they may well preserve the melodies and even the meaning of the words of the hierophants of Teotihuacan.

Were the Teotihuacan paintings, or some of them, executed while the painter was under the influence of the entheogen? They tell us vividly what the Mesoamerican saw and sensed when he was bemushroomed. They are done with such disciplined control that one would think they must have been accomplished by sober artists working in the full flood of their immediate memories. But this may be a Western point of view: the discipline that the bemushroomed acquires with practice is a marvel, and the artist (himself a hierophant?) m ay have prided himself on having painted them under the immediate dictation of the entheogen.

There was no vast edifice for corporate worship in Teotihuacan, no 'cathedral' or ' temple'. If there was human sacrifice, this was performed in the open, atop either of the two pyramids, the one to the sun and the other to the moon. These pyramids antedated by centuries the time of which we are speaking, and the cathedral of Teotihuacan was truly these pyramids set against the heavenly panorama of the hills and sky encircling the vast theater of that wondrous sanctuary.

I am sorry Arthur Miller did not know our writings for he would then have answered his own questions and rounded out his impressive work. By an heroic feat of disciplined imagination an occasional Mesoamerican scholar with the soul of a poet might be able to enjoy the shadow of a velada without ingesting entheogens. But why make this effort? For most there is no substitute for the real thing. The day is arrived when no one who would learn what Mesoamerican culture meant to the Mesoamericans, what the murals of Teotihuacan meant, what the picture writing of the codices meant, what the surviving Nahuatl poetry meant,

195

what the intoning of the chants meant that is to say, no aspiring Mesoamerican scholar, will deny to himself the key to this understanding.

TEOPANCAXCO AND THE WATER GLYPHS

One of the earliest murals of Teotihuacan to become known, in the late 1880's, is in a chamber - a cenaculum, as I believe - of a structure called Teopancaxco. On one wall of this small chamber is a mural painting that we reproduce in our Fig 2. There can be no doubt that its reconstruction by Agustin Villagra Caleti conveys the effect of the original mural. Damage through the centuries and neglect since it was rediscovered had taken their toll. In our reproduction the darker field shows the portions that were well preserved when Villagra undertook his task, and he also had access to paintings of other hierophants in procession. Almost all of the border had disappeared, and of the murals that had originally covered the other three walls there was virtually nothing left. When we visited Teopancaxco in the middle fifties we noticed, on the wall to the right as one faced the surviving mural, a small stretch of the original border (including an angle) of the lost mural of that wall.

Though m any must have seen it, no one had yet copied it. At our request Eduardo Noguera took the task in hand and gave the commission to Villagra. This border fragment will be found in Fig 1, and as that portion of the mural is an authentic Teotihuacan painting, in no way retouched, it serves well to demonstrate my thesis. We discover here the glyph for water in Mesoamerica at an earlier stage of its pictographic evolution.

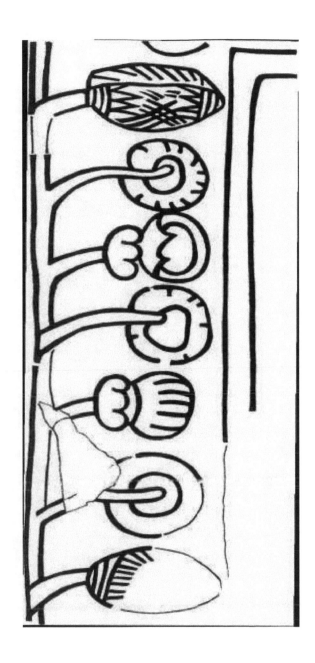

Fig 1. Teopancaxco mural. Detail reduced.

Fig 2. Teopancaxco mural, in the valley of Mexico.
From the Teotihuacan III period
AD 300-600

Working down from the top, first we find a well delineated marine snail. I think no one has ever disputed this identification. Next comes what is for me plainly the undersurface of the cap ('pileus') of a mushroom showing the gills ('lamellae'). The stem ('stipe') emerges from the center of the cap and runs like an umbilical cord to a stream of water, the waters of life, the waters that one links inevitably with shells and mushrooms. In the mural itself there survived the faintest traces of green paint on the mushrooms, signifying holiness. As for the third and fifth glyphs, prevailing opinion is that they are bivalves, but in the glyph for water do they ever recur in Mexico? The murals of Teotihuacan are clearly the product of a long evolution in picture writing of which no one has yet found examples, and these two 'shells' may well have been obsolescent elements in the water glyph. The marine snail, however, often accompanies the mushroom, even in post Conquest times, as we saw in the pictogram for water in the mid-sixteenth century *Codice Indigena* No 27, p110. But the mushroom is always present, simplified, reduced finally to two concentric circles or even to a circle around a dot. The overwhelming importance of the divine mushroom in pre-Conquest Mesoamerica finds fitting expression here in the link between water and mushroom, in the glyph for water, in a glyph that sanctifies water by tying it to the divine flower, a flower that is green for holiness.

Alfonso Caso accepted our identification of the symbol as a mushroom, and I think this is hard to challenge. Why should it not be the mushroom that plays so big a role in Mesoamerica? Some have suggested in conversation that it might be the leaf of a water-lily. But the water-lily, as we see in Fig 3, has a deep cleft where the stem leads off and the veins of the leaf assemble. The water-lily belongs to the genus Nymphaea and all species of that genus have the cleft leaf. A pictographic artist catches the significant lines of the model. Those lines persist through generations and no artist portraying the water-lily could miss the distinctive cleft. What the artist does catch are the radiating gills of the entheogenic mushroom around a blank center where the round stipe is reduced to a circle.

How different would be the veins in the water-lily leaf gaining strength as they assemble at the point where the stem leads off! Some ask why the 'mushroom' could not b e a flower or seashell, but they do not suggest the species and are idly guessing. Why is there this reluctance to recognize the Wondrous Mushroom when the pictogram is so consistently displayed? A survival of the age-old mycophobic syndrome?

Fig 3. Nymphaea tuberosa

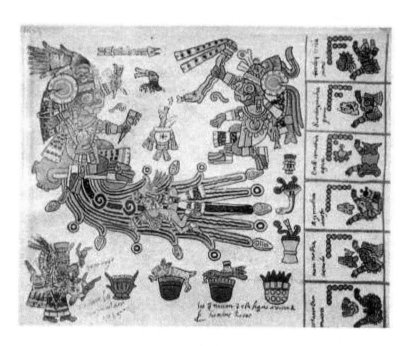

Fig 4. Codex Borbonicus: Tlaloc
Note symbol for water at end of streamers.

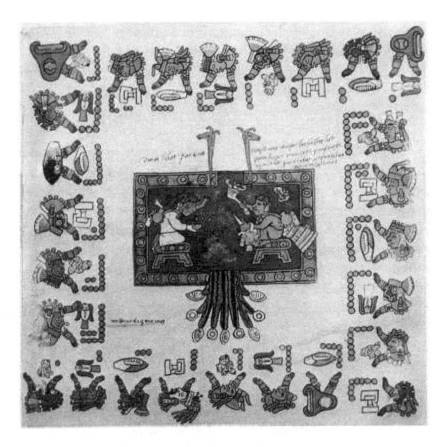

Fig 5 *Codex Borbonicus*: Two Ancients

Every pictogram has its origin in a specific object and here we have the sacred mushroom. Much later, when his reading clientele had become used to the lines, the scribe simplifies them until at last the lines are so abbreviated as to make the glyph obscure for the outsider. At Teopancaxco we possess a pictographic artist's work when the mushroom was still easy to recognize. In the evolution of the pictogram the stipe disappears, leaving a round inner ring, and the gills disappear, leaving the outer ring. The two rings persist to the end, but the inner one is sometimes reduced to a dot, as we saw in Co'dice Indigena No 27, p110.

Why did the hierophants and pilgrims stress seashells in their murals? The sea is hundreds of miles from Teotihuacan. There seem to be no midden heaps in the ruins of that ancient city. Perhaps the pilgrims took

201

shells back home as a lasting souvenir of their pilgrimage. But such a practice would be a by-product of the main use, and might relate only to the elaborate and beautifully structured shells that are frequently seen in many of the Teotihuacan murals. The main use would be different: lime, ground fine, is mixed with Nicotiana rustica to make the bright green pisiete, widely used in Mesoamerica for rubbing on the body in healing rites and often held as a wad in the cheek. The shells may have supplied lime for adding to pisiete. Lime was naturally available close at hand but to get lime from either sea - Pacific or Caribbean - from the clean pure shells in their amazing and endless shapes, abundantly illustrated in the murals of Teotihuacan, would be a telling refinement in the entheogenic rite. No honor was too great for the sacred mushrooms or morning-glory seeds.

In the surviving mural of Teopancaxco two hierophants are facing each other and chanting. Their singing scrolls are adorned with flowers. We assume that they are bemushroomed and chanting to a tiny band of suppliants also enjoying their 'dream flowers', *temicxoch*. They are pouring a libation including seeds on the ground but what it is we do not know. With our Western fixation on alcohol, some have said it was pulque. On excellent authorities, contemporary and historical, alcoholic inebriants and the divine inebriants were not mixed and the hierophants were certainly not under the influence of alcohol. Skipping now forward a thousand years, let us look at a few instances of the water glyph in pre- and post-Conquest codices, where the examples are innumerable. In Figure 4 we show a representation of Tlaloc, the god of rain, taken from the pre-Conquest Codex Borbonicus. The water with which he is identified carries our glyph repeatedly, shell and mushroom alternating at the end of the streamers leading to the flowing water. In Figure 5, again from the Codex Borbonicus, two ancients are casting kernels of grain in a cave from which a stream emerges, the stream being similarly identified by shell and mushroom. Our third, Figure 6, is post-Conquest, in the Atlas of Diego Duran. It shows the founding of Tenochtitlan Mexico City, and the lake where the city was built carries on its edges the glyph now reduced to nine 'mushrooms', insignificant in size, but seemingly necessary; the shell has vanished. The mushrooms in these codices no longer wear the color green. In the post-Conquest Cadice Indigena No 27 (p 111) we follow the evolution of the glyph for water from (1) the shell-and-concentric circles to (2) the concentric circles alone, and finally to (3) a mere dot in the center of a little circle.

Fig 6 Diego Duran: Founding of Tenochtitlan (Mexico City)

TEPANTITLA

Perhaps the best-known of the murals of Teotihuacan are those of the building complex called Tepantitla, restored by Agustin Villagra Caleti, now displayed for all to see on a wall of the *Museo Nacional de Arqueologia* in Mexico City. The word 'restoration' calls for a word of explanation. When Mexican murals some 1500 years old are discovered, they are never in prime condition. At best the colors are faded beyond the layman's understanding, and the lines are obscure. It takes long experience to read the lines and colors. In those murals that lend themselves to restoration, the specialists familiar with the colors that the ancient painters had at their command can often say precisely which colors were used. By minute inspection they can read the original outlines and also the colors of what survives and give us again the artist's intention. There lies the duty of the restorer and beyond that limit, if he is a good restorer, he will not go. Villagra is an experienced, conscientious painter who does not invent motifs: here is the verdict of outside judges who have minutely examined his work at Teotihuacan. He makes the murals live again for us in the colors close to or perhaps the same as the pilgrims in A D 500 saw. His restoration of Tepantitla took place almost twenty years before our 'hallucinogenic mushrooms' came to be discussed.

Some years ago, Dr Efren del Pozo and I visited Villagra in his studio-home. Sr Villagra was glad to show us the stages of his restoration of Tepantitla, a series of draft-studies that he had made immediately after the archeologists had uncovered the originals. (The murals, when exposed once again to daylight and the atmosphere, deteriorate rapidly.) In the upper register of the main mural of Tepantitla there is the massive divinity that George Kubler, Peter Furst, and others take to be female (Fig 7) and above her head is the 'Tree-in-Flower', a '*tree*' painted in Teotihuacan perhaps fifteen hundred years ago, which Diego Duran describes when he tells us of the celebration of the Feast of Xochipilli and which we link to the texts of Nahuatl poetry given us by Father Garibay.

Fig 7 Female Divinity, Tepantitla

It is a '*tree*' made ad hoc, not a living tree. This interpretation seems to be the consensus of informed belief today. Dr del Pozo photographed some of Sr Villagra's early drafts and we reproduce them in Figures 8-11, showing something of the many stages by which he arrived at his '*Tree-in-Flower*'. First, he restores the patches where colors and lines are unmistakable. He studies those lines and colors and extends them, helped by vestiges and by the artist's grasp of the original artist's conception. Where there is nothing left, he leaves nothing.

Figs 8-1 1 Villagra's intermediate paintings after a Tepantitla mural and details thereof

205

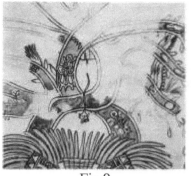

Fig 9

Fig 10

Fig 11

To the right of the divinity, a hand of a lost hierophant or deity protrudes and from it gushes a stream of falling water. (Fig 10) That this is indeed water is proved by the glyph to which we are now accustomed, alternating shells and mushrooms. The mushrooms are green. In the stream itself are seeds among which I recognize entheogenic seeds of *Rhynchosia sp.*

In the lower register of this mural we see the 'Playing Fields of Paradise' or Tlalocan as Caso has suggested. The lower right-hand corner of this mural shows a newcomer arriving in Tlalocan, waving a branch and shedding tears of nostalgia: so, they interpret the picture. He sings an elaborate canticle, with five turnings in his speech scroll ornamented with flowers. Underneath this scene a stream emerges from the mouth of a frog. In the lake where he squats we see three times the symbol for water - shell and mushroom - and as the stream courses along 'disembodied eyes' mark its path. The whole scene is of the real world of the entheogenic vision of the Mesoamericans (Fig 12), unsuspected by Dr Caso or Sr Villagra.

Fig 12 Tepantirla mural, derail: soul arriving on the Playing Fields of Paradise

Figs 13 and 14 Tepantitla, details

207

Fig.14

Fig 15 Tepantitla: further details

Dr Henry B. Nicholson also photographed for me a few details in the borders, often serpentine, of the Tepantitla murals. We show these in Figures 13-15. From a jaguar's mouth hangs a mushroom, green for holiness, and from the top of his head bursts forth a fountain, dividing into two streams that fall on each side of his face. Drops of fluid, obviously entheogenic, emerge from the streams and a score or more of 'disembodied eyes' attend their fall. Nicholson gives us also another detail showing strange aquatic figures swimming with the familiar water glyph in their mouths - shell-and-mushroom. In a further detail there is the mushroom flanked on each side by a shell, the shells being of different species.

Figs 16 and 17 Tepantirtla: derails

Fig 18.   Fig 19.

Margaret Seeler has supplied me with four black-and-white reproductions of the Teotihuacan murals that appear here as Figures 16-19. In two, flowers (perhaps highly stylized morning-glories) drip wondrous fluid, the flowers and the drops being accompanied by 'disembodied eyes'. In another, three creatures are proceeding upstream each with a mushroom in its mouth - a flying fish, a turtle(?), and a heron. Especially striking is the fourth: drops of fluid, obviously hallucinogenic, are giving birth to 'disembodied eyes' as they fall.

ZACUALA

In all the glyphs for water that we have seen, mushrooms were the telling ingredient. But mushrooms figure also in isolation, away from water. Mme Laurette Sejourne and her archaeological team discovered a mural on the front, perpendicular part of a step (it might be called a 'predella' in Western ecclesiastical architecture) in a structural complex known as Zacuala, which we reproduce in Figure 20. In the central cartouche of this mural there is a 'radiant mouth', and from this cartouche four unmistakable greenish mushrooms emerge. Beyond the mushrooms on either side are three 'disembodied eyes'. Could there be more eloquent expression in paint of the Word, of Sacred Song, under the potent influence of the divine mushrooms? How could any single picture tell us more clearly what Teotihuacan was all about? Our painting was a reconstruction by Abel Mendoza based on the surviving fragments, which amply justified his restoration. Some sherds found in the debris of Zacuala permitted Mendoza to paint a terracotta bowl decorated with a row of mushrooms encircling it and a second row, behind the mushrooms, of seashells. (Figure 21) I like to think this was a utility vessel to carry the mushrooms to the *cenaculum* where they were needed.

Fig 20 Zacuala: 'Predella'

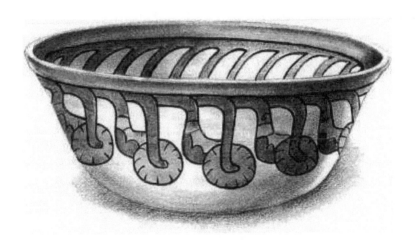

Fig 2 1 Zacuala: Painting of reconstructed bowl

CHALCHIHUITL AND TONALLO: A SPECUALATION

Small rings of jade played a prominent part in pre-Conquest Mesoamerican culture. Scholars seem to think this was because of the high value placed on the jade. Green, the color of jade, was always a symbol of enhancement, as we have often seen in the color given to the sacred mushrooms. But surely the mushroom comes first. It is ·colored green because its divinity merits the color of the most precious stone known to the Mesoamericans, though for the awesome mushrooms it was contrary to nature. The jade rings are precious, of course, because they are of jade but basically because they exemplified the sacred mushrooms. Agustin Villagra in his chapter on the 'Mural Painting of Teotihuacan' in the *Handbook of Middle American Indians* (1971, Vol 10, p 141) shows us the surviving elements in the facade that is peopled with *chalchihuites*, jade-green rings, which he has kindly reproduced for us. (Fig 22) He is right: they are the representations of jade-green rings. But surely, they represent something infinitely more precious, the divine mushrooms. There is an intimate reciprocity between the jade rings, shaped to represent the glyph for mushroom and carved from the most precious stone, and the mushroom painted green like jade, the acme of holiness. A chalice designed by the finest goldsmith and jeweler, a Cellini-conceived cup, merely aspires to be worthy of the blood of Christ that it is destined to hold. The green chalchihuites to which Villagra calls our attention in the Road of the Dead are only a symbol of the jade rings that in turn speak for the wondrous mushrooms.

Again, let us take the tonallo symbol. (p 64) What is the derivation of that symbol? What is it ultimately but four mushrooms, the sacred number four? And what of the series of concentric rings that we have seen encircling the tablero of our statue of Xochipilli? (p 64) Why are they not the glyph for mushrooms rather than solar symbols? The mushrooms signify of course all the other beneficent manifestations of a favorable Nature - solar warmth, gentle rains and life-giving showers, butterflies, hummingbirds, flowers waving in the breeze, music, laughter, singing and dancing, poetry. However alien it be for us of an alien culture, the sacred flowers breathed life, breathed reverence and joy, into all these other pleasant aspects of existence on this earth.

The superior entheogens of Mesoamerica - primarily the mushrooms and morning-glory seeds - all interrelated chemically, at the outset of the visions that they bring, more often than not start with abstract designs, for me mostly angular but for others often sinuous, curving, serpentine. They are breathtaking in their clarity, three-dimensional, in color, constantly shifting, changing, as it were dancing. We have already pointed out that these motifs recur in the finest of the Mesoamerican codices. I think this explains their haunting beauty that many have felt when contemplating them. We have suggested that this was why the codices were venerated beyond any reason that the Spaniards' mentality could grasp: the characters were inspired by the divinity that dwelt in the entheogen.

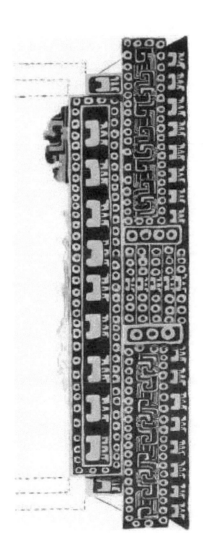

Fig 22. Teotihuacan: surviving elements of façade in Road of the Dead, painted by Villagra Caleti.

The architects of pre-Conquest Mexico let themselves go in complicated '*frets*', borders usually with angular designs endlessly repeated, or else in rhythmically curving lines, and in Figures 23 and 24 we show photographs of these '*frets*' from the ruins of Mitla. The same theme can be seen in Teotihuacan but the Mitla '*frets*' serve to show how widely scattered they are in Mesoamerica. The '*frets*' in Spanish are called grecas as they are also in Italian. Greca simply means 'Greek'. Is this not odd? Why 'Greek'? The grecas of Mitla could not have been inspired by Greece, nor did the Greeks learn to design their *grecas* from Mexico. Both, I suggest, were inspired by their respective entheogens, in Mesoamerica by the entheogens that by now we know well, in Greece by the sacred potion drunk at Eleusis and certainly elsewhere, coming from entheogenic mushrooms called Claviceps parasitic on barley or other grasses.

Fig 23

Figs 23 and 24 Mitla: grecas in ruins of the pre-Conquest temple

Fig 24

There have been arguments about the swastika, which occurs in remote parts of the world to all appearances autochthonously. Or is diffusion the explanation? The answer surely lies rather in the natural diffusion of the plants producing entheogens instead of the diffusion of art motifs. To illustrate this, we show in Figure 25 an amphora of the archaic period (ca B C 640) from Eleusis. Interspersed among the figures there are many ornamental 'fillers', as the art historian is apt to call them, which are simply our 'grecas' broken down into isolated art motifs. The Greek art historian has generally said that this vase gives no clue to what took place once a year in the sacred precincts of the Temple to Demeter.

But as he was not present on that night of revelations he of course does not know, and now that we are familiar once again with the abstract designs engendered by the entheogens, this new evidence tells us with certainty that the artist was drawing his inspiration from the potion of Eleusis. Such designs were the common property of initiates everywhere in the Age of Entheogens. Mari ja Gimbutas has revealed to us a wealth of such designs from artifacts running back to the fourth and fifth millennia B C, mostly from what she properly calls 'Old Europe' but what we know today as the Balkans. (The inhabitants of Old Europe, whoever they were, possessed cultivated barley and wheat and therefore ergot was available to them, in addition to several other entheogenic mushrooms.)

She also reproduces the design (Fig 26) of a gold ring recovered near Knossos, ca B C 1500, showing a vision of five whirling females (Maenads?) with insect heads and 'hands', and a 'disembodied eye', which I suggest is the eye of the hallucinating observer. Teotihuacan belongs to prehistory. We cannot even be sure what language was spoken by the natives of that vast city-sanctuary. But its dimensions are so great that I suggest it was the religious capital of all Mesoamerica, and that for many centuries. Here is the explanation of the cultural amalgam that united so many peoples of diverse linguistic families, of diverse origins, living in widely different climates and ecosystems: that explanation lay in the entheogens and specifically in the Wondrous Mushrooms. For the native they were miraculous.

Fig 25 Archaic Greek amphora found in Eleusis

Fig 26 Gold Ring of Isopata near Knossos. Goddess on right and worshippers. Note disembodied eye. Much enlarged.

Miller in his book on Teotihuacan even points out the plunging god that I think was Piltzintli, an aspect or manifestation of Xochipilli. The veladas that were sung in those chambers have their direct descendants in veladas being sung over wide areas of Mexico today, of which we possess full recordings in the chants of Maria Sabina. In 1960 I wrote:

What you are seeing and what you are hearing appear as one: the music assumes harmonious shapes, giving visual form to its harmonies, and what you are seeing takes on the modalities of music - the music of the spheres. ' Where has there been greater rivalry between seeing and hearing?' How apposite to the Mexican experience was the ancient Greek's rhetorical question!

It is indeed surprising to discover in Mexico a common denominator with ancient Greece - in the *veladas* that were there sung the key to the Mysteries of Eleusis, in the 'ornamental fillers' that decorate the vase from archaic Attica and the frets of Mitla! There were two mushroom potions, in Greece derived from a Claviceps, in Mexico from a Psilocybe. The effect was the same and it was prodigious.

217

CHAPTER 9

THE MUSHROOM STONES OF THE MAYA HIGHLANDS

Many now know about the mushroom stones of the Guatemalan highlands. They first emerged into the world's consciousness on 29 May 1898, when the famous German geographer Carl Sapper published a picture of one in Globus. (Figure 1) They had been discussed for some years in Guatemala in circles interested in the archaeology of that country, and now finally they were breaking into print in journals of the outside world. Sapper pointed out that the mushroom stones were ' mushroom-shaped' but, strangely, failed to consider whether the sculptors might be carving mushrooms. He saw that these stones were religious. He dismissed a suggestion that they were phallic but, in the end, he left their purpose in the air. He was right in dismissing the erotic notion: the fungal world is filled with erotic symbolism, male and female, but when an artist sets out to present a phallus, he starts with a phallus in mind, not a mushroom, and the figurines are all mushroomic, not phallic. Sapper ends by urging that specialists in neighboring cultures be consulted to see whether they might shed light on these 'unique' figurines. But his appeal went unanswered until the Wassons linked the mushroom stones with the mushroom cult in Mexico in the early 1950's.

Two months after Sapper, on 29 July 1898, Daniel Brinton reverted to the mushroom stones in Science:

> I would offer a suggestion. They resemble in shape mushrooms or toadstools, and why should not that be their intention?
>
> [n. s., vol 8, no 187, p 127]

He then advanced a linguistic justification, discovering (as he thought) that the sounds in one of the Mayan languages for the words 'mushroom' and 'moon' were almost the same. Mayan scholars dismissed his idea, but let it be now noted that he was the first to tie mushroom stones with mushrooms. In this he was right but wrong in his follow-through. He had clearly never heard of the mushroom cult in Mesoamerica.

Archaeologists in the Guatemalan highlands have been finding additional mushroom stones and many others have slid into the market from surreptitious sources, until today some three hundred are known to exist. They are in private collections and museums throughout the world. I have selected from the finest of them to illustrate this chapter. When

Valentina Pavlovna and I came on the Mesoamerican scene in 1952, we at once assumed that the mushroom cult reported by the friars in Mexico found full expression in the mushroom stones of the highland Maya.

Fig 1 Earliest mushroom stone published. Now in Rietberg Museum, Zurich. Ht 32.5 cm

Fig 2 Second view of Rietberg mushroom stone

Fig 3 Hans Namuth artifact.
Early photograph taken in middle 50's

We propounded this thesis in *Mushrooms Russia & History* and other publications in the late 1950's, failing however to stress our surprise and puzzlement that it took us, outsiders, to see the obvious. True, we were specializing in the role of mushrooms in human cultures, but still we were astonished at the seeming blind spot of all scholars of European ancestry in failing to consider what the sixteenth and seventeenth century friar-chroniclers had stressed, though inadequately. In *Mushrooms Russia & History* (pp 181-2) we drew attention to a reference to mushrooms in the pre-Conquest Mayan *Popol Vuh* in a religious context, and likewise to one in the *Annals of the Cakchiquels*, also Mayan, also religious. There are no other references to mushrooms in these pre-Conquest sources.

The late Stephan F. Borhegyi thought he discerned a tie linking the mushroom stones and the Mesoamerican ball game, for reasons that I will not enter into here. The ball game was a religious event alike in Guatemala and Mexico. (This may seem odd to some, but one need only attend a sumo match in Japan to see a survival of such a feeling in the ritual of those wrestling matches; and in ancient Greece the Olympic games breathed religion.) There is nothing incompatible between the mushroom stones and the ball game. Those who have mastered the mushrooms arrive at an extraordinary command of their faculties and muscular movements: their sense of timing is heightened. I have already suggested that the players had ingested the mushrooms before they entered upon the game. If the mushroom stones were related to the ball game, it remains to be discovered what role they played.

We were constantly on the lookout for evidence of the tie between the mushroom stones and mushrooms. The difficulty was that the last carvings, extremely crude, were made some centuries before the Conquest and it looked as though the stones were being abandoned at that time. We hardly dared hope to find a continuity with post-Conquest Mesoamerica.

Early in our pursuit we became acquainted with a mushroom stone in New York owned by Mr. and Mrs. Hans Namuth. He is a photographer and she had been born a Herrera of Guatemala. A striking piece, it came to be known as the Namuth artifact, and Mr. Namuth graciously photographed it for us. (Figure 3) An elderly woman (as we thought her then) was bending over an inclined plane in front of her. The figurine was admirable but it meant nothing more to us than that.

Late in June 1960 Robert Ravicz and I made a field trip to the Mixteca together and in Juxtlahuaca we put up in the home of Robert's friends, Guadalupe Gonzalez Vega and his family. On the night of 5-6 July, we attended a *velada,* the aunt of our host serving us as *sabia.*

Fig 4 Young girl grinding sacred mushrooms in Juxtlahuaca, Oax., in the Mixteca

The notable feature of this *velada* was the preparation of the entheogenic mushrooms: Juventina, the youngest daughter of the family, a child, a maiden (*doncella*), ground them on a metate over which she leaned. She ground them, as is customary, with a *mano*, a hand roller also made of stone. It was at once clear to me that the *doncella* was performing the religious office of the female figure in the Namuth artifact. There could be no doubt about it. The composition of the figurine was as close as the medium would permit the sculptor to go. (Figure 4)

I returned to New York and on Steve Borhegyi's next visit we rushed around to the Namuth studio together: we perceived for the first time that the figure displayed the budding breasts of a virgin. We ordered new photographs that would highlight this feature. (Figure 5) In his letter dated 14 June 1962 to Mr. Namuth, Borhegyi explained why we needed them:

I am now completely positive that the figure on this mushroom stone represents a young female working on the metate.

[Carbon copy in my Borhegyi file]

Later we learned that grinding the mushrooms on the metate and drinking the pulpy crushed mushrooms in water was far more widespread than we had known at the time: before the Conquest it may have been the general practice. I have given the evidence for this on pp 31-32. Juventina in Juxtlahuaca was, all unknowing, the key to the highland Mayan doncella some 2000 years before.

Fig 5 Second photo taken of Hans Namuth artifact in 1962

A little later, reinforcing our Mixtec evidence, there emerged into the market place from the archaeological site of Kaminaljuyu a remarkable find: nine miniature mushroom stones with nine miniature *metates* and *manos*. (Figure 6) The miniature mushroom stones were linked by physical association with the *metates* and *manos*. They supported the testimony of the Namuth artifact and of Juventina.

Fig 6. Miniature mushroom stones and metates, now in the Nottebohm Collection, pictured with a mushroom stone of normal size.

For three weeks in 1953 Steve Borhegyi, his wife Susie, and we scoured the Guatemalan highlands seeking a contemporary use of entheogenic mushrooms. We did our best and we found none. The practice seems to have died out, but there is always a question: the Maya are more reserved than the Mexican Indians and we were less experienced then than later. We have always hoped for a breakthrough. There have been reports of the use of the sacred mushrooms among the Maya on both sides of the Guatemalan-Mexican border but the reports are not so far substantiated. Now the trails are muddied by the activities of trippers and hippies.

Inexperienced observers have often remarked that no entheogenic mushrooms have been reported from Guatemala. They should realize that in Mexico Professor Heim and we had won the confidence of the Indians who brought the mushrooms to us and us to the mushrooms. To embark on a mycological survey of the highlands is an altogether different matter, much more arduous and prolonged. No reason exists to think the entheogenic species fail to grow there in abundance. Geologically the Guatemalan highlands are a continuation of the Sierra Madre in Mexico and we have always taken it for granted that the mycoflora would be the same. Bernard Lowy, Professor of Mycology at the State University of Louisiana in Baton Rouge, has been devoting a few weeks in each year to such a survey and he has lately found *Ps. Mexicana Heim* in the heart of the Pokoman country. Pokoman is one of the Mayan-languages. (Fig 7) Professor Lowy is the first mycologist on record to make field trips in Guatemala.

Fig 7

That the highland Maya knew the inebriating mushrooms is proven by a number of Mayan word lists for the Cakchiquel linguistic area around Guatemala City and Antigua. The lists that I have seen are mostly handwritten and experts date them from the end of the seventeenth century, though they bear no date. In the Tozzer Library at Harvard, I discovered a photographed copy of a *Vocabulario Castellano-Cakchiquel* in which there are a number of entries for mushrooms. One reads: *hongo que emborracha*, 'mushroom that inebriates'. This word list was compiled, according to the library listing, by 'Calepino Franciscano', 'and there is an almost identical copy in the Bibliotheque Nationale, Man. Americana, No 41, folio 106, linked with no name and written by a different and I think later hand. I am indebted to Karl-Herbert Mayer for discovering the Paris copy: he is assembling a notable collection of Mayan lexicons wherein the mushrooms figure. Then there is the Vocabulario compiled by the Franciscan friar Thomas Coto, to which Peter Furst drew my attention. It also lists *otros* [hongos] *que embriagan*, 'others that inebriate'. The Maya highlands and the highlands of what is now Mexico are essential areas of Mesoamerica, where there was an active give-and-take in warfare and trade throughout history and prehistory. Here is for me conclusive evidence that the use of entheogenic mushrooms existed in the highlands of what is now Guatemala. An anthropological trait as important as the use of entheogens would inevitably characterize the whole of the cultural entity known as Mesoamerica.

As though supporting this conclusion, Donald B. Lawrence, Professor emeritus of Botany at the University of Minnesota, has turned up ancillary evidence in the portals to the patio of the Church of San Francisco in Antigua. This evidence is noteworthy in associating the complete pattern of entheogenic use in Mexico with such use in Guatemala. The columns of these portals were originally covered with stucco molded to represent a climber and that climber was a *morning-glory*. The colors are lost and only fragments remain of the climber. In Figures 8 and 9 we reproduce two views of this portal, one to place it in relation to the church, and the other, Joya Hairs' photograph of a detail. That the Indians were molding the entheogenic *morning-glory* seems to me evident. This was in the second half of the sixteenth or perhaps more probably in the seventeenth century. Did the Franciscan friars know what the Indians were doing? I should like to think so.

For readers who would pursue further the mushroom stones, I would draw their attention to Figures 10-13. In Figure 10 from the mouth of a giant toad a mushroom stone is emerging. In another, Figure 11, a mushroom rises from the back of a toad with an anthropomorphic face. In front the toad is indicated by the four toes on each of the front feet and the characteristic squat is seen from the side. We show two more mushrooms with the toad theme reiterated, Figs 12 and 13.

Fig 8 Church of San Francisco in Antigua seen through portal

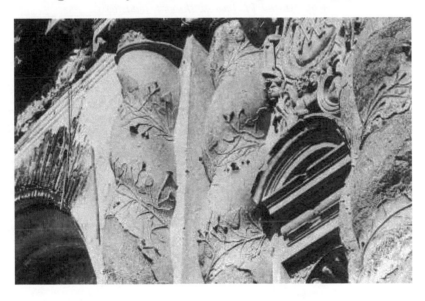

Fig 9 Detail of morning-glory carved on columns of portal

Figs 10 and 11 Two mushroom 'toadstools'

Figs 12 and 13 Two additional mushroom 'toadstools'

Strangely moving is the sporadic recurrence throughout the northern hemisphere of this chthonic deity, the toad, with the entheogenic mushroom. It survives to this day in the Basque language (*amoroto*, 'toad mushroom', *A. muscaria*), in
rural France (*crapaudin*, *A. muscaria*), in Chinese (*hama chun*, 'toad mushroom', *A. muscaria*). In Old French *l e bot* was a toad, the Devil, and a mushroom. (By 'mushroom' did the lexicographer mean any mushroom or a specific kind that he did not identify? A crapaudin perhaps?) The same association survives in far wider circles in those mycophobic lands where through taboo the handsomest of all our mushrooms has lost its name and what had been its name is become the designation ('toadstool') of every mushroom that the seeker distrusts, above all *A. muscaria*, which he knows he should distrust. How far back into the stone age must this association carry us! In Mesoamerica *A. muscaria* has been replaced by the superior Psilocybe species.

In our 1953 travels throughout the Maya highlands we discovered a convergence of three ideas in one Mayan word: 'toad', 'mushroom', and for the external genital organs of the woman. (*Mushrooms Russia & History*, p 280) Borhegyi sent us afterwards a chart in diverse Mayan languages and dialects giving us supporting evidence for this in Quiche and we reproduce that chart here. This linguistic pattern is not confined to Mayan languages. How widespread it may be, I do not know.

Among the Kogi of Santa Marta, in the Sierra Nevada of Colombia, Gerardo Reichel Dolmatoff writes:

For a Kogi the toad symbolizes the feminine sexual organ in an aggressive and insatiable sense. Linguistically the words 'toad' and 'vagina' are identical (*maukui*) and on occasions a man may refer to his wife as 'my toad '. * Mention of the word or the mere sight of a toad provokes hilarity and disgust. Young people laugh and the elderly become angry. It is a 'bad word'. The 'toad is ugly'. The toad is a woman, is the feminine sex. 'The toad eats worms', is a very common obscene phrase which being interpreted means the way that the feminine organ 'eats' the masculine.

* In the dialect of the Sanca, no word exists to designate the feminine organ and a hybrid is used: sapi or the euphemism soma = 'flower'.

[Los Kogi, vol 1, p 268; 1950, Bogota. Translation mine: RGW]

Richard Evans Schultes tells me that the toad is also linked with the female genitalia in southern Colombia and Ecuador. How odd is this association of ideas throughout the northern Hemisphere! Perhaps the toad in Figure

10 is swallowing the mushroom, not giving it birth. We see our Mesoamerican toad in Hieronymus Bosch in his Seven Deadly Sins in the Prado (Figure 15) and we see it also in the mosaic of the ceiling in the Baptistery of Florence. (Figure 16)

Fig 15 Hieronymus Bosch. Seven Deadly Sins. Detail: 'Superbia'. Madrid, Prado Museum

In the association of these ideas we strike a vein that must go back to the remotest times in Eurasia, to the stone age: the link between the toad, the female sex organs, and the mushroom, exemplified here in the Mayan languages and the mushroom stones of the Maya highlands. Man must have brought this association across the Bering Strait (or the land-bridge that replaced it in the ice ages) as part of his intellectual luggage.

When we look at the mushroom stones we must always remember that in pre-Conquest times most art, if not all, was religious, as it once was in Europe. And we must remember that the hold on the inner life of the Mesoamerican peoples of the entheogens, notably the entheogenic mushrooms, was all-powerful, as it is to this day in remote corners of highland Mexico. Those who have not explored the role of the entheogens in the cultural past of Mesoamerica easily overlook that role or assume that it was of minor importance, solely because for us it is of no importance.

Fig 16 Toad. Detail from a mosaic. Florence, Battistero, in ceiling

MUSHROOM STONES OF THE MAYA

In the association of these ideas, we strike a vein that must go back to the remotest times in Eurasia, to the stone age: the link between the toad, the female sex organs, and the mushroom, exemplified here in the Mayan languages and the mushroom stones of the Maya highlands. Man must have brought this association across the Bering Strait (or the land-bridge that replaced it in the ice ages) as part of his intellectual luggage.

When we look at the mushroom stones we must always remember that in pre-Conquest times most art, if not all, was religious, as it once was in Europe. And we must remember that the hold on the inner life of the Mesoamerican peoples of the entheogens, notably the entheogenic mushrooms, was all-powerful, as it is to this day in remote corners of highland Mexico. Those who have not explored the role of the entheogens in the cultural past of Mesoamerica easily overlook that role or assume that it was of minor importance, solely because for us it is of no importance.

To sum up our argument, then, and without suggesting the use to which the mushroom stones were put, I have shown, thanks to the Namuth artifact, that the sacred mushrooms were crushed on a metate by a maiden. It is certain that the entheogenic mushrooms flourished in the Maya highlands and that they and (thanks in this case to Donald Lawrence's keen eye) *ololiuhqui* were there used. The friars learned of the use and included the entheogenic mushrooms in their word lists of the Cakchiquel language. We have arrived at verbal associations of ideas - toad, pudenda muliebria, and mushroom - that link them, long long ago, with the same verbal associations in Eurasia.

There came to light in the late 1950's a terracotta artifact representing an Indian woman, seated cross-legged on the floor, with her right hand on a plain hollow pottery mushroom and the left hand raised in air: she might be supplicating or giving voice to an oracular utterance. (Figure 24) This figurine is until now unique. The late Stephan F. Borhegyi said that it came from Tenenexpan in the State of Veracruz and it is, appropriately, in the style of a *Remojadas* piece, with the exposed sections of the woman's legs and arms covered with black asphalt paint (*chapopote*). The woman wears a turban-like headdress, a *quexquemitl* (a kind of shoulder cape), a beaded necklace, and a wrap-around skirt. In the middle of her back is a hole (Figure 25), which communicates with two round apertures in her upper lip under her nose, serving as nostrils, and one can blow smoke of tobacco or copal or aromatic plants through this hole in her back and out of her upper lip. Our figurine fits well into the pattern of mycolatry that I have given in the pages of our book. It is a superb expression of the religious faith of a people who held the entheogenic mushrooms in awe, both for their ecstatic potency and their divinatory powers. It dates from the classic period, ca A D 300.

Fig 17 Mushroom stone in Garcia Collecrion, Guaremala City

Fig 18 Second view of the same

Figs 19 and 20. Mushroom stones with
Plunging Figure motif

Figs 21 and 22 Late Classic mushroom stone
with carved head

235

Fig 23 Mushroom stone with geometric design and jaguar head

Figs 24 and 25 Terracotta figurine, Remojadas style, found in Veracruz

29 July 1977

I had reached this point in writing my chapter when there reached me by post a copy of the doctoral thesis on the mushroom stones submitted by Dr Richard M. Rose to the Department of Anthropology of Harvard University in June 1977. In it he advances the novel thesis that the mushroom stones served a 'utilitarian' purpose in the making of the rubber balls used in the pre-Conquest ball game in the Maya highlands. He assembles evidence of the widest diversity to support his position and I think he makes good his case. I also hope he is right for he has supplied the missing copestone to support my mushroomic interpretation of the mushroom carvings of the Maya highlands. Somewhat strangely, Dr Rose does not see this, perhaps because his concentration on his voluminous and diverse evidence, all of it pertinent, has blinded him to the larger view. He has opened the door to a fresh discussion of Maya culture and the mushroom stones. What is 'utilitarian' is often also religious: designing and shaping a superb chalice is both a 'utilitarian' and a religious act. All art in pre-Conquest Mesoamerican society, or virtually all, is inspired by religious beliefs. At that time there was no 'art for art's sake', no genre art. The Maya ball game was, in essence, a religious observance.

From the beginning it has been known that the ball game of Mesoamerica was played over a much larger area than Mesoamerica: throughout the Caribbean islands and northern South America. Rose has explored the sources for this ball game over the whole area including the parts of Mexico that are north of the cultural entity known as Mesoamerica. He has come up with relevant data of fascinating kinds. The ball was of course of rubber. As the Maya did not know the vulcanizing process, a new ball presumably had to be made for every game. In making the ball, strips of latex were stretched on a round and roughened surface, the cap of our volcanic-stone mushrooms, and when the strips had hardened to the proper point they were removed and molded into the rubber ball. The pottery 'mushrooms' of El Salvador and Tabasco are smooth but the cap is skillfully roughened by pecking to the required degree, making the cap surface comparable to the mushroom stones. Rose enlists further evidence of a surprising kind: it has long been known that 'mushroom' caps have been found, not fragments of mushroom stones, but deliberately carved caps without pedestals. Until Rose no one could explain 'these beautifully carved caps and little attention had been paid to them. These caps date from the early phase of mushroom stone carvings. Rose thinks they were held in the hand and served the same purpose as the mushroom stones. Here then we find a use for these caps, until now unexplained.

Thus, through more than a millennium and a half the mushroom stones apparently served the purpose of making rubber balls for the ball game, the artisan sitting on the ground, his legs encircling the mushroom stone, and applying by hand the latex in strips to the round mushroom cap.

We know something of the paraphernalia that the players in the ball game wore but of the rules and practices of the game we know little. The stakes were high, in the great games the very life of a player being the forfeit. We of modern European provenience naturally assume that the captain of the losing team was decapitated. In a society where the standards were utterly different, I am not so sure. The divinity to whom the game was dedicated deserved the sacrifice of the best, not the second best. The glory of winning the game and the plaudits of the attending throngs, plus his own transcendental beliefs, might well have led the captain of the winning team to offer himself to the sacrificer with the physical courage before certain death that was the crowning glory occasionally open to the Mesoamerican and North American natives. We see a parallel in the deaths of those Christian martyrs who presented themselves of their own volition to judges who would surely send them to the stake.

Henry Munn and I, independently of each other, have pointed out the extraordinary control, the precise timing, that the mushrooms generate in the shamanic ingester. It is the neophyte who staggers, who even steps off a cliff or out of a window into space. I now ask anew whether the ball player did not take the entheogenic mushrooms (or infusion of ground morning-glory seeds) before the game started and play under their influence. For the players as for the attendance the emotional tension of the game must have been awesome, each side fighting to win and the winning side (as I believe) having the honor of surrendering their captain to certain and quick death. Naturally in our pusillanimous, self-indulgent, permissive society such standards are inconceivable.

Those of us who have spoken for a conscious mushroomic use of the mushroom stones have never known what that use was. Twenty years ago, we ventured the guess that they had served a ritual purpose in such veladas as Maria Sabina has sung throughout her life. No supporting evidence for this hypothesis has been discovered. Lately I have explored the activities of the Princes and Nobles of the Nahua with the divine mushrooms and have now recorded these doings in the preceding chapters. We can be certain that when they s ang their poetry, when they entered upon the dance, they did not stammer, they did not stagger like drunken men. Their words glow with the wondrous religious passion that most - not all - of us in the West have lost. But the anthropologist, though he need not share in these beliefs, fails in his duty when he does not allow fully for them in studying Early Man, whether long ago or among his survivors in our own times.

When the child Juventina crushed the sacred mushrooms on the *metate* in *Juxtlahuaca*, s h e w a s performing a religious a c t a s well a s a utilitarian one. When the sculptor carved the beautiful Namuth artifact, he was depicting the same performance in stone as faithfully as the limitations of his medium permitted, and his carving expressed religious belief. The nine miniature mushroom stones with the nine miniature metates and manos speak for themselves in the same way. The toad effigy mushroom stones express a tripartite association of ideas that link in a common embrace Early Man throughout the Northern hemisphere. The craftsman who carved the stone shown in Figs 17, 1 8 must have been aware that he was carving a mushroom, as well as an artifact to serve in making the rubber ball. Dr Rose sets forth fairly the evidence offered us by the Namuth artifact but then fails to discuss it and draw conclusions. He fails to see the import of the miniature mushroom stones lying in a common cache with the miniature metates and manos. He ignores the toad symbolism in the toad effigies carved on four mushroom stones. He gives only a sentence to the terra cotta figurine, a woman with her right hand on a mushroom, her left hand raised in a speaking gesture, the Remojadas artifact found in Veracruz and dating from the time of Christ or shortly thereafter. (Figs 24-25)

If the mushroom stones of Guatemala were carved primarily for the making of rubber balls for the ball game - and Rose may well be right in thinking so – this in no way diminishes the relevance of the mushroom to the stone: Early Man was accustomed to see in superficial resemblances profound meanings. Similarities in the sound of distinct words are today dismissed as fun puns or as sources of confusion in the ambiguities that they provoke. But in preliterate times paronomasia, as such verbal identities are called, led to deeper misinterpretations, mistaken folk etymologies, as in the case of 'Soma '. And this was even truer in semiotics - communication through means other than words - as is to be seen in the (for us) absurd meanings placed on the forked root of the mandrake. From earliest times the stone cutter carving his volcanic rock to serve for making rubber balls must have associated this holy stone with the holy plant that it resembled, its sacral meaning being vastly enhanced by the overlapping of the two shapes. In fact, the mushroom may well have been, in this case, a prime motive in leading to the evolution of the cap into the tripartite mushroom stone.

Rose concedes, though grudgingly, that the hallucinogenic mushrooms were used in the Maya highlands. He fails to allow for the way the mushrooms permeated Mesoamerican life, for which the signs have been available to all though they have not been read. He fails to see the breathtaking beauty of his rubber ball – fashioned on a *mushroom* stone, thus redoubling the religious potency of his act. Probably the fashioning was attended by religious rites before, during, and after; and thereupon the ball was thrown into the game played by both teams with skilled fury for the highest of stakes.

CHAPTER 10

THE HISTORICAL RECORD

In *Mushrooms Russia & History* (1957) Valentina Pavlovna and I gathered together and published a dozen extracts from early sources illustrating the use of inebriating mushrooms in Mesoamerica. We also cited early lexicons composed by friars for the Zapotec and Tarascan languages giving native words for these mushrooms, just as we have now done in the preceding chapter for Cakchiquel, an important highland Mayan language. In *Les Champignons hallucinogenes du Mexique* (1958) the quotations rose to above a score. Today, if I am right in my interpretations contained in this book, it is useless to count the pre-Conquest and later references to the divine mushrooms, so many are they, and more are sure to be discovered, especially in Nahuatl and Mayan texts not yet translated. The blind spot of the scholarly world for the entheogens manifests itself with peculiar force here in Mesoamerica precisely because their role was so important.

Chronologically the divinatory mushroom first appears in a tradition preserved for us in Fray Antonio Tello's chronicle when (according to this tradition) 'Teopiltzintli' led the Aztecs to their new 'Promised Land' back in the early centuries of our Christian era. No one can say that this took place but the folk memory may well be right, for the function attributed to the divinatory mushroom was a normal one for it to perform. Much later, one of the legendary 'founding fathers' of Tenochtitlan-Mexico was Nanacatzin, the 'mushroom' (*nanacatl*) with an affectionate and reverential suffix, - *tzin*. A number of lists of the founding fathers survive and Nanacatzin's name occurs in at least two, in Fray Juan de Torquemada's *Monarquia Indiana*, at the end of Chap 3, Book 2, and in the famous *Historia Antigua de Mexico* published in Italian by the Jesuit Francisco Javier Clavijero in 1780-1. The list of the twenty legendary founders appears only in that first edition, as a footnote in the first volume of the Italian text at the beginning of Chapter 3.

For these two historical citations I am indebted to Gutierre Tibo'n of Cuernavaca, that questing scholar in the byways of Mesoamerican history. He is imbued with a sense of the poetry, the mystery, the drama of Mexico's past.

DIEGO DURAN, O. P

Among the friars the Dominican Diego Duran supplies us with unique evidence of the pre- Conquest use of mushrooms in his superb *Historia de las Indias de Nueva Espana.* (I shall use the two-volume text edited by Father Garibay, 1967.) This work was written in the 16th century and survives in the author's own manuscript. Here is a remarkable account of the history of the Aztecs, an account that no Spaniard could have assembled on his own, an intimate inside story of the rulers of Mexico-Tenochtitlan, their entourage, their traditions and practices, their wars, religious beliefs, diversions, successes and failures. Duran cites constantly the '*Historia*' that he is using or sometimes certainly translating, and scholars seem agreed that when he wrote he had before him a narrative in Nahuatl but in Latin characters written or dictated by someone highly placed in the pre-Conquest regime who had enjoyed the confidence of the sovereign and who was steeped in the oral traditions of his people. This unidentified personage, intelligent and able, was clearly a partisan but as we do not possess comparable narratives by others, scholars can usually do no other than let his stand alone. As its author concerned himself solely with the doings of the kings and aristocrats, he tells us only by inference about the conditions of the farmers, the artisans, and the women folk. This '*Cronica X*' (as it is called) may still exist and its discovery would be a sensational event in Mesoamerican studies.

According to *Cronica X,* in the festivities following the coronation of the sovereign Tizoc in 1481, at the end of the great banquet, inebriating mushrooms were served to the guests. Duran does not say whether this had happened on the occasion of previous coronations but from his context it seems probable that it was habitual on all grand occasions. Here is what Diego Duran writes:

Y todos los senores y grandes de las provincias se levantaron y, para mas solemnizar la fiesta, comieron todos de unos bongos monteses, que dicen que hacen perder el sentido, y asi salieron todos muy aderezados al baile.

[n Cap XL 40]

And all the lords and grandees of the provinces rose and, to solemnize further the festivities, they all ate of some woodland mushrooms, which they say make you lose your senses, and thus they sallied forth all primed for the dance.

Tizoc's reign was a failure: he was pusillanimous and he died, probably poisoned (according to *Cronica X*), in 1486, whereupon his brother Ahuitzotl was elected his successor.

243

Not a word is said about mushrooms in the detailed and glowing account of Ahuitzotl's coronation feast, but in an important aside that Diego Duran makes on the text before him we gather by implication the general role played by the mushrooms on all such occasions.

He notado una cosa en toda esta historia: que jamas hace memoria de que bebiesen vino de ningun genero para embriagarse, sino solo los hongos monteses, que los comian crudos, con los cuales, dice la historia, que se alegraban y regocijaban y salian algo de su sentido, y del vino nunca hace memoria, sino es para los sacrificios o mortuorios; solo hace memoria de la abundancia de cacao que se bebia en estas solemnidades.

[II Cap XLII 16]

One thing I have noticed in all this Historia [= *Cronica X*]: that never is mention made that they drank wine [i.e. fermented drinks] of any kind to get drunk, but only the woodland mushrooms which they ate raw, with which, says the Historia, they would rejoice and grow merry and become somewhat tipsy; and mention is never made of wine save only for sacrifices or funerals; mention is made only of the abundance of chocolate that would be drunk on these exalted occasions.

In this pregnant aside Duran is telling us several things:

a) by strong implication the *Cronica X* speaks often of inebriating mushrooms but Duran as editor has chosen to omit all save four or five such citations and he is now summarizing all the references that lay before him;

b) he observes that fermented drinks were never taken with the mushrooms: fermented drinks were beneath the dignity of the Aztec aristocrats on occasions such as Duran is describing. (The Aztecs tried to confine the use of fermented drinks to the superannuated men and women whose active role in life had ended.) It seems to have been considered an offense to pollute the pure effect of the mushroom inebriation with alcoholic inebriation; and

c) an abundance of chocolate was however consumed in these great banquets: chocolate was a beverage served cold with maize, poyomatli, other flowers, and almost certainly spiked with the juice of entheogenic mushrooms or an infusion of ground morning-glory seeds.

We come now to the coronation of Moctezuma II in 1502 when no one in the Aztec country had yet heard of the Spaniards. For four days there was feasting and celebration and then on the fourth day came the coronation followed by human sacrifices in numbers. Then follows this paragraph where the sacred mushrooms enter:

Acabado el sacrificio y quedando las gradas del templo y patio banadas de sangre humana, de, alli iban todos a comer hongos crudos; con la cual comida salian todos de juicio y quedaban peores que si hubieran bebido mucho vino; tan embriagados y fuera de sentido, que muchos de ellos se mataban con su propia mano, y, con la fuerza de aquellos hongos, veian visiones y tenian revelaciones de lo porvenir, hablfodoles el demonio en aquella embriaguez.

[II Cap LIV 24]

The sacrifice finished and the steps of the temple and patio bathed i n human blood, they all went to eat raw mushrooms; on which food they all went out of their minds, worse than if they had drunk much wine [i.e. fermented drinks]; so drunk and senseless were they that many killed themselves by their own hand, and, with the force of those mushrooms, they would see visions and have revelations of the future, the Devil speaking to them in that drunken state.

Duran's tone here is so out of harmony with what he had previously said that, were we not dealing with the holographic manuscript in his own hand, I would ask whether we had to do with an interpolation of a priestly redactor. Such a violent statement - many men drunk and senseless killing themselves! is repeated by white men unacquainted with the hallucinogenic mushrooms, or who have possibly been ill-prepared for the experience and been drunk from alcohol when they took them. In Father Garibay's three volumes of Poesia Nahuatl we see time and again the glowing ecstasy, the awe-struck and reverential attitude, of the Nahuatl aristocrats, speaking to us in person about the wondrous mushrooms.

The coronation of Moctezuma is the occasion for another passage strange for us, founded on *Cronica X* but with Duran's comments added, in which we learn that the princes and lords of the enemy states were invited to the festivities and that they accepted the invitation, where among other items on their social agenda, they witnessed from specially built blinds the sacrifice on one of the lofty pyramids of their own kin and compatriots captured in past 'wars'. Here we see to what extent those 'wars' were purely ceremonial, to capture prisoners for sacrifice. Afterwards Moctezuma sent the enemy delegations home laden with jewels and other presents, and he gave them powerful escorts back to their own borders so that they would not be waylaid as hated enemies by Aztecs or their allies. [See II LIV 23; also, XLII 17 and elsewhere.]

Such passages in the chronicles of the Aztecs astonish us: the number of human sacrifices that are set forth in detail, the way in which they are keyed to the religious calendar, the variety of methods used in taking the lives of the victims many of them cruel taxing belief and, perhaps strangest of all, the presence at their deaths, on the invitation of the victorious Aztec king, of their kin and friends. All these elements leave us in a quandary. A well-known mycologist has expressed the view that the victims, to prepare them for sacrifice, were fed massive doses of mushrooms:

Il devient comprehensible maintenant comment les fetes sacrificielles de l'ancien Mexique ont pu ne susciter aucune defense des milliers de victimes humaines choisies qu' on y sacrifiait de maniere cruelle et sanglante: ell es obtenaient la pleine cooperation des victimes, selon toute apparence apres des orgies massives de champignons.

[Bulletin Suisse de Mycologie, June 1958]

It now becomes comprehensible how the sacrificial feasts of ancient Mexico were unable to provoke any defense from the thousands of chosen human victims that were sacrificed in a cruel and bloody manner: they won the full cooperation of the victims, according to all appearances after massive orgies of mushrooms.

There is no support for this conclusion in either Duran's *Cronica X* nor in the testimony of Sahagun's Nahuatl informants nor anywhere else. This mycologist was giving circulation in a scientific journal to his own idle fancies. He did not know his sources, readily available though they were to him.

A point has now been reached in Mesoamerican research where we can begin, hesitatingly and with all reservations, to sum up this advanced culture of Early Man, evolved out of its own innards, with no sure trace of external influence, and define the outlines of its distinctive even though unexpressed objectives. Their intelligent and thoughtful leaders might not have formulated the objectives in my terms but I think these were at least subliminal in all that they did.

The highest goal of Mesoamerican Man, his greatest achievement, was to display physical and moral courage in the face of imminent death. Those mushrooms, had the victims eaten of them, would have deprived their behavior of merit: it would have been cheating. Imminent death may also have confronted the winner in the Maya ball game, when I think he would proudly rise to the occasion. The prospect of imminent death, always a possibility, lies like a shadow over the thinking of the poets that Father Garibay has given us. The presence of their kin and compatriots at their sacrifice must have imbued these victims with pride as they climbed the long, steep, shallow steps without balustrade of the pyramid to meet death when they reached the top. The enemy delegations, sad though they were, were a moral support for them and made their courageous behavior easier. We must not forget that slaves scheduled for sacrifice, from the moment when they were chosen and dedicated to the gods, received honored treatment, being given the best of clothing, the best of foods, and treated with utmost respect. Tlaxcala and that city's allies were habitual losers to the Aztecs at the moment of the Spanish conquest, but there is every reason to think that, if the tide had been reversed, they would have inflicted identical penalties on the Aztecs.

In accounts of the native North Americans I have read that prisoners destined to die would take pride in taunting their captors, insulting them ingeniously to infuriate them, even as their captors were torturing them and slowly putting them to death. May not this practice, where physical courage in face of certain death was exalted to the highest degree, have found its supreme, most sophisticated expression in the religious sacrifices of the Mesoamericans?

Moctezuma in his pride tried to carry yet further his ambivalent relations with those who were his enemies though his efforts were unsuccessful:

Desde este dia, cuenta la historia, que tres v eces en el afio convidaba Motecuhzoma a los reyes y sefiores enemigos y les hacia gran fiesta. La una era en la fiesta que ellos llamaban de los sefiores, y la otra en la gran fiesta de las banderas, y la otra, cuando comian todos hongos, que la llamaban la fiesta d e las revelaciones. Las cuales fiestas hallaran en la Segunda Parte de este libro [Vol 1 of this edition] escritas a la larga.

Este orden tomo Motecuhzoma de convidar a sus enemigos, el intento del cual no lo pone la historia; empero, concluire con decir que Motecuhzoma convidaba a susenemigos; lo cual no hicieron los demas reyes sus antepasados, sino solo su abuelo el primer Motecuhzoma. La cual costumbre duro mientras reino. Y lo mismo guardaron los tlaxcaltecas en convidarle a el a sus solemnidades y a las veces iba o enviaba sus grandes; iban sin ser sentidos de sus genres, ni de los tlaxcaltecas, aunque, segun la historia, muy pocas veces fue el en persona, ni se hallo en estas fiestas ni solemnidades.

[II Cap LIV 27, 28]

From this day on, according to the Historia, three times a year Moctezuma would invite

247

the enemy Kings and Lords and give them a big feast. One was the feast that they called 'of the Lords', and the other was the great 'Feast of the Flags', and the other when they would all eat mushrooms, which they would call the ' Feast of the Revelations'. The which feasts will be found in the Second Part of this book written out at length. Moctezuma took this decision to invite his enemies, but the History does not say what his intention was; however, I shall conclude by saying that Moctezuma invited his enemies, which was not done by the other kings his predecessors, save only by his grandfather the first Moctezuma. The which custom lasted as long as he reigned. And the same observed the Tlaxcaltecas inviting him to their solemnities, and sometimes he went or sent his grandees; they went without their people's noticing it, nor the Tlaxcaltecas, although, according to the History, very seldom did he go in person, nor did he attend the festivities nor the solemnities.

The Feast of the Lords and the Feast of the Flags are indeed described in what Duran calls the second part of his book. (In Father Garibay's edition he has reversed the two volumes, so that the relevant Chapters XI and XVIII are now in his Vol 1.) But the Feast of the Revelations, 'when they would all eat mushrooms', is alas missing in its entirety. Was it perhaps suppressed by Duran's religious superiors? This lost section of *Cronica X* would certainly have proved an invaluable document for us.

There is one further reference to mushrooms in Duran:

[Moctezuma] despues de estos oraculos y plegarias, hacia comer a los viej os y sacerdotes antiguos, hongos verdes y otros brebajes supersticiosos, que les hacia beber, para que supiesen en aquellas embriagueces que aquellas comidas y brebajes les causaban, de tener victoria o n o. Y desdichados de los que le anunciaban mal suceso, porque luego eran mandados matar, sin ningun remedio.

[II Cap L X V 26]

[Moctezuma] after these oracles and supplications, made the old men and former priests eat green mushrooms and other superstitious potions that he made them drink, so that they would learn in those drunken states that were caused by those foods and potions whether he would win victory or not. And woe betide those who predicted a bad outcome, for forthwith he ordered them to be killed without help for it . . . [Italics mine]

'Green mushrooms': we already know what the green mushrooms are, the sacred ones, which in paintings are green to suggest the most valuable of jewels, the rings of jade.

BERNADINO DE SAHAGUN

The Dominican Diego Duran and the Franciscan Bernardino de Sahagun towered above the other friars in sixteenth century Mexico in their intellectual curiosity about the natives, their history and culture. According to Father Garibay, they almost surely sprang from Jewish families lately converted to Catholicism. If so, it must be no mere coincidence that these two able men devoted their lives to the study of the conquered and downtrodden race. Sahagun spent more than half a century taking down in Nahuatl the testimony of numbers of carefully selected informants - selected for their knowledge and connections - and in 'rendering' or paraphrasing (not translating) in a Spanish version their depositions. The Sahagun corpus is immense, only now coming to be fully known. It lies in Madrid and in the Biblioteca Laurenziana in Florence. *The Florentine Codex*, as this latter manuscript is commonly called, is bilingual, the Nahuatl depositions with Sahagun's rendering, profusely illustrated. In the 1960's Dr Charles E. Dibble and Dr Arthur J. 0. Anderson brought to term the immense task of translating the Nahuatl text into English and the University of Utah published it in thirteen large volumes, the Nahuatl text and their English translation in parallel columns.

In the light of its size, what is contained in the Sahagun corpus about the hallucinogens and the mushrooms in particular is meager, and what there is seems written with studied detachment leaning on the pejurative side. There is nothing of the free-flowing enthusiasm of the Nahuatl poets rendered for us by Father Garibay, but we must also point out Sahagun does not indulge in vituperative condemnation of the sacred mushroom such as we see in the writings of Motolinia and De la Serna. The longest passage that Sahagun's informants ever give us of the formal use of mushrooms is in an account of a celebration of some prosperous merchants who are making a display of their wealth in their neighborhood. We are grateful to Dr Dibble and Dr Anderson for having granted us permission to offer our readers their translation of this and other passages relating to the mushrooms, which are mostly new to the scholarly world. Here is the Nahuatl account of the merchants' mushroom celebration put into English:

At the very first, mushrooms had been served. They ate them at the time when, they said, the shell trumpets were blown. They ate no more food; they only drank chocolate during the night. And they ate the mushrooms with honey. When the mushrooms took effect on them, then they danced, then they wept. But some, while still in command of their senses, entered [and] sat there by the house on their seats; they danced no more, but only sat there nodding. One saw in vision that already he would die, [and] there continued weeping.

One saw in vision that he would die in battle; one saw in vision that he would be eaten by wild beasts; one saw in vision that he would take captives in war ; one saw in vision that he would be rich, wealthy; one saw in vision that he would buy slaves - he would be a slave owner; one saw in vision that he would commit adultery - he would be struck by stones -he would be stoned; one saw in vision that he would steal - he would also be stoned; one saw in vision that his head would be crushed by stones - they would condemn him; one saw in vision that he would perish in the water ; one saw in vision that he would live in peace, in tranquility, until he died ; one saw in vision that he would fall from a roof-top -he would fall to his death. However, many things were to befall one, he then saw all in vision: even that he would be drowned.

And when the effects of the mushrooms had left them, they consulted among themselves and told one another what they had seen in vision. And they saw in vision what would befall those who had eaten no mushrooms, and what they went about doing. Some were perhaps thieves, some perhaps committed adultery. Howsoever many things there were, all were told - that one would take captives, one would become a seasoned warrior, a leader of the youths, one would die in battle, become rich, buy slaves, provide banquets, ceremonially bathe slaves, commit adultery, be strangled, perish in the water, drown. Whatsoever was to befall one, they then saw all [in vision]. Perhaps he would go to his death in Anauac.

[Florentine Codex, Dibble & Anderson, Bk 9 pp 38-39]

The Nahuatl original differs in one striking particular from Sahagun's Spanish rendering in the familiar Florentine text: The Codex says explicitly in Spanish that the mushrooms *aun provocan a lujuria*, they 'even provoke lust'. This is an interpolation for which there is no justification in the Nahuatl source. Was Sahagun responsible for adding these words? Why were they inserted? To excite the sixteenth century readers seeking always the Fountain of Youth and new aphrodisiacs? Or to incite his pious readers against the mushrooms?

The well-known passage where Sahagun in the Florentine Codex uses the word teonandcatl appears afresh in the Dibble & Anderson translation of the Nahuatl:

NANACATL

It is called *teonandcatl*. It grows on the plains, in the grass. The head is small and round, the stem long and slender. It is bitter and burns; it burns the throat. It makes one besotted; it deranges one, troubles one. It is a remedy for fever, for gout. Only two [or] three can be eaten. It saddens, depresses, troubles one; it makes one flee, frightens one, makes one hide. He who eats many of them sees many things which make him afraid, or make him laugh. He flees, hangs himself, hurls himself from a cliff, cries out, takes fright. One eats it in honey. I eat mushrooms; I take mushrooms. Of one who is haughty, presumptuous, vain, of him it is said: 'He bemushrooms himself'.   [Ibid Bk 11 p 130]

BOOK 10 OF SAHAGUNS HISTORIA GENERAL

In Dibble & Anderson 's translation of Book 10, we discover five references to the inebriating mushrooms where none is cited in the Spanish rendering. These five citations are parallel: indeed, they resemble each other so closely that one asks oneself whether they were not dictated by the same informant. Much of this Book 10 is given over to a particular kind of exercise, primarily linguistic: scores of types of people are succinctly abstracted - people chosen by their occupation, worthy and unworthy, by kinship roles as eg the 'grandmother', by social rank, etc: hundreds of such types are offered to us. Until Dibble & Anderson gave us their translation, this wealth of information about the Nahuatl vocabulary and the Nahuatl social organization was accessible to us only in the inadequate Spanish version of the Florentine Codex. Here follows a mere sprinkling of the hundreds of individuals described:

The lazy mother
The goldcaster
The maguey syrup seller
The mason with plumb
The bad farmer
The good nephew
The sodomite
The seller of salt
The green stone seller
The seller of tamales
The bad nobleman
The buffoon
The lapidary
The harlot
The thief

The reader of these abstractions inevitably thinks back to that minor form of literature known to the literary historian as 'Characters', first delineated by Theophrastus in ancient Greece and developed most subtly in the seventeenth century by Jean de la Bruyere in France and Sir Thomas Over bury in England. These two men came after Sahagun and one m ay assume that he did not know Theophrastus. Sahagun was simply intent on finding ways to elicit systematically from his informants an immense range of vocabulary that would otherwise have escaped him, and a range of social circumstance that will prove an inexhaustible mine for scholars to pore over. Here then is one character:

NOBLEWOMAN

The noblewoman [is] of nobility, belongs to the order of rulers, comes from rulership whether she is legitimate or a bastard child.
The good noblewoman [is] one who is bashful, ashamed [of evil], who does things with timidity, who is embarrassed [by evil]. She is embarrassed [by evil]; she works willingly, voluntarily.
The bad noblewoman [is] infamous, very audacious, stern, proud, very stupid, brazen besotted, drunk. She goes about besotted; she goes about demented; she goes about eating mushrooms.

[Ibid Bk 10 p 49]

The Harlot; the Carnal Woman is described at length. Put briefly, she is the whore of the itching buttocks. She lives like a bathed slave, acts like a sacrificial victim, 'goes about with her head high - rude, drunk, shameless, eating mushrooms. [Ibid p 55] The Lewd Youth is a drunkard, foolish, dejected; a drunk, a sot. He goes about eating mushrooms. [Ibid p 37] The One of Noble Lineage when he is a bad nobleman is a flatterer - a drinker, besotted, drunk. He goes about becoming crazed on both kinds of Daturas; he goes about eating Daturas and mushrooms. He becomes vain, brazen. [Ibid p 20] The Bad Youth goes about becoming crazed on both kinds of Daturas and mushrooms; he is dissolute, mad; he goes about mocking, telling tales, being rude, repeating insults. [Ibid p 12)

From these citations we learn that the inebriating mushrooms had been abused under the old regime, as would be natural in any community freely using them. By accepted standards of the Nahua and other Mesoamericans, the mushrooms were imbued with sanctity and were to be ingested only where the glow of religious belief accompanied the act. In our five citations the repellent context was fortunate for Sahagun's informants: they could truthfully and gladly excoriate those who in former times had abused the mushrooms, and the friars would also approve such excoriation though they naturally were condemning all use of the mushrooms as a mortal sin, trafficking with the Devil. Even if friars as intelligent as Diego Duran and Sahagun were asking themselves searching questions about what the inebriating mushrooms really did, they could not afford to experiment with them, especially so if Father Garibay is right in thinking they were of Jewish origin: this racial origin must have been known to their conventual colleagues and extreme circumspection must have been the undeviating rule of their lives.

There remains one further citation of mushrooms in Book 10: in the description of *The Smoking Tube Seller*, the tobacco tube seller. (This would correspond to our tobacco pipe dealer but our tobacco pipe differs so much in appearance from the tobacco tube of the Nahua that Dibble & Anderson are well advised not to use our misleading term in their translation.) At the end of the description, which is rather lengthy, the informant gives a list of the ingredients that the seller offers with the tobacco for the 'tube'. [Ibid p 88] Amongst others there are mushrooms and *poyomatli*, the flowers of *Quararibea funebris*, with which we are already familiar. In my own experience in Mesoamerica I had not known that the sacred mushrooms were smoked and was skeptical when I read in Carlos Castaneda's *The Teachings of Don Juan* (entry for Sunday 10 Sept 1961) how Don Juan added *los honguitos* to his pipe mixture. Now there is the best of authority for Castaneda's text.

THE HOLY OFFICE OF THE INQUISTION

In the notes at the end of Dr Aguirre Beltran's *Medicina y Magia* there i s a wealth of references to the court records of the Inquisition held in the Archivos Generales de la Nacion (= AGN) dealing with hallucinogens and in my files, I hold copies of many of the cases that he cites. One arresting fact emerges from these files of the Inquisition: Spanish housewives of the lower classes seem to have consulted the hallucinogens often, not personally, but through their Indian servants and slaves who would know the curandero to consult, the hallucinogen to take. In my perusal of these files lasting for weeks I found no evidence that any Spaniard, male or female, had ingested the mushrooms but that many of them did not hesitate to enlist a surrogate from among the Indians. To this generalization there was one possible exception.

1

The earliest reference to the sacred mushrooms in the story of the Conquest came in 1537, when the first Bishop of Mexico, the Franciscan Juan de Zumarraga, presided over the trial in Mexico City of two Indians, brothers, called in Nahuatl Mixcoatl and Tlaloc and in Spanish Andres and Juan. They were charged with organizing resistance to the Spaniards,

253

arming their fellow Indians, and invoking their Indian divinities for help in the struggle. These activities were aggravated by the fact that they had been baptized and were apostates, backsliders. They seem to have enjoyed considerable success, and as the Spaniards had been on the scene at that time for only two decades, the rulers may well have been fearful of an uprising. The record is lengthy and the mushrooms are mentioned five times, each time briefly, as though the Spaniards were not altogether familiar with them, but the Spaniards knew well that the mushrooms were served by the Indians in what they considered a simulacrum of the Holy Eucharist. The brothers were convicted and sentenced: they were to be mounted on asses or other beasts of burden equipped with packsaddles, they were to be paraded through Mexico City, Tulantzingo, and other centers where they had carried on their agitation, and each was to receive one hundred lashes in each community, with a crier going before proclaiming their offense. Their hair was to be shorn, they were to renounce their heresies, and they were to be remanded for a year to live in the monastery of Tulantzingo, listening to the Doctrine and doing penance for their misdeeds. Their property was to be sold for the benefit of the Exchequer of the Holy Office. All this having been done, the Guardian Father of Tulantzingo was empowered to absolve them and reconcile them to Holy Mother Church.

This trial must have caused a stir among the Indians at the time. The sacred mushrooms figure in it certainly but it would be a mistake to exaggerate their importance. The gravamen of the charge was that the accused were apostates stirring up the Indians with inflammatory talk, denouncing the Spaniards, mobilizing arms, encouraging rebellion, and professing the power of the gods of the old religion. But the Holy Office was fully aware of the parallel between the bread and wine of Holy Communion - the flesh and blood of Christ - and the mushrooms that, according to the Indians, gave them visions.

In the light of the terrifying cruelties inflicted commonly on prisoners in the sixteenth century, let it be noted that Andres and his brother Juan came off lightly.

[Archivo General de la Nacion: Vol III Procesos de Indios, Idolatrias y Hechiceros pp 53-78, Mexico City, 1912]

2

The files of the Inquisition disclose another episode, amusing as well as instructive, that took place in 1629 in Michoacán, some distance west of Mexico City. A young woman named Ines Martin had left her husband Gonzalo. In despair he sought her in the woods. There he met an Indian named Joseph who advised him to ingest certain mushrooms (raices = roots) that would reveal her to him in a vision. He followed this advice with startling effect: they showed her to him in a vision half a league away, underneath a tree in a garden where a relative was delousing her. It is noteworthy that no one disputed the miraculous power of the mushrooms: the inquisitor himself tacitly accepted the story as told. The gravity of the case was not Gonzalo's credulity but that he had recourse to the Devil for a miracle. Gonzalo may have been entirely Spanish in origin, and if so, he is the first and only known instance where a non-Indian ingested the mushrooms until the Wassons came on the scene in 1955. Still today the mushrooms serve to find objects or animals or persons that one seeks, and here we have, in testimony before the Inquisition i n 1630, a classic instance of this kind. The translation of some of the testimony of Gonzalo follows:

In the town of Taximaroa, 11 May 1630, before Father friar Cristoval de Vaz, Commissary of the Holy Office of the Inquisition in this jurisdiction . . . at about 4 o'clock in the afternoon, there appeared without having been summoned and duly sworn to tell the truth a man who said that his name was Gonzalo Perez and that he was married to Ines Martin, both domiciled in this town . . . who to clear his conscience accused and denounced himself in this wise : he says that about two years ago, his wife having fled from him , and as she was his first love he was profoundly touched by her absence, and going into the woods to look for her he found an Indian named Joseph, a servant of his father, who said to this witness that he would give him an herb that they call *nanacates* with which he would see where she was, and having given him two little roots he saw nothing and afterwards this witness said to this Joseph, ' Get away from me, for you are a witch for you have done nothing for me nor have I seen anything', to which said Indian said he should take five of those as it were roots and he would see her, and this witness without knowing what he was doing with the desire that he had to see his said wife took them at about the hour of vespers and ate them and within two hours having bedded down in the woods, he saw a snake that said to him, ' Turn your head and you will see your wife', and turning he saw her in the house of a first cousin of this witness named Petrona Gutierrez who was delousing her, being half a league from that hacienda without being able to see said hacienda ; and that this witness really saw her, and from where he was this witness went to the house of his parents and said to his mother he had seen his said wife and confessed that he had taken said herb because his mother already knew it, who threw a rosary around his neck, and said mother went in search of his said wife and she found her there where this witness had seen her and brought her to his house . . . He was asked whether he firmly believed that the herb had shown him his said wife and that it had been by the craft of the Devil, whereupon he said yes.

[Audience of the Holy Office of the Inquisition, AGN, Mexico City, vol 340, fol 3 54-359, transcribed for us by the late Sra Maria de la Luz Viamonte]

3

Our third episode tells of a curandero who narrowly escaped the clutches of the Holy Office. A seventeenth century cleric, Jacinto de la Serna, composed a guide for priests ministering to the Indians. His work was entitled *Manual de Ministros de In dios para el Conocimiento de sus Idolatrias y Extirpación de Elias*. He was a garrulous busybody, zealous in rooting out and extirpating all expressions of the Indians' old religion, and eager in his narrative to leave a record of his own zeal. Chapter IV of his work continues a recital of incidents that had happened to the author proving (as he says) that idolatry was still rampant among the Indians in his own time. In Section 3 of this chapter, he is discussing native physicians and midwives, especially the role of 'witchcraft' in their practices, and certain goings on in his own household that had aroused his liveliest suspicions. A certain Indian, master of the native lore, had lately arrived in the village and had officiated at a religious rite in which the intoxicating mushrooms had been a central feature. The description of the religious ceremony reaches us through don Jacinto by hearsay only, as of course he was not present, but it carries a ring of authenticity.

And what happened was that there had come to the village an Indian, a native of the village of Tenango, great master of superstitions, and his name was Juan Chichiton, which means 'little dog', and he had brought the red-colored mushrooms that are gathered in the uplands, and with them he had committed a great idolatry, and before I tell of it, I wish to describe the property of said mushrooms, which are called in the Mexican language *Quautlannamacatl,* and having consulted the Licentiate Don Pedro Ponce de Leon, the great Minister and Master of Masters as I said in Chapter II, he told me that these mushrooms were small and golden, and to gather them it was the custom for the priests and old men deputized as ministers for this kind of hum buggery to go up into the mountain, and they remained almost the whole night in prayer and superstitious entreaties, and at dawn, when there sprang up a certain breeze that they knew, then they gathered the mushrooms, attributing divinity to them, possessing as they did the same effect as *ololiuhqui* [*Turbina corymbosa* (L.) Raf.] or *peyotl* [*Lophophora Williamsii* (Lem.) Coulter], because whether eaten or drunk, it intoxicates them and deprives them of their senses, and makes them believe a thousand foolish things. And so, this Juan Chichiton, having gathered the mushrooms on a certain night, in the house where everyone had gathered on the occasion of a saint's feast, the saint was on the altar, and the mushrooms with pulque and a fire beneath the altar, the *teoponastli* [a percussion instrument peculiar to Mesoamerica] and singing going on the whole night through, after most of the night had passed, said Juan Chichiton, who was the priest for that solemn rite, to all those present at the fiesta gave the mushrooms to eat, after the manner of Communion, and gave them pulque to drink, and finished off the festivities with an abundance of pulque, so that what with the mushrooms on the one hand and the pulque the other, they all went out of their heads, a shame it was to see.

De la Serna goes on to relate how he had made utmost efforts to ferret out and lay his hands on Chichiton. There was a hot chase, but by the skin of his teeth the 'Little Dog' eluded his pursuer's clutches.

THE MYCOPHOBIC SYNDROME

Our book has undertaken to show how the White Man at first tried to play down, then ignore, the entheogenic mushrooms of Mesoamerica, until, having fully accomplished this purpose, even the scholars specializing in the field, spokesmen as it were for our Western civilization, did not give them a thought. Here follows an enlightening illustration of this mental block from the very citadel of Mesoamerican studies.

In the late 1920's there was found lying in the library of the University of Texas, a manuscript entitled:

> Coloquio de la nueua conbersion y bautismo
> de los cuatro ultimos reyes de Tlaxcala

> 'Colloquy of the new conversion and baptism
> of the four last kings of Tlaxcala'

The 'Colloquy' is written in crude verse, a piece of religious propaganda devoid of literary merit. The participants in the 'Colloquy' are twelve: Hernan Cortes Marques del Valle and his interpreter Marina, two 'Ambassadors', the cleric Juan Diaz, the four 'kings' (as they are called) of Tlaxcala, *Hongol demonio ydolo*, and two angels who raise their voices in triumphant singing as the four 'kings' are baptized with Christian names suggested by Cortes. The utterances of the four 'kings' are saturated with talk of Hongol: at first, they are under Hongol's domination but they lend themselves readily to conversion and baptism. Though Hongol delivers three lengthy speeches, he of course loses out to the Christian appeals. The manuscript bears the date 1619 which gives us a *terminus ad quern*: it was composed in the early seventeenth century or the final years of the sixteenth.

Hongo is 'mushroom' in Spanish and it takes no perspicacity to see that Hongol, the Demon and Idol, is our *teonandcatl* or *xochinandcatl*.

Whether this 'Colloquy' was ever performed we do not know. But this 'Colloquy' does declare and ratify one lesson that our book brings out: the preoccupation of the friars for generations after the Conquest with the divine mushroom (as the Nahua called it), a powerful rival to the Holy Eucharist.

The Coloquio was published for the first time in 1935 by Jose J. Rojas Garciduenias in Mexico City in a volume entitled: *El Teatro de Nueva*

Espana en el Siglo XVI. Father Garibay in Vol II of his *Historia de la Literatura Nahuatl* devotes two pages of comment to the *Coloquio* because of the possibility that it represented an imitation of a lost original in Nahuatl. However, that may be, Father Garibay makes one comment on the pagan divinity Hongol that is chilling:

Bastara decir que los cuatro reyes, como el autor los llama, hablan a la continua de un dios ONGOL, HONGOL, perfectamenta desconocido en Tlaxcala y en todo sitio en que se habla nahuatl, pues sabido es que esta lengua carece de G. [pp 157-159]

Suffice it to say that the four kings, as the author calls them, speak continually of a god *ongol, hongol,* completely unknown in Tlaxcala and everywhere else where Nahuatl is spoken, since it is well known that this language lacks the letter G.

Father Garibay did not see that hongol was simply a translation of teonandcatl with the terminal I of Nahuatl added. The sacred mushrooms of the Nahua were absent from his mind. But how much did he differ from other Mesoamerican specialists? In 1843 Prescott, in his Conquest of Mexico, omitted all mention of the sacred mushrooms. In 1898 Carl Sapper and also Daniel Brinton showed that they had never heard of the mushrooms in Mesoamerica. Walter Lehmann, when he edited the Codex Vindobonensis in 1929, remarked on the resemblance to mushrooms of the curious objects therein portrayed, but it did not occur to him that they might be what they looked like: he had failed to note the mushrooms in the writings of the friars. Father Garibay, reaching the height of his scholarly activities in the fifties, did not perceive the teonandcatl of the Nahua when editing his Sahagun (published in 1956), when he commented on the seventeenth century Colloquy featuring '*hongol*', nor ten years later when editing his version of the Nahuatl poets in the 1960's. He did not know about the worries of his fellow clergy and their struggles against what they had considered the travesty of the Holy Eucharist that the Indians were accustomed to perpetrate with mushrooms. Indeed, did he not learn of the existence of the sacred mushrooms of the Nahua from the publicity that attended the discoveries of Heim and the Wassons?

Alfonso Caso, albeit with some reluctance, was the first and only Mesoamerican scholar to concede recognition to the potent entheogenic mushrooms in his paper on the *Codex Vindobonensis*. In it he declared at the outset that the paper owed its genesis to Heim and the Wassons. Even that paper of Dr Caso's, which appeared fifteen years ago, has had no reverberations in scholarly circles.

Safford's blunder in 1915 drew no protests from eminent scholars or scientists. Reko's persistent protests fell on deaf ears and he died a disappointed man in 1953. Weitlaner's efforts, and Jean Bassett Johnson's, and Schultes's passed unnoticed, perhaps because of the war. Until Valentina Pavlovna and I assembled and recapitulated their activities in an article that appeared in the *journal* of the New York Botanical Garden, Jan-Feb 1958, few thought of them or of *teonandcatl*. Sahagun, Diego Duran, De la Serna, Motolinia, Hernandez, etc etc - they might as well not have mentioned mushrooms. The sacred mushrooms of the Mesoamericans had fallen into oblivion. Safford was victorious, almost.

Strange, how most Mesoamerican scholars slough off as of no interest to them (or us!) an area of experience that for thousands of years irradiated the lives of the people they study. Our original and daring and eccentric hypothesis, my wife's and mine, that the peoples of Western Europe (except those speaking Catalan and the *langue d'oc*) were steeped from birth in darkest mycophobia to the point where their minds, all unawares, were invincibly closed to mushrooms, may well have been right! To my amazement, let it be said: was ever wild conjecture more stunningly ratified than ours by the extraordinary Mesoamerican evidence? But our strictures are not confined to Mesoamerica. The use of fungal entheogens was once circumpolar. The Claviceps at Eleusis, the fly-agaric linked with birch and conifer, and also (increasingly probable) with the famous *Soma* of the Aryans, along with the teonandcatl of Mesoamerica, seem to have evoked boundless awe and obeisance from our Eurasian ancestors and their New World descendants.

THE RANGE OF MUSHROOM USE IN MESOAMERICA

In Fig 1 we offer our readers a map of the areas over which I think it is fair to say that the cult of the divine mushroom probably prevailed at the moment of the Conquest. This is an approximation, perhaps on the conservative side. The map is built on linguistic areas as those areas probably stood in the fifteenth century. Trade was flowing constantly throughout Mesoamerica, the merchants travelling with their stocks of goods on their b acks and, for mutual protection, in bands. There was also warfare in which slaves and goods were captured. It stands to reason that throughout this cultural area the mushrooms were known and used wherever they grew and perhaps slightly beyond. Their fame must have been wider than their use. There was no secrecy about the mushrooms. How could there be?

1. The Nahua in the Valley of Mexico have left us rich documentation on their use and abuse of inebriating mushrooms and the exalted status accorded to them by the aristocrats. Father Garibay in his rendering of the two anthologies in his *Poesia Nahuatl* 1-3 leaves us in no doubt about this and Diego Duran in brief but pungent references agrees. The Nahua were widely distributed over what is now central and southern Mexico and bands had emigrated to Guatemala on the Pacific Coast and into the Highlands where they were known as Pipil.

2, 3, 4. The *Otopamean* linguistic group: *Otomi, Matlatzinca, Mazahua. In Les Champignons hallucinogenes* . . . (1958) I traced back to 1543 the evidence for the use of the mushrooms in Otomi country and also cited an Otomi lexicon dated 1640 in the Biblioteca Nacional de Mexico that cites Otomi words for the inebriating mushrooms. Karl-Herbert Mayer of Graz has lately discovered an Otomi lexicon in the Bibliotheque Nationale (Paris) dated 29 October 1605 giving similar words for the inebriating mushrooms in that language: these are both manuscripts, and the 1640 dictionary may have been copied from the original of the 1605 version. No one seems to have reported a present day use of the sacred mushrooms: perhaps no one has looked for it.

Similarly, in the Matlatzinca country, in *Les Champignons hallucinogenes*, a manuscript lexicon of 1642 composed by Diego Basalenque lends support for the use there of the mushrooms. We called attention also to a document of 1579 that recorded the payment of tribute in kind in the old days to the Lord of Mexico, and among those deliveries were mushrooms. One anthropologist has drawn attention to the fact that in the records of tribute paid in kind under the kings of the Aztecs mushrooms are never mentioned. He had overlooked this passage, but it is true that so far as we now know it is unique. Is not the explanation simple? When we went down to Mexico in 1953 and began our exploration of the mushroom complex, we discovered that mushrooms did not figure in the market squares: they changed hands privately, they were carried out of sight through public thoroughfares, one did not speak of them. Was not this even truer in the old days before the Conquest?
The Matlatzinca language survives to this day in one town: San Francisco Oxtotilpan. Dr Gaston Guzman and A. Lopez-Gonzalez, the former a mycologist and the latter an anthropologist of the Escuela Nacional de Antropologia e Historia, succeeded in documenting the use of *Psilocybe Wassonii* among the inhabitants of that village. Leonardo Manrique, Chief of the Department of Linguistics of the Museo Nacional de Antropologia, says that the name of these mushrooms in Matlatzinca today is *netoc'hutata,*

ne- being the plural, *-to-* a reverential diminutive, *-c'hu-* the root for sacred, and - *tata* being lord; ' the most holy little Lords'.

For the Mazahua, we have no contemporary information. Robert Weitlaner and I visited them briefly but failed to arrive at any positive information. On the other hand, in *Mushrooms Russia & History* we cited a manual prepared in Mexico and published in 1637 entitled *Doctrina y Enseñanza en la lengua Macahua de Casas muy Utiles, y Provechosas para* las *Ministros de Doctrina* by the Licentiate Diego de Nagera (or Najera) Yanguas, incumbent of Xocotitlan. This is a manual to guide the clergy serving the Mazahua population and specifically guiding them in asking questions of the faithful in the confessional. The Father confessor on folios 27-29 catechizes his penitent as to whether he has eaten mushrooms and got drunk on them and if so why, whether to find lost objects or for illness. The following extract shows the tenor of the questions, the column in English being added by us:

SPANISH

por que querias comer essos hongos? por que estaba enfermo queria comer hongos para ver lo que perdi quantas vezes? no los comiste? no los comi solamente queria comerlos

MAZAHUA

yoqhenangueze daguiminernaha toguica mayho yocho nangueze darimichoye dariminemaha rogoza yocho maqheranuu maqhe peqherobexi hanchanixi? que higuiza? hiroza anguechco dariminemaha togoza

ENGLISH

Why didst thou want to eat those mushrooms? Because I was ill I wanted to eat mushrooms to see what I had lost how often? didst thou not eat them? I ate them not I only wanted to eat them.

Mushrooms Russia & History p 221

5. *Tarascan.* A lexicon compiled by Maturino Gilberti and published in 1559 gives the word in Tarascan for the mushroom that inebriates. Furthermore, in the episode before the Inquisition that we told at length on pp 210-211, the scene took place in 1629 in Michoacán and Joseph the Indian was presumably a native Tarascan speaker.

6. *Huastecan.* This tongue descended from the Mayan stock is spoken along the Gulf Coast, the most northern of the languages that we are tempted to place among those using the entheogenic mushrooms. Our only written evidence is a letter discovered by Guy Stresser-Pean to the clergy of Huasteca written by the Archbishop of Mexico in 1726 in which he deplores the pagan practice of taking mushrooms and possibly other substances to obtain visions. Three of the poems in Poesia Nahuatl (numbers 12, 13, and 14 in Vol 3), riotous drinking songs, were said by the anthologist in the sixteenth century to be Huastecan in inspiration. In our inquiries in the mid-twentieth century we have not found the use of mushrooms in low lying territory, and as the Huasteca is partly low lying, if the practice was native there, this might extend the range of their use.

7. *Totonac.* Some linguists suggest that this language is remotely related to Mayan. It is spoken by the people living on the Gulf of Mexico south of the Huasteca. Our terracotta figurine showing a woman with her right arm on a mushroom and her left arm raised in what I interpret as a speaking gesture, is from what is now the Totonac country but dates from the beginning of our Christian era. We assume that the Totonacs knew the mushrooms that abound there.

8. *Mixe.* We visited this area twice and found abundant evidence that the entheogenic mushrooms were known to everybody, both in the eastern stretch of the Mixe country and the western. This Mixe region is a remote and conservative country and the usage must go back long before the Conquest.

9. *Zoque.* We have not visited this area and we have no information about it, either historical or contemporary. It is contiguous with the Mixe country to the West and with the Mayan peoples to the East and North. I do not see how they could avoid practicing the mushroom cult, but as I have no information I designate it with a question mark.

10. *Mazatec.* There seems to be no historical information but we have uncovered an abundance of contemporary tradition. Maria Sabina has been our ever-flowing source of information, and the tradition is strong and obviously ancient.

11. Zapotec. This major group of mutually unintelligible dialects is in an area where the inebriating mushrooms are common and where the people know them intimately. In a lexicon published in 1578 and compiled by Fray Juan de Cordoba there are words for 'mushrooms that they say give

you visions'. There is additional testimony of considerable interest. It is to be found in Paso y Troncoso: *Papeles de Nueva Espana, 2nd Serie, Geografia y Estadistica*, Vol IV: *Relaciones Geograficas de la Dio'cesis de Oaxaca*. The manuscript from which it was printed was dated 15 April 1580. The document begins on p 109 and deals with a Zapotec town called Teticpac, four leagues west of Antequera and 40 leagues from Tehuantepec. In the course of Paragraph XIV, we read:

Adoravan al demonio haziendo a su figura ydolos e caras de piedra muy feas a las quales sacrificavan perrillos e yndios esclauos y esta hera su adoracion e a quien tenian por dioses; e despues que hazian algun sacrificio tenian por costumbre bailar e ynbriagarse con vnos hongos en tal manera que vian muchas visiones e figuras espantables.

They would worship the devil making in his likeness idols and faces of stone, very ugly to which they would sacrifice little dogs and Indian slaves and this was their worship and whom they took for gods; and after they had made some such sacrifice it was their custom to dance and get drunk on some mushrooms in such a manner that they would see many visions and fearful figures.

12. *Chatino.* This is a linguistic enclave in the Zapotec country. The language is called 'Zapotecan'. When Roger Heim and I went there in 1956, introduced by Bill Upson of the Instituto Lingtuistico de Verano, we found many species of sacred mushrooms in use. As the Chatino country is entirely surrounded by Zapotec speakers, it is safe to assume that the practice is ancient.

13. *Mixteca.* The use of mushrooms in this important linguistic area is documented in the *Codice de Yanhuitlan* edited by Jimenez Moreno. On 15 October 1544 in proceedings before a Spanish scribe and notary, three Indians, notables, gave testimony concerning their ostentatious worship of the gods of the old religion. As they had been baptized, they were of course apostates. The principal Indian gave his testimony in Mixtec. It seems that he had taken inebriating mushrooms to invoke divine help in various circumstances. The pre-Conquest Codex Vindobonensis and the post-Conquest *Lienzo de Zacatepec* both include the same glyph for the sacred mushrooms. Both were Mixtec in origin. I visited the Mixteca twice, in 1960 and 1961, accompanied by Robert Ravicz and on the second occasion also by Roger Heim. Our mushroomic experiences have been published.

14. Chinantla. Robert J. Weitlaner and Thomas MacDougall learned of the use of inebriating mushrooms in Comaltepec and Yolox, Chinantec towns, in 1960, and in a letter to Weitlaner from Guadalupe M. Calderon,

263

Chinantec Indian, dated 8 August 1963, he gave details about their use. Later Arthur J. Rubel and Jean Getterfinger-Krejci published a paper in Economic Botany, July-September 1976, submitted September 1974, giving an account of a *velada* that they had attended in Santiago Comal tepee. In that paper they also documented the use in the Chinantla of inebriating mushrooms in the 18th century.

15. *Chantal de Oaxaca.* Evidence of a unique character seems to support the supposition that inebriating mushrooms were used in the small enclave, close by Tehuan tepec, of speakers of this language classed as a Hokaltecan tongue. ('Chontal de Tabasco' is a Mayan language utterly unrelated.) Occasionally anthropologists working in remote villages in Mexico come across texts written on paper giving details, often liturgical, in the native language. They used to be most highly valued and handed down from generation to generation. When the paper was wearing out, it was recopied. No one can say how far back the text goes. Now that the hold of traditional values is breaking down, these papers are drifting into the hands of anthropologists and linguists and usually end up in the Department of Ethnology in the Museo Nacional. In the summer and fall of 1968 such a document was made available to Robert Weitlaner by Juan Ramirez, an informant who is wholly Chontal. In its text there occur the words '*mescal de hongo*': apparently the mushroom is thrown into boiling mescal. Later German Placencia of the Department of Ethnology found another manuscript where '*mescal de hongo*' is cited. In the light of the hold that the inebriating mushrooms have on the native peoples among whom these Chontal are living, I think we are justified in assuming that these documents refer to the use of inebriating mushrooms in the religious practices of the Chontal of Oaxaca.

16. The Highland Mayan languages. I have dealt with these in the preceding chapter.

CHAPTER 11

THE SHAMAN AND THE MUSHROOM:

NEW PERSPECTIVES

The fascination of the Mesoamerican culture for the modern world lies in its strange (for us) traits, in the vast and ever-expanding documentation permitting us to explore those traits always making discoveries, in the refinement of its thinking and its high artistic craftsmanship contrasting with human sacrifice and cannibalism on a scale unknown to us elsewhere, and in its chronological and geographical proximity to us. Here we possess an unrivalled opportunity to study Early Man in a pure culture, and also his head-on collision with sixteenth century European civilization.

How odd then is our failure until now to have grasped the hold on this culture of the entheogenic mushrooms. There was no secrecy about them before the Europeans arrived on the scene. How could there be? They grew almost everywhere in the highlands of southern Mexico. There would have been no secrecy after the White Man arrived on the scene, were it not that we, knowing nothing about them, seemed aggressively determined to learn nothing. Though living in the age of science, we regarded ourselves as inhibited from trespassing on this legitimate area of inquiry.

I have sometimes asked myself whether the unlettered ages, stretching back through aeons of time, were not those belonging peculiarly to the entheogens, the Age of entheogens. The Mysteries of Eleusis began in the unlettered past of the amazing Greek people, then persisted for a few centuries under a hermetic seal of secrecy into an age of glorious letters, whereupon they finally and completely petered out. The Soma of the Vedic Hymns knew its heyday before the Aryans learned their letters but it disappeared with the coming of the alphabet, and it lingers on to this day among the Hindus (and some Sanskrit scholars!) only as an unsubstantial dream plant. Can these coincidences be dismissed as cases of *cum hoc ergo propter hoc*? Among the northern tier of peoples in Siberia the divine mushrooms flourished as a focus of devotion so long as they knew no alphabet, until the Russians and specifically the Soviets, precisely like the friars of Mesoamerica, tried to rub it out before studying it.

Has the advent of the alphabet with its slow progress among the languages of the world been studied in all its aspects? The coming of

265

literacy and writing was the profound cultural event of our human civilization: this much we all know. Perhaps that event exerted a significantly different impact on different elements in the community. From my observations in Mexico, in the Algonkian country, in India, I think the unlettered herbalists possessed a body of knowledge, commanding an infinity of empirical subtleties, that has escaped our botanists and anthropologists. In the prehistory of all cultures including those still existing, the herbalists are a repository of knowledge acquired through centuries of intensive observation and experience which they pass on from generation to generation by word of mouth from master to apprentice. This was a self-contained system and largely secret. These practitioners were hardly the ones to quicken with excitement and curiosity when the talk of the alphabet was abroad in the land. On the other hand, those who took to the new-fangled writing were the aggressive intellectual leaders and scribes, including sometimes priests for their own reasons and some of the aristocracy, all of them beings from a different world, and the hidden knowledge of the herbalists would hardly have come their way, their corpus of knowledge not lending itself easily to writing. Here is why Theophrastus and Dioscorides are disappointing for us: they were the heralds of the New Dawn in botany but were beginning virtually from scratch. They would have failed to win the trust of the herbalists in their midst. I am not dogmatic about these trends of long ago but am suggesting a plausible framework to explain what may have happened. The herbalists' knowledge was secret but of different degrees of secrecy. In Mesoamerica the entheogens were known to everyone, but in Greece secrecy was the rule.

In Mexico I have seen how quickly the coming of the alphabet (i.e. primary schools), the spread of literacy, changes the outlook of a village almost overnight. The old world of the sabia, the herbalist, the shaman, lingers on for a few more seasons in rapidly shrinking circles. Here is what Marfa Sabina, the shaman in her eighties, said as translated from the Mazatec by Alvaro Estrad a little while ago:

Es cierto que antes de Wasson nadie hablaba con tanta soltura acerca de los ninos. Ningun Mazateco revelaba lo que sabia de ese asunto . . .. Los ninos son la sangre de Cristo. Cuando los mazatecos hablamos de las veladas lo hacemos en voz baja y para no pronunciar el nombre que tienen en mazateco [nti'xi'tho'] los llamamos cositas o santitos. Asi los llamaron nuestros antepasados . . .. Desde el momento en que llegaron los extranjeros . . . los ninos santos perdieron su pureza. Perdieron su fuerza. Fueron profanados . . .. De ahora en adelante ya no serviran. No tiene remedio. Antes de Wasson, yo sentia que los nifios santos me elevaban. Ya no lo siento asi.

[Alvaro Estrada: La Vida de Maria Sabina, pp 103, 119-20]

Certainly, before Wasson no one spoke with such freedom about the 'children'. No Mazatec would reveal what he knew on this subject. The 'children' are the blood of Christ. When we Mazatecs speak of the *veladas*, we do so in a low voice and so as not to pronounce their name in Mazatec *['nti'xi'tho']* we call them 'Little Things' or 'Little Saints'. Thus, were they called by our forebears. From the moment when the strangers arrived the 'Holy Children' lost their purity. They lost their strength. They were profaned. From now on they will serve no purpose. There is no help for it. Before Wasson I felt that the Holy Children elevated me. I no longer feel so.

These words make me wince, but I was merely the precursor of the New Day. I arrived in the same decade with the highway, the airplane, the alphabet. The Old Order was in danger of passing with no one to record its passing. The Old Order does not mix with the New. The wisdom of the *Sabia*, genuine though it was, has nothing to give to the world of tomorrow. I think it was ever so with the arrival of the alphabet. Now the young generation is intent on the new learning, wants to forget the mushrooms that only yesterday evoked their awe, chooses the young doctor from the medical school in the city in preference to the wisewoman, and is not learning or is forgetting the language of his ancestors. Alvaro Estrada, Mazatec born in Huautla, writes me under date of 24 August 1977:

Los jo'venes huautecos hoy dia se avergtuenzan de su origen indio y tratan de que sus hijos no hablen el mazateco.

The young of Huautla are ashamed of their Indian origin and try to see to it that their children do not speak Mazatec.

Whether these trends are good or bad is not the question: they are inevitable.

We know that the shamanic practice of Maria Sabina is ancient. The evidence for this is diverse and I think overwhelming. The architectural arrangement of the immense building complexes of Teotihuacan and their murals, hitherto unexplained, make sense for the first time when interpreted by her practices. Ruiz de Alarco'n's writings as illuminated by Alfredo Lopez Austin's studies point to strikingly similar *veladas* in the Nahuatl-speaking country in the early seventeenth century, and we have listened to identical shamanic chants deep in the Zapotec country, though we did not tape them. The mushroom stones of Guatemala, the carvings of ecstatic figures of parallel age found in Mexico, the mythological genesis of the role for mushrooms elucidated for us in the Codex Vindobonensis - all speak with the same voice. We possess no starting

267

point for this use of the divine mushrooms: the trail disappears from sight in the remotest past. Shamanism is the term customarily used to describe one aspect of the religious life of communities, mostly preliterate, where individuals known to us as 'shamans' claim to possess, and are recognized by their neighbors as possessing, extraordinary powers for communicating with the unseen world, the world of departed spirits, which they enter through an ecstatic trance. The shamans are not organized in priesthoods: each is on his own, and the following he enlists is in proportion to the charisma that he enjoys. If, as is commonly believed, Homo sapiens began his domination of the world some 50, 000 years ago, then it is possible, perhaps even a fair assumption that shamanism has been the highest vehicle for the expression of man's religious yearnings for more than nine-tenths of his domination of this earth, and it still survives with diminishing vigor in the world's outlying communities. If our Neanderthal (Homo sapiens neanderthalensis) and other predecessors were of comparable intellectual capacities, shamanism may well be far, far older.

In discussions of shamanism there has been much nonsense uttered about the role of inebriants. Distilled alcohol could never have been important. In the West distilled alcohol seems to have been a discovery of the School of Salerno about the year AD 1100, and it was kept a secret restricted to alchemical and monastic circles up to the Reformation four centuries later. In the East the Chinese were earlier, especially by the 'freezing-out' process, perhaps as early as the fourth century AD. But even so this is late in the long history of shamanism. I question whether fermented drinks -mead, wine, beers -were ever much used in shamanism: in most persons they cloud the brain and render muscular responses unreliable. Many are so primitive where the psyche is concerned that for them states of alcoholic inebriation are landmarks for judging mind-altering drugs. Alcohol and the entheogens are worlds apart. Their effects are different in kind. We must divorce alcohol from the entheogens: this is the first and great commandment. The entheogens, whose secrets the modem world is only now learning (chiefly from what I call 'Early Man' regardless of the chronological age) are a key to shamanism and the Mystery religions, a key that students have yet to evaluate at their full worth. In every case the use of these entheogens goes back as far as history, linguistics, and archeology carry us, and we must assume much further. Their use seems to be older than our oldest information. Not that the entheogens are needed to induce an ecstatic trance. Some people practicing shamanism do not know them. By dint of frenzied dancing, singing, shouting, and percussive music, chiefly drums, the shaman arrives at the desired state of ecstasy and finally falls down in a stupor, whereupon communication with the other world is established.

The Hindus, perhaps inspired by a potent memory of their divine but inaccessible Soma, have evolved techniques - austerities, postures long maintained, physical exercises, mental concentration - that permit them to arrive at a state of 'contemplation' without the aid of plant hallucinogens. This state is of a different nature from the ecstasy we are discussing, and certainly its adepts rate its quality as superior, indeed as the ultimate in human achievement.

Botanists and anthropologists sometimes ask why we are discovering so many entheogens in use in the contemporary New World cultures, among Indian peoples of Mexico and southwards, as contrasted with their relative scarcity in Eurasia. Surely the answer lies in our being able to examine in the New World the many living cultures at the precise moment when they are entering the stage of their own proto-history from their prehistory. We catch these cultures when, so far as the entheogens go, they are still pure, thanks to the strange determination of our race through centuries not to trespass on this field - a boon certainly for us present day inquirers! In Eurasia we are dealing for the most part with cultures that emerged into history long ago, that have therefore left behind shamanism with its trappings, that have lost the secrets of their own herbalists of the remote past. Entheogens were always secret preparations in Greece and large parts of Eurasia, the secret spontaneously guarded by those privy to it. We must remember that the Indians of the New World have led our botanists by the hand to the entheogens. It would have been a lengthy, costly, perilous journey if we had had to rely on trial and error to arrive at those plants that, when properly handled, offer us psychotropic effects.

In his trance the shaman goes on a far journey the place of the departed ancestors, or the nether world, or there where the gods dwell - and this wonderland is, I submit, precisely where the entheogens take us. They are a gateway to ecstasy. Ecstasy in itself is neither pleasant nor unpleasant. The bliss or panic into which it plunges you is incidental to ecstasy. When you are in a state of ecstasy, your very soul seems scooped out from your body and away it goes. Who controls its flight? Is it you, or your 'subconscious', or a 'higher power'? Perhaps it is pitch dark, yet you see and hear more clearly than you have ever seen or heard before. You are at last face to face with Ultimate Truth: this is the overwhelming impression (or illusion) that grips you. You may visit Hell, or the Elysian fields of Asphodel, or the Gobi Desert, or Arctic wastes. You know awe, and bliss, and fear, even terror. Everyone experiences ecstasy in his own way, and never twice in the same way. Ecstasy is the very essence of

269

shamanism. The neophyte from the great world associates the mushrooms primarily with visions, but for those who know the Indian language of the shaman the mushrooms 'speak' through the shaman. The mushroom is the Word: *es habla*, as Aurelio told me. The mushroom bestows on the curandero what the Greeks called Logos, the Aryans Vac, Vedic kavya, 'poetic potency' as Louis Renou put it. The divine afflatus of poetry is the gift of the entheogen. The textual exegete skilled only in dissecting the cruces of the verses lying before him is of course indispensable and his shrewd observations should have our full attention, but unless gifted with kavya, he does well to be cautious in discussing the higher reaches of Poetry. He dissects the verses but knows not ecstasy, which is the soul of the verses.

The shaman exercises his calling according to his lights. Every shaman puts on a different performance, and the extraordinary shaman is entitled to be called a virtuoso. His voice, his verses filled with traditional ('formulaic') phrases, his dancing, his percussive effects - these he works up in response to his little audience and in fulfillment of his genius, and there can be no doubt that sometimes the effect is telling. The reputation of a good shaman extends over a wide radius and some villages are famed for the shamans they produce, shamans with conviction, self-confidence, who *cantan recio*, 'sing stoutly', as they say. I believe villages exist in Mexico where there is such a strong tradition of shamanism that one may speak of a 'school' of shamanism associated with their names; not of course an organized school but a tradition of shamanism permeating the village life and in which the villagers take quiet pride. While the shaman is not confined to any fixed liturgy, he is naturally a product of the cultural ambiance of his and the neighboring villages. He will be a prisoner of the conceptions of the universe and the beliefs that they possess, the practices that are habitual in the community. He may introduce personal variations into his performance, striking effects, but it is hardly possible for him to do violence to the framework of the world in which he has lived his life. He can only stretch that framework.

But what do we mean by 'stretching that framework'? In his ecstasy the shaman invokes in fervent verse and hymns the spirits that his neighbors know, gives utterance to the community's beliefs mythological and eschatological. When he is a man of intellectual power and moral prestige, will he not introduce grace notes into the common stock of those beliefs, variations and elaborations and deviations, within the confines that he senses are permissible and perhaps conforming to the inchoate notions already dimly felt by some in his gathering? Such deviations might consider the heroic doings in war or hunting or when fishing on the high seas of the mighty men of his own generation, whom all have known, or natural catastrophes that have overtaken the village, or a migration to a new environment with strange and uncertain neighbors . These deviations will be accepted, and successive generations of shamans will bring innovations, which accounts for the fluidity of oral traditions among related peoples. For we speak of a world where there is no writing, where the corpus of cosmological and historical beliefs, the whole culture of the people and their vocabulary, lies in the minds and on the tongues of the living generation and nowhere else. Later, when the age of writing has arrived, a Herodotus comes along who puts down all the various recensions - 'some say this and some say that and yet others tell another story, but I think the truth is so-and-so'. Surely the shaman preceded in time the itinerant bard, for the bard presupposes kings with their audience chambers and patronage and a degree of sophistication. The shaman knows only his neighbors among whom he has lived from the beginning. When possessed, he bears in his person the charisma of a village mediator with the spirits of the invisible world. How extraordinary that in this nuclear age so ancient a form of religious expression still survives, for a few more years, in the remote regions of the world!

THE FLY AGARIC IN THE NEW WORLD

In 1968 in my *Soma* I said that we should be thankful for the data we had assembled on the *fly-agaric* cult of Siberia but warned against exaggerating their importance. For a shamanic practice that had lasted we know not how many millennia our soundings reached back only three centuries, ripples on time's surface. Moreover, those three centuries of cultural upheaval and chaos saw the end of the practice: it could be observed only when it was in extremis.

Some of the observers [I wrote] were supercilious and none of them saw the implications of their observations. None of them seems to have been prepared in botany and none probed the questions that are compelling for us. The circumstances that brought them on the scene were at the same time bringing about the end of the beliefs and performances for which they were to be the sole witnesses. They were observing the fly-agaric cult only in its dying phase, when the area of its diffusion was being lopped away, when in some places the integrity of belief in it had been undermined, and when the tribes themselves were mostly in a pitiful state of physical and psychological disarray. There is ample evidence that the

271

ethnic movements, often gradual and more or less peaceful, in the inhospitable tundra and taiga of Siberia have been continuous, and we are far from unraveling them. In recent centuries the peoples practicing the fly-agaric cult have been living in areas to the north of where they were in their heyday, some of them on or close to the Arctic Ocean. They have been displaced from their former homes by Altaic tribes who do not, apparently, take the fly-agaric but who have absorbed into their shamanic practices the corpus of beliefs that go with the fly-agaric, beliefs that seem to accompany the ecology of the forest belt, especially the reverence for the birch. For the historian of human cultures, it is a matter of regret that the impact of the modern world is inevitably brutal, bulldozer-like, in its disregard and contempt for the beliefs and ways of life of primitive peoples whom our industrial civilization wrenches from their traditions and tries, usually without success, to bring into step with our contemporary ideas. This holds true for the communist as well as the capitalist world. When I wrote the foregoing paragraph about Siberian shamanism and the fly-agaric, I did not anticipate the denouement. True, almost twenty years ago Claude Levi-Strauss had given me a lead in a Jesuit's letter to his brother written in the early seventeenth century, and in Levi-Strauss's detailed review of Soma he expanded on other leads in the North American native cultures, but preoccupied as I was in a different direction and lacking the needed personal contact, those leads, though never forgotten, lay fallow. In 1975, through a combination of circumstances, I came to know, at first only by correspondence, a remarkable Ojibway herbalist and shaman, Keewaydinoquay, 1 living on a lovely island in Lake Michigan, the only resident on an island that had once belonged to her ancestors. There quickly unfolded before us an account of the fly-agaric cult that was breathtaking, not only for itself but for the fact that for centuries, millennia, the Ojibway, and in varying degrees the other peoples of the Algonkian nation, had looked to the fly-agaric for consultation about the most serious matters in their lives. The cultural trait that in Siberia we discerned dimly had been preserved for us, live and pure, as though in a time capsule, owing to the peculiar state of social relations between Whites and Algonkians during these last four hundred years.

And so, quite unexpectedly, we discover the cult of the fly-agaric in full panoply here in North America. No one knows when the Algonkians arrived here. The European settlers found them occupying a large part of North America, the Amerindian nation that is most widespread. Presumably they came across the Bering Strait, or else the land bridge that replaced the Strait during the successive Ice Ages. But if it should develop that they came from the north of Europe, in remote ages when the geography may have been different and stepping-stone islands permitted such transit, it would make no difference, for I think I have shown that the fly-agaric cult in former ages was circumpolar in extent, wherever the birch or appropriate conifers thrived.

As in Mexico, we owe the preservation of the cult into these modern times to the total lack of interest displayed by the White Man. It was an important and precious secret for the Ojibway, and they were not inclined to tell anyone about it who would sneer and scoff. How ironic it is that in Michigan and thereabouts, where the mycological faculties have considered themselves strong, the miskwedo (= *Amanita muscaria*) has played its age-old role among the Algonkians until now without so much as a nod from our mushroom men! (There needs be no incompatibility between our mycologists and our ethnomycologist: witness Roger Heim.) Anthropologists and linguists have overlooked that role in spite of obvious clues in their standard sources and in spite of the widespread interest aroused by the anthology of Siberian source materials in my SOMA: Divine Mushroom of Immortality.

Those in the Great Lakes area who take a professorial interest in the humane letters pass by on the other side when a poor Indian people not yet at home with the alphabet manifest their faith in a toadstool. Yet these same scholars will sit up straight at the mere mention of Eleusis or the Vedic Hymns, far removed though they are in time and space, or is it precisely because they are so removed?

Prof Bernard Lowy, mycologist of Louisiana State University, may well have uncovered exciting evidence in his ethnomycological investigations in Chiapas and t h e nearby Quiche-speaking area of Guatemala. There *Amanita muscaria* is common and well known but avoided. In Quiche, Dr Lowy tells us, it is called *kakuljd*, which carries the terrifying sense of *rayo* in Spanish, *foudre* in French, *parjanya the thundergod* in Sanskrit. Lightning in Spanish is commonly *relampago* but this word is devoid of any aura of supernatural associations, free of mythological meaning. The Quiche speakers do not know why *A. muscaria* is the lightning-bolt and no longer think of the word's meaning when they use it. But *kakuljd* was the god of the lightning-bolt and this Quiche term is to be found in the Popol Vuh. How did this association of ideas, to which we are accustomed in Eurasia and among the *Ojibway*, arrive in the mountains of southern Mesoamerica? In Chichicastenango an alternative name for the *kakuljd* is *itzel ocox*, evil or diabolical mushroom. *A. muscaria* in Tuxtla Gutierrez and San Cristobal de las Casas is called *yuyo de rayo* when the native is speaking Spanish, again the mushroom of the lightning-bolt. For the Tzeltal-speakers in Zinacantan the fly-agaric is the *yuy chauk,* with the same meaning.

273

In folklore throughout Eurasia and Mesoamerica we are well acquainted with the tie that binds together the entheogenic mushroom and the lightning-bolt. Everywhere that tie is strong, but in Mesoamerica it generally belongs to the entheogenic Psilocybe and Stropharia genera: Dr Lowy has discovered one part of that area where the lightning-bolt impregnates the soft earth with the 'toad mushroom'. Does this word *kakuljd* come from a time when the ancestors of the Quiche knew the secret of *A. muscaria* and used it? Did they abandon it because? long ago, they found the Psilocybe species preferable? Or because the friars in post-Conquest times drove it out?

New perspectives in ethnomycology are beckoning to us.

CPSIA information can be obtained
at www.ICGtesting.com
Printed in the USA
BVHW032149291121
622844BV00018B/606